On Endings

ON ENDINGS

American Postmodern Fiction
and the Cold War

DANIEL GRAUSAM

University of Virginia Press
CHARLOTTESVILLE AND LONDON

University of Virginia Press

© 2011 by the Rector and Visitors of the University of Virginia
All rights reserved
Printed in the United States of America on acid-free paper

First published 2011

9 8 7 6 5 4 3 2 1

LIBRARY OF CONGRESS CATALOGING-IN-PUBLICATION DATA

Grausam, Daniel, 1975–
  On endings : American postmodern fiction and the Cold War / Daniel Grausam.
    p. cm.
  Includes bibliographical references and index.
  ISBN 978-0-8139-3161-6 (cloth : acid-free paper)
  ISBN 978-0-8139-3162-3 (pbk. : acid-free paper)
  ISBN 978-0-8139-3166-1 (e-book)
  1. American fiction—History and criticism—Theory, etc. 2. Postmodernism (Literature)—United States. 3. Cold War—Influence. 4. Cold War in literature. 5. Barth, John, 1930–Criticism and interpretation. 6. Pynchon, Thomas—Criticism and interpretation. 7. Powers, Richard, 1957–Criticism and interpretation. I. Title.
PS374.P64G7 2011
813'.5409—dc22

2011008422

A book in the American Literatures Initiative (ALI), a collaborative publishing project of NYU Press, Fordham University Press, Rutgers University Press, Temple University Press, and the University of Virginia Press. The Initiative is supported by The Andrew W. Mellon Foundation. For more information, please visit www.americanliteratures.org.

Contents

	Acknowledgments	vii
	Introduction: On Endings	1
1	Institutionalizing Postmodernism: John Barth and Modern War	23
2	*The Crying of Lot 49*, circa 1642; or, Pynchon, Periodicity, and Total War	42
3	The Time of the Nation, the Time of the State	59
4	Unthinking the Thinkability of the Unthinkable	76
5	Trying to Understand *End Zone*	104
6	The Dominant Tense: Richard Powers and Late Postmodernism	124
	Afterword: Critical Conventions / Postmodern Canons	149
	Notes	163
	Bibliography	179
	Index	191

Acknowledgments

An earlier version of chapter 2 appeared in *Clio: A Journal of Literature, History, and the Philosophy of History* (2008), and a shorter version of chapter 4 (Copyright © 2011 The Johns Hopkins University Press) appeared in *ELH* 78, no. 3 (Fall 2011). I'm grateful to both journals for permission to revisit those essays, and for the very helpful input of their anonymous readers.

I owe many thanks: Mitchell Breitwieser prevented my sophomore self from a full-time defection to the philosophy department, and a course in my junior year convinced me that graduate school might be in my future. And when that future arrived, it was Mitch who guided me through it, with just the right combination of support and insight. I owe him more than I can say. John Bishop and Fred Dolan also provided crucial feedback and help as I began to conceptualize this project. Washington University in St. Louis proved to be a hospitable home to think about the Cold War, and to bring this book to completion. Thanks are especially due to the two department chairs under whom I've been fortunate enough to work. David Lawton took the chance on hiring me, and made me feel immediately welcome; Vincent Sherry's own work on war and literature has been enormously inspiring, and this book benefitted in many ways from his attention. Guinn Batten and Dillon Johnston helped me feel at home, and have remained the best of friends; Joseph Loewenstein's comments on the abstract for this book sharpened my thinking, as did Bill Maxwell's, and Steven Meyer supplied several key sources. Lara Bovilsky, Dillon Brown, Benjy Kahan, Anca Parvulescu, and Jessica Rosenfeld read chapter 4 with great care; and Bill McKelvy guided me through the late stages of this project with characteristic cheerfulness and warmth. Outside the English Department, Rob Henke has been incredibly supportive, and a long rainy-day conversation with Angela Miller helped me to think about this project in new ways. My students have been an extraordinary resource, and though they all deserve thanks, two graduate students deserve special recognition: Katie Muth has patiently listened to and helped improve these ideas more times than she can count, and Dustin Iler was especially helpful on Richard Powers.

I am delighted to have the chance to thank friends and colleagues whose support enabled me to bring this project to a close. David Widmark and Paul Morrison kept me honest, and kept me fed. Mark Pedretti and Mitchum Huehls were there from the beginning with careful feedback and constant good cheer. Steve Belletto, Mike LeMahieu, Benj Widiss, Matt Wilkens, and Joe Jeon have offered warmly appreciated camaraderie and advice. At crucial points, conversations with Deborah Nelson, Franny Nudelman, Deak Nabers, Priscilla Wald, and Andrew Hoberek were helpful and inspiring in equal parts, and Franny's reading of the entire manuscript was a gift I will not soon forget. My thanks as well to the wonderful staff at the University of Virginia Press: Cathie Brettschneider, Ellen Satrom, and Raennah Mitchell have made what I imagined would be a stressful process a joy. Jason Harvey's cover design was a dream come true. Alan Nadel and an anonymous reader reported on the manuscript for the press, and their comments were invaluable. Tim Roberts at the American Literatures Initiative has been wonderful to work with, and I'm grateful to Susan Murray for her copyediting.

If this book has a single origin, it can no doubt be traced back to a childhood in the San Fernando Valley, just a few miles down the road from the defense contractor satirized in *The Crying of Lot 49*. While those early years certainly have something to do with my interests, more vitally it was the family tradition of intense conversation with my parents, Anne and Jeff, and my sister, Elizabeth, that set me on this path, and I dedicate this book to them. Finally and most importantly, my love to Marina MacKay, who both prevented and bandaged many an intellectual paper cut of mine, and suffered more than a few physical ones of her own during her countless, and transformative, rereadings of this manuscript.

On Endings

Introduction: On Endings

No one encountering a book review that castigates an author as the "worst writer of his generation" would be surprised to find further incendiary claims, but Dale Peck's poisonous 2002 review of Rick Moody's *The Black Veil* is worth quoting because it so economically restates one powerful narrative about the American novel after 1945.[1] A scathing critique of Moody's novel becomes a denunciation of the whole strand of contemporary fiction to which it belongs: these writers are "heirs to a bankrupt tradition," a tradition that "burst into full, foul life in the ridiculous dithering of Barth and Hawkes and Gaddis, and the reductive cardboard constructions of Barthelme, and the word-by-word wasting of a talent as formidable as Pynchon's; and finally broke apart like a cracked sidewalk beneath the weight of the stupid—just plain stupid—tomes of DeLillo." This is, in Peck's mind, "a tradition that has systematically divested itself of any ability to comment on anything other than its own inability to comment on anything"[2]

Peck's account of "the most esoteric strain of twentieth-century literature" or "what some people think of as the highest of high canonical postmodernism" suggests that something went horribly wrong when the stylistic extravagance of modernism—an extravagance still tied to reference and empathy—decayed into a words-for-words'-sake postmodernism, which "turned the construction of a novel into a purely formal exercise, judged either by the inscrutable floribundity of its prose or the lifeless carpentry of its parts."[3] And so it was that the early twenty-first century declared a new open season on high postmodernism: Peck's attack would be reiterated in Jonathan Franzen's public airing of his agonized relationship with William Gaddis's work.[4]

But for all the heat of Peck's review, and notwithstanding the oddity of seeing these debates played out in the nation's magazines (Peck was writing in the *New Republic*, Franzen in the *New Yorker*), the reaction of many academic readers might have been nothing more than a slightly embarrassed yawn: at most, we simply note the minor differences between this moment and its original, as if we were watching a deferential Hollywood remake of a classic movie. After all, the most surprising thing about these early-twenty-first-century attacks on postmodern experimentation was not their novelty but their familiarity, their repetition of claims made about postmodern fiction in the 1960s, 1970s, and 1980s by the generation of scholars that included Gerald Graff, John Gardner, and Charles Newman.[5] And Ben Marcus's 2005 defense of experimentation, published as a lead essay in an issue of *Harper's* ("Why Experimental Fiction Threatens to Destroy Publishing, Jonathan Franzen, and Life as We Know It: A Correction"), could just as easily have been written by an updated John Barth or William Gass, valuing as it does the productive potential of difficult fiction for smart readers.

This enduring categorization of postwar fiction divides writers into those who are committed to mimesis and the representation of "real" people with "real" problems and those who are not. In this story, a body of aesthetically innovative work ("postmodernism" in the most restricted sense) is set against fiction committed to the reality of lived experience. Depending on the critic's commitments, "postmodernist" fiction becomes either powerfully world-making and ontologically rich or hopelessly narcissistic and autotelic, and the "realist" tradition either an expression of the possibilities of representation or evidence of imaginative failure.[6] And if we can now laugh at the rasher claims made by partisans on both sides—Gardner, for instance, wondering whether Pynchon and Barth, with their "intellectual blight, academic narrowness, or fakery," would still be read in the next century; Barth dismissing much fiction by women as nothing more than "secular news reports"—we are reminded by the debate in America's highbrow press of how little the fundamental categories have changed for a substantial number of readers: there is metafiction and there is realism, the making of other worlds or the committed representation of our own.[7]

This repetition of claims from earlier decades is surprising not least because a substantial body of work has built on Linda Hutcheon's assertion advanced over two decades ago in *A Poetics of Postmodernism* that much of what we have called postmodern fiction is actually seriously engaged in debating and representing recent history, albeit in far from straightforward ways. For Hutcheon, Fredric Jameson's account of the historical depthlessness of postmodern fiction looks untenable when one considers works such as E. L. Doctorow's *Ragtime* or D. M. Thomas's *The White Hotel*, manifestly antirealist novels whose complex narratives can scarcely be seen as uninterested in history or interested in history only as depoliticized pastiche or nostalgia. "Historiographic metafiction" is the influential term Hutcheon coined for this body of fiction when she saw in it not ahistorical or dehistoricized navel-gazing, but a serious engagement of what it means to write history: "Historiographic metafiction both underlines its existence as discourse and yet still posits a relation of reference (however problematic) to the historical world, both through its assertion of the social and institutional nature of all enunciative positions and through its grounding in the representational."[8] And while Hutcheon is perhaps guilty of a certain circularity—in order to prove the historical interests of literary postmodernism she suggests that literary postmodernism *is* historiographic metafiction, labeling as eminently "late modernist" the more extreme forms of metafiction so as to avoid having to account for them as putatively postmodern—her influential reading of postwar fiction has usefully attuned us to how complex the dialogue between narrative experimentation and historical reference is in this period, and has helped us to produce nuanced readings of those profoundly experimental texts that yet seek to represent historical events.[9]

Olive Branches

Despite their substantial disagreements about the ultimate political value of postmodern fiction, what Jameson and Hutcheon share is an idea that would surprise no reader of these texts: that postmodern fiction has, at the very least, a complicated relationship to history and historical representation. Hutcheon's critique of Jameson assuredly doesn't take the form of a rejection of textual difficulty or a belief that these texts straightforwardly represent historical events in the mode of the realist novel, nor is she out to recover some incidental content "exterior" to the narrative experimentation; rather, "what postmodernism does is to contest the very possibility of our ever being able to *know* the 'ultimate objects' of the past. It teaches and enacts the recognition of the fact that the social, historical, and existential 'reality' of the past is *discursive* reality when it is used as a referent of art" (24, italics in original). And while

Jameson and his followers have usefully advanced a historical account of his notion of a problem of historiography, seeing postmodern culture as what Jameson has called the "cultural logic of late capitalism" in which the depthlessness of that culture is a symptom of life in an era of finance capital, much work remains to be done on *historicizing* the complicated relationship between postmodern fiction—especially less obviously historiographic texts—and history. That is to say, somewhere behind Jameson's wholesale rejection of the idea that postmodern texts might be capable of representing history as anything other than depoliticized pastiche and Hutcheon's celebration of postmodernism's historiographic interests is a story waiting to be told about the historical pressures that led to this complicated relationship to history in the first place.

There is no doubt that fiction from the 1960s forward was taking into account revolutions in historiographic practice; indeed, the crisis that Moses Herzog faces in Saul Bellow's 1964 novel *Herzog*—although he needs to finish his book project, he is no longer sure of the historiographic underpinnings of his work—is revealed across the fiction of the period, which takes apart the idea of a positivist, linear, and teleological history (Pynchon's fiction, filled as it is with amateur historians, is here exemplary, as is DeLillo's *Libra*), and Hutcheon and Amy Elias have certainly developed nuanced accounts of how those revolutions showed up in postwar fiction.[10] But this is only half the story, I would argue, because it doesn't take into account a radical change in the collective understanding of historical *time*—especially a newly vexed relationship to futurity—distinctive to the period, and which posed difficult questions for narrative. By this I mean that the historiographic revolutions of the era surely challenged the idea of a unitary, fully knowable past, and revealed the problematic assumptions that undergirded history as a discipline, but accompanying them was the understanding of a new relationship to the *future*, a relationship conditioned by the Cold War's nuclear threat. That new relationship, I argue, was explored at length by the writers considered in this study.

On Endings thus participates in the recent and ongoing rethinking of what Amy Hungerford has called "the period formerly known as contemporary" by suggesting that the narrative experimentation of American postmodern fiction is an effect of, and, increasingly, an attempt to understand, life lived under the threat of total nuclear war: Postmodernist fiction is, in short, the literary symptom of new understandings of space and time produced by the nuclear age with which it coincided.[11] These texts reflect a paradigmatic change in understandings of historical time and finitude brought about by the invention and widespread deployment of atomic and then thermonuclear weapons.[12] Those weapons made newly possible—at least in the imagination—an ending at once secular and instantaneous, an ending so final that it would preclude any position from which it could retrospectively be represented. This unwitnessable fact of nuclear ending haunts these novels and leads, I argue, to their signature textual difficulties.

A central question drives this book: What does narrative look like when the possibility of an expansive future has been called into question? While fiction always, by virtue of having an end, might be said to reflect on finitude—a point usefully theorized in the work of Walter Benjamin and Peter Brooks—and while fears of the end of the world are scarcely restricted to post-Hiroshima culture, thermonuclear weapons, especially in the missile age, offer a radically new conception of what ending might mean.[13] As we shall see, the possibility of global thermonuclear war changed authors' conceptions of historical time, and it is this altered understanding of the future that I highlight in the pages that follow; these complex novels are attempts to imagine literary forms appropriate to new conceptions of temporality and historicity. While the presence of the Cold War and nuclear threat as a thematic interest in these texts, and in other texts from the period, has been amply noted—and would surprise few readers of, especially, Thomas Pynchon and Don DeLillo—the role that the bomb has played in *shaping* their experimentation has gone underexamined, and what follows is an attempt to correct that omission. Brian McHale is surely correct when he describes the shift from modernism to postmodernism as a shift in the dominant questions fiction asked: a modernist concern with epistemological questions morphs into a postmodernist concern with ontology, but the shift has a complex history, and understanding the dialogue these novels enact with the nuclear age and the Cold War historicizes changes in representations of reality and history.[14] Indeed, what is striking about this fiction is that it emerged simultaneously, as both McHale and Tony Jackson have pointed out, with a new concern in academic literary criticism with narrative as a subject; if the mid-1960s brought a host of experimental narratives, these years also elicited much scholarly work—in narratology and narrative theory—that made questions of narrativity central, and recovering the dialogue this fiction enacts with problems of nuclear representation thickens our understanding of these parallel developments.[15]

Perverse as it initially sounds, we might even designate postmodern fiction a form of realism, insofar as it tries to find models of representation adequate to the Cold War's changed understanding of historical time; what I argue here is not that experimental postmodern narrative thematically represents nuclear anxiety and nuclear threat—it surely does, as does much cultural production of the period—but that the changed relationship to futurity introduced by the bomb in part produces the complicated relationship to reference that these novels employ. Indeed, as I shall show, the "reality" of the nuclear referent was so complicated that even in those circles most committed to making it thinkable—the worlds of the Department of Defense and the think tanks it sponsored—representation took forms that suggest an affinity with experimental fictional narrative rather than with straightforwardly referential prose.

On Endings is thus part of the historicist turn in analysis of the postmodern. Both Hungerford and Wendy Steiner have argued that the dividing line between a multicultural canon committed to social justice and an experimental canon committed to aesthetic jouissance is untenable: the politically committed work of Kathy Acker, Toni Morrison, and Ishmael Reed is as formally inventive as anything produced by the supposed residents of Peck's Ivory Tower. And the corresponding idea that a "postmodernist" like Pynchon is primarily interested in narrative experimentation, and therefore categorically uninterested in history and politics, has begun to look even sillier than Pynchon's worst jokes. The historical distance we now have from the fiction produced in the second half of the twentieth century has made it possible to see the continuities of both style and subject across what once seemed diverse strains of American writing.[16] Mark McGurl's recent *The Program Era*, for instance, is able to tell an inclusive story of postwar American fiction that links high postmodernism, minimalism, and the multicultural canon by highlighting the central role played by the university—as sponsor, and sometimes setting—in the fiction of the period.[17]

The subject of this book is a tradition of writing whose commitment to formal innovation is axiomatic, and in my arguments about John Barth, Robert Coover, Thomas Pynchon, Donald Barthelme, Don DeLillo, David Foster Wallace, and Richard Powers I take for granted that there is a self-conscious and recursive tradition at work here that is still identifiable as a unique subcategory of the larger postwar literary field, identifiable through its self-consciousness and metafictive qualities (different only in degree rather than in kind from many other novels).[18] But this is not to say that its formal accomplishments make it more valuable than other canons or traditions. Now that much of what we still call "contemporary" fiction is no longer meaningfully contemporary, the work of literary history can properly begin, and aesthetic innovation can be seen as symptomatic of larger historical pressures. Although my hope is that this book will contribute to an ongoing conversation about the shape of postwar American fiction, it is useful to still consider this experimental tradition *as* a tradition for a little while longer—long enough, at least, for us to identify the historical provocations out of which this strand of postmodernity emerged. The limits of this inquiry are clear: the archive here is constituted of all white and all male authors. But this tradition has certainly been identified as a tradition since the 1960s, and to reveal the historical conditions out of which it emerged is, emphatically, not to endorse its exclusions.

The Present's Future

Jameson's formulation of postmodernism as a present unable to think of itself historically has been enormously influential, and has tended to produce readings that uncritically reiterate his claim that the concerns of postmodern fiction are primarily spatial, in keeping with an era of globalization and instantaneous communication.[19] Temporality, in contrast, is properly the domain of modernist scholars, working as they do on a body of fiction attuned to the elasticity of narrative and psychological time. But as Elias, Elizabeth Ermarth, Ursula Heise, and Mitchum Huehls have all demonstrated, much postmodern fiction also makes temporal experience important, and in the pages that follow I extend this project of making time central to postmodern culture by focusing attention on how the history of narrative experimentation is intertwined with the history of the nuclear age.[20] Indeed, the argument of this book reveals the substantial continuities between Hutcheon's account of the postmodern as eminently historicist and Jameson's account of its depthlessness. To pay full attention to the historical situation out of which these texts emerged is to realize that these two accounts are more related than we might otherwise have thought: in what follows I argue that the historiographic complexity of postmodern fiction is a representation of, and an attempt to come to terms with, a radically changed understanding of historical time that *potentially* makes historical consciousness impossible. I say "potentially" quite deliberately: the bomb, of course, hasn't been used in conflict since 1945, and the agonized torsion between reference and reflexivity that these novels record is in part the realization that time might, and hopefully will, go on well past our deaths, but that the human ability to record time's passage might also disappear so quickly that we could not even record its disappearance. Jameson's statement of the postmodern as "an attempt to think the present historically in an age that has forgotten how to think historically in the first place," the claim so comprehensively critiqued by Hutcheon, might usefully be rewritten: in my analysis of the texts that follow, texts central to most accepted literary histories of the postmodern, I uncover their own self-definitions as something like attempts to think the present historically in an age that has invented and deployed a technology that, if used, would make historical thinking impossible through its nearly instantaneous obliteration of the world.[21]

Albert Einstein famously remarked at the dawn of the atomic age that "the unleashed power of the atom has changed everything save our modes of thinking."[22] Early attempts to understand what kind of paradigm shift occurred in 1945 reflect this sense that everything had changed, but changed in ways that made it far from clear how this transformation might be represented and understood.[23] This book proposes that what we have come to call postmodern fiction was in fact part of the new mode of thinking for which Einstein called. In his Nobel Prize acceptance speech in 1950, William Faulkner argued that literature risked disappearing in the nuclear age: "Our tragedy today is a general and universal physical fear so long sustained by now that we can even bear it. There are no longer problems of the spirit. There is only the question: When will I be blown up? Because of this, the young man or woman writing today has forgotten the problems of the human heart in conflict with itself which alone can make good writing because only that is worth writing about, worth the agony and the sweat."[24] Faulkner's solution, to ignore the contemporary threat of mass death so as to return to matters of "the human heart," is assuredly not the tactic pursued by the generation of writers I discuss. And while they cannot be "good" according to Faulkner's definition of what is "worth writing about," they certainly look different when we recover their own meditations on the problems of life in the nuclear age.

Without Society or Spectacle

We can begin to understand the links between postmodern form and the nuclear age by looking at a short story that makes the connection between postmodern mediation and the nuclear its very subject. The British author J. G. Ballard's story "The Secret History of World War 3" (1988) illustrates perfectly some of the paradoxes of writing the history

INTRODUCTION / 9

of future war in the nuclear era by suggestively offering, only to retract, one of our most common understandings of postmodern culture.

An otherwise average suburban pediatrician, Ballard's narrator claims to be the only normal person who has noticed that World War Three has happened. In the aftermath of the Reagan years and the total failure of Reagan's unnamed successor, the world political situation has fallen apart: a second Iran-Iraq war, a new energy crisis, and near-revolution in the "Asiatic" Soviet republics all create a global state of emergency, and so the necessary constitutional amendment is passed to get Reagan elected in 1992 to a third term by a joyously optimistic American public. But Reagan's return to office does little to calm the world: the problems that have motivated his re-reelection prove stubbornly resistant even to his renewed presence on the political scene, and the Iran-Iraq war threatens to engulf Turkey and Afghanistan. Furthermore, the now-elderly president is showing signs of advancing senility when he appears in public. A stroke of marketing genius on the part of his handlers saves the situation: they have his doctors increase the frequency and detail of their reports on the president's health. After the first broadcast, which includes details of pulse, respiration, blood pressure, and white and red blood cell counts—in short, details typically relevant only in times of illness, and which are meaningless as raw data to an average person—the global political situation improves dramatically: Gorbachev reaches accords with Ukrainian separatists, interest rates fall, and the world's stock markets shoot through the roof.

Having seen the power of these reports, Reagan's staff starts issuing much more detailed updates (first weekly, then daily) on the president's health, and these updates carry the Republican Party to huge midterm congressional gains. Alongside this massive news interest in the president's health, however, political problems are deepening around the world, and especially along the Pakistani border, where treaty obligations threaten to pull the United States into war with the Soviet Union. But very few, if any, Americans notice, obsessed as they are with the health updates. At a particularly crucial moment, when tensions on the Pakistani border have reached the boiling point, the president's handlers decide on round-the-clock coverage:

> A curious pattern had appeared along the bottom of the screen, some kind of Christmas decoration, I assumed, a line of stylised holly leaves. The rhythmic wave stabbed softly from left to right,

> accompanied by the soothing and nostalgic strains of "White Christmas."
>
> "Good God . . . " Susan whispered in awe. "It's Ronnie's pulse. Did you hear the announcer? 'Transmitted live from the Heart of the Presidency.'"[25]

Not transmitted live from the heart of the president, but from the Heart of the Presidency. The transformation of the office into one coextensive with "Ronnie's" body has finally taken place, and Ballard suggests that this heartbeat is in excess of the particular heart that generates it. Needless to say, the updates continue until details of Reagan's health constitute almost the entire news agenda. When World War Three finally erupts, it is virtually squeezed out by a presidential cold contracted from a visiting grandchild. You can now imagine why Ballard's narrator is the only witness to the "event" of World War Three; everyone else is too wrapped up in the media spectacle of Reagan's health to notice.

Ballard's story could be assimilated into any number of narratives about postmodern culture. The era that produced the power to totally destroy itself has also developed the technology to anesthetize public awareness; this is so fully a society of the spectacle that representative democracy is now eclipsed entirely by representation in a quite different sense. Except that reading is wrong, and wrong because, much like the anesthetized viewers uncritically following TV events, it is a reading that takes the short story wholly at face value. Ballard so completely inhabits—and has so helped to create—our notions of the postmodern that to read him against the grain may seem odd, but we might begin by asking one very simple question: Why is this suburban pediatrician the only civilian who seems to notice that World War Three has happened? What marks him, makes him special? The answer: nothing really, except that he is hopelessly deluded:

> Now that World War 3 has safely ended, I feel free to comment on two remarkable aspects of the whole terrifying affair. The first is that this long-dreaded nuclear confrontation, which was widely expected to erase all life from our planet, in fact lasted barely four minutes. This will surprise many of those reading the present document, but World War 3 took place on 27 January 1995, between 6:47 and 6:51 p.m. Eastern Standard Time. The entire duration of hostilities, from President Reagan's formal declaration of war, to the launch of five sea-based nuclear missiles (three American and two

Russian), to the first peace-feelers and the armistice agreed by the President and Mr Gorbachev, lasted no more than 245 seconds.²⁶

We learn later that the missiles landed in uninhabited Alaska and Siberia. World War Three? The universal assumption that a third world war would inevitably involve the two global superpowers has here been converted by the narrator into the fallacious supposition that *any* conflict between those two superpowers is World War Three.

The insight that Ballard's story affords is that World War Three hasn't happened at all, and in fact could never happen within the confines of narrative. From almost the very moment when atomic weapons were first used in 1945, World War Three has named an imagined event that can never be recorded as an event because it would be the total war that could wipe out life altogether.²⁷ The final sentence of Ballard's opening paragraph is thus chilling for how right and wrong it simultaneously is: "World War 3 was over almost before anyone realised that it had begun."²⁸ Well, yes, of course in this case, but more importantly, World War Three as a proper name marks the event that is so sudden, so immediate, and so destructive that there is no time to give it the status of an event, which presupposes a time of reflection that could make it one. It will indeed be the war that is over before anyone realizes it has begun—an instantaneous and total moment of destruction that leaves no witnesses and no record. This "Secret History of World War 3" teaches us, in fact, that all histories of World War Three are secret, precisely because the historical agents that would be required to render the event historical—to witness, remember, and write that history—have already been annihilated by the "event" they would name. Thus, total thermonuclear war is simultaneously the event that we must collectively think about and the event we have no narrative means to engage. Its seriousness as an event is in conflict with the fact that it can't be accorded event status.

The problems Ballard associates with narrating world war in the nuclear age recall those raised by Jacques Derrida just four years earlier in his 1984 manifesto "No Apocalypse, Not Now (full speed ahead, seven missiles, seven missives)." Derrida begins his essay by asking whether the possibilities of war in the nuclear age are different by degree or by kind from previous imaginations of destruction. In answering that question, Derrida distinguishes between a war in which nuclear weapons have been or will be used, and what he terms "total" nuclear war, which, as "a fantasy, or phantasm, conditions every discourse and all strategies"; in Derrida's account, such a war can never occur and then be represented because it will be a war that leaves no witnesses, and hence no archives in which its occurrence will be documented.[29] Total nuclear war, in other words, *cannot* be apocalyptic ("apocalypse," of course, entails revelation or unveiling); rather, it is relentlessly anti-apocalyptic because it cannot promise a future from which its implications might be assessed. As James Berger usefully puts it, "The apocalyptic event, in order to be properly apocalyptic, must in its destructive moment clarify and illuminate the true nature of what has been brought to an end," and as a result that "end is never the end" because if it were, the apocalyptic event couldn't have brought clarity and illumination.[30] To be properly apocalyptic, then, a text must, in Berger's formulation, be postapocalyptic; this is the very possibility threatened by thermonuclear war, which could produce what Jonathan Schell in 1982 called "the death of death."[31] And so, for Derrida, fiction cannot ever be mimetically "about" total nuclear conflict, because no literature that takes seriously the possibility of total destruction could offer speculative postapocalyptic representations of life after nuclear war, which would require survivors to do the representing. In contrast, Derrida argues that only formally complex modernist works that test our notions of textual finitude, and make visible the possibility of ending without revelation, can engage the unthinkability of total nuclear war, even though, ironically, they predate the era in which it was possible.

The body of nuclear representation against which Ballard and Derrida are writing is best exemplified by John Hersey's *Hiroshima* (1946), a work that virtually defined early American literary responses to the nuclear age, and did so by trying to contain and describe the origins of the atomic age within preexisting literary forms. Robert Jay Lifton and Greg Mitchell have described its initial appearance as an issue of the *New Yorker* as "an immediate sensation," which sold out on newsstands, was reprinted numerous times, and was read out loud over the radio: "The mayor of Princeton, New Jersey, asked every citizen to read it," and many called "it the best reporting job of its time."[32] The book has gone on to have a long life as a staple of American high school and college syllabi, and, as Paul Boyer points out, "has always been rediscovered as a primary text" during periods of American nuclear anxiety.[33] *Hiroshima* is, in short, the ur-text for American nuclear writing, though, as we will see, this power potentially only obscures the threat posed by nuclear war.[34]

Before arriving in Hiroshima, Hersey had been reading Thornton Wilder's *The Bridge of San Luis Rey* (1927), the story of a bridge collapse in Peru that kills the five characters whose lives Wilder explores over the course of the novel. Hersey found in Wilder's format "a possible way of dealing with this very complex story of Hiroshima; to take a number of people—half a dozen, as it turned out in the end—whose paths crossed each other and came to this moment of shared disaster."[35] *Hiroshima*, then, is an attempt to represent the origin of the nuclear age via the resources of disaster fiction.

But Hersey's opening paragraph unwittingly reveals the limits of that chosen form when it mentions the equation needed to turn his six survivors into representative victims: "A hundred thousand people were killed by the atomic bomb, and these six were among the survivors. They still wonder why they lived when so many others died. Each of them counts many small items of chance or volition—a step taken in time, a decision to go indoors, catching one streetcar instead of the next—that spared him [sic]. And now each knows that in the act of survival he lived a dozen lives and saw more death than he ever thought he would see. At the time, none of them knew anything."[36] Although Hersey's text was widely praised upon its release, these kinds of substitutions (six survivors, who each lived a dozen lives, standing in for one hundred thousand dead) generated a vocal minority opinion. Witness, for example, Mary McCarthy's 1946 letter to *Politics*:

> What it did was to minimize the atom bomb by treating it as though it belonged to the familiar order of catastrophes—fires, floods, earthquakes—which we have always had with us, and which offer to the journalist, from Pliny down to Mr. Hersey, an unparalleled wealth of human interest stories, examples of the marvelous, and true-life narratives of incredible escapes.... But with Hiroshima, where the continuity of life was, for the first time, put into question, and by man, the existence of any survivors is an irrelevancy, and the interview with the survivors is an insipid falsification of the truth of atomic warfare. To have done the atom bomb justice, Mr. Hersey would have had to interview the dead.[37]

McCarthy's argument is also subject to the problem it identifies, because having realized that what was at stake was no less than "the continuity of life," McCarthy still anticipates a surviving journalist who might "interview the dead." All the same, McCarthy's objection to Hersey's survivor stories is prescient as well as astute: if redeploying the tropes of disaster fiction was already grotesquely inadequate to the devastation of Hiroshima (what Derrida would call a nuclear end to a conventional war), it would be less adequate still to the prospect of representing war between nuclear-armed superpowers. McCarthy is already writing about a potential next war, part of the substantial postwar reaction that immediately understood that these weapons would proliferate, and become more destructive.[38]

But even Hersey would come to see the limits of his formal choices in *Hiroshima*. The author who had once equated the death of one hundred thousand people with a bridge collapse would start to sound rather like Ballard or Derrida when he turned his attention decades later to the ongoing development of nuclear weapons. The final paragraph of the 1946 version of *Hiroshima* opens with the statement, "It would be impossible to say what horrors were embedded in the minds of the children who lived through the day of the bombing in Hiroshima." (90). But Hersey turned that statement into a question when, years later, he returned to the subject. The result was a new final chapter for *Hiroshima* prepared for the reissue of the work on the fortieth anniversary of the bombing.

In a persuasive and sophisticated reading of the 1946 version, Alan Nadel pays close attention to the techniques Hersey employed in order to narrate the details of the bombing to an American audience: "But the span between six dozen lives and innumerable deaths neither delimits adequately the subject nor makes it adequately representative, a point emphasized by Hersey's immediate need to distance his 'historical' perspective from his subjects' limited knowledge ('At the time none of them knew anything'). Because those limitations are circumscribed temporally and spacially, the representative authority of Hersey's text comes not from his witnesses but from his rhetorical position as omniscient narrator."[39] Nadel moves between focused narratological readings and their broad implications, finding in the work a continual tension between its journalism and its more literary qualities, and seeing the 1946 version as figuratively cracking under the pressure of trying to write history in the nuclear age. In his 1985 addition, Hersey would seem to make this explicit. The new final section adds a third layer to the movement between witness and narrator, by introducing as separate italicized sections the ongoing history of the nuclear age. One example: "*On February 13, 1960, France tested a nuclear weapon in the Sahara. On October 16, 1964, China carried out its first nuclear test, and on June 17, 1967, it exploded a hydrogen bomb*" (150). Here we encounter the limit of Hersey's position as narrator, the place where the bomb trumps even his ability to record it within the omniscient narrative voice that has dominated the text. The italicized sections present the key post-1945 events of proliferation: the Bikini Atoll tests; proliferation by the Soviet Union, Great Britain, France, China, and India; the development of hydrogen bombs by the

United States, the Soviet Union, Great Britain, and China; and the Lucky Dragon incident, in which Japanese fisherman were exposed to heavy doses of fallout from a distant bomb test.

The arithmetical maneuvers with which Hersey began are now impossible. If the six survivors, who each lived a dozen lives, can in no way account for the one hundred thousand dead, yet are Hersey's only way of capturing the story, then what kind of mathematics—and what form of narrative—could record the use of a weapon that was now up to several thousand times more powerful than the weapon used at Hiroshima, was stockpiled in the thousands, and was at the command of multiple world powers? This perhaps suggests why Hersey thought it necessary to mark these italicized sections as stylistically distinct from the narrative proper, as if the narrative form that *Hiroshima* previously took couldn't possibly deal with the reality of expansion and proliferation.[40]

If one narratologically interesting feature of the 1946 version of the text is the consistent incorporation of individual perspectives into Hersey's omniscient narration, now we have a reality—that of the weapon's historical evolution—that thwarts Hersey's position and ability to frame individual stories. This move forty years later suggests just how difficult it might be to find a perspective adequate to new possibilities of destruction. Hersey's 1985 additions can thus be read as both a defense of his original decisions and an acknowledgment of McCarthy's critique. For what stands out in McCarthy's letter is that she isn't talking about Hiroshima at all, but about what Hiroshima might come to mean: an event that marked the birth of an epoch that made possible a man-made and instantaneous global end. Hersey's refusal to frame the story of proliferation within the narrative voice of the 1946 text implies that even Hersey had come to see the limits of his formal choices, a point confirmed in a *Paris Review* interview granted by this notoriously reticent author on the publication of the revised version of *Hiroshima*. There he claimed that the problem of multiplication was central to his vision of the role of Hiroshima (and *Hiroshima*) in historical memory: "The demonstrations at Hiroshima and Nagasaki were so powerful that we have been able, so far, to extrapolate from them what it would be like to have a much bigger bomb dropped on a center of population. But if memory had been fully active, fully functional, we would long since have had some agreement on the use—or rather the non-use—of these weapons, some curbs on their manufacture and deployment. For some, the memory is certainly still there; but it seems to me very spotty in the centers of power. A Caspar Weinberger or a Richard Perle, it seems to me, must never have grasped the meaning of the Hiroshima bomb, the way they go on about a future with bigger and better nuclear weapons."[41]

Inadvertently, perhaps, *Hiroshima* might have been the problem, at least if we pursue McCarthy's line of attack; in his focus on survival, Hersey may have helped those who, like Weinberger and Perle, would see nuclear weapons on a continuum with other weapons, and containable in the way any "disaster" might once have been. But in refusing even to *try* to extrapolate from Hiroshima, Hersey reveals that whatever the power and failure of *Hiroshima*, we have now entered an era that rendered this historic document the history of an age definitively left behind; if in the future there were another Hiroshima, there could be no *Hiroshima*, however problematic, to record it. Nadel is certainly correct in seeing the 1946 version of *Hiroshima* as an "uncanny anticipation of postmodern writing," and the 1985 version suggests that Hersey would agree with Nadel's later assessment of his 1946 text.[42]

Collectively, then, Hersey and Ballard suggest that any fiction that tries to think seriously about the possibility of narrative in the thermonuclear age *must* be a form of metanarrative that reflects on the very possibility of narrating an event that would leave no narrator.[43] We might see a novel like Nevil Shute's *On the Beach* (1957) as a transitional text, one written in an era that understood the terrible destructive power of the weapons, but that could still imagine a temporary delay or lag in total destruction, at least in part because stockpile size had yet to swell to the capacity of massive overkill, and the weapons weren't yet capable of being deployed on operational ICBMs. After a nuclear war in the Northern Hemisphere, the novel imagines that parts of the world survive the initial exchange only to succumb inexorably and inevitably to fallout. In this respect, *On the Beach* is a postdisaster novel that nevertheless accepts the total destruction that the weapons would lead to even as it allows for the retrospection that makes narration possible. The story of "the short, bewildering war . . . the war of which no history had been written or ever would be written" can imagine a character reflecting on the impossibility of writing the history of that war because it is written on the cusp of the missile age (1957, the year of its publication, was also the year of the Sputnik launch).[44]

Claiming that texts that seek to represent total nuclear war must be experimental isn't to say, of course, that all metafictional texts are "about" World War Three, but only to suggest that a sustained attempt to answer the representational challenges posed by thermonuclear war, especially in the missile age, would have to take a metafictional form, and that this point goes some way toward explaining the increasing self-reflexivity of narrative in the period: the key texts of a metafictional and postmodern turn in American culture make just this move. Understanding the links they propose between history and narrative form means seeing postmodern fiction as a reflection of a culture that saw itself not as the prehistory of another age, but as contemporaneous with new technologies that might have made it a *last* age. The frequently remarked upon awkwardness of the term "postmodern" might not be so awkward after all, naming as it does an age that introduced the possibility of there being no future from which it might be reassessed; "postmodernism" introduces the possibility that it only comes after, never before.[45]

Writing World War Three

To identify the historical connection between postmodernism and the nuclear age is not to claim that critics have been uninterested in Cold War culture, or more specifically in how literature from the period represented possible nuclear war.[46] On the contrary, a substantial body of work has investigated the literary representations of fictional nuclear war and nuclear threat, and critics have addressed some of the more indirect ways in which life in the nuclear age influenced cultural production. Nadel's seminal *Containment Culture*, for instance, in describing how a political culture sought to police dissent, suggests that this was at least in part a response to the immense pressures of life in the atomic age. And, although some have noted the links between key concepts of postmodern theory and the atomic age, while others have acknowledged the spectral presence of the bomb in some of the key texts of American postmodern fiction,[47] much of the work on Cold War culture has bypassed the nuclear age, focusing instead on the domestic political phenomena of McCarthyism, containment, and the chastened culture of postwar liberalism.[48] Indeed, Cold War culture has become almost synonymous with containment or, even more narrowly, with McCarthyism and its aftermath. And because the metaphor of containment has proved so powerfully flexible, a backlash movement has suggested that the omnipresence of containment has resulted in a reductive view of the 1950s, and even of the entire Cold War epoch.[49]

Perhaps underlying these priorities—containment over the bomb, domestic over global questions—is the fact that, unlike McCarthyism, a thermonuclear war did not happen, at least not as conventionally understood.[50] And so much of the fiction directly imagining a thermonuclear war is relegated to the status of speculative or science fiction, with the associated loss of prestige that such genre designations always entail: Paul Brians's *Nuclear Holocausts: Atomic War in Fiction* lists nearly a thousand texts, though very few of them have even precanonical status. These are texts that by virtue of being representations of nuclear war and its aftermath never engage the problems I have been describing about narrating the unnarratable. That these texts have tended to cluster around the periods of most pronounced nuclear fear—the early years of the conflict, the Cuban Missile Crisis, the Reagan Years—makes for less than subtle understandings of the relationship between text and context.[51] Critics have thus largely followed Gertrude Stein's reaction to the bomb: asked what she thought about the weapons, she replied that she couldn't be interested in anything so powerfully destructive since there would be "nothing" and "nobody" left after their use.[52] But this claim, naming as it does a limit to thinking, has had any number of psychological effects, and the body of narrative I discuss in the chapters that follow reveals symptoms of an event that, properly speaking, could never produce symptoms (a temporal paradox I most fully engage in chapter 6).

The important exception to this very literal understanding of nuclear culture was the short-lived phenomenon of "nuclear criticism" that emerged during the Cold War's second phase in the 1980s, after the conference proceedings of a Cornell symposium (which included the Derrida essay discussed above) were reprinted in the journal *Diacritics*. In the introduction to that issue, the editor proposed that the work of nuclear criticism would be to understand how critics of discourse can intervene in policy debates, and also to uncover the presence of the nuclear in texts and contexts that don't initially seem to be directly about the bomb. But at the very moment when this work might have been expected to produce the series of monographs, collections, and essays that invariably follow the inauguration of a new theoretical paradigm, the Cold War came to an end. And while in retrospect it seems naïve to have assumed that the end of the Cold War meant the end of the nuclear age, work published in the early 1990s typically opened with passages of self-justification, defending itself against the perception of anachronism.[53] With the special urgency attendant on the threat of global total war now relaxed, and with a sense that the recent cultural past was still too present to be fully historicized, the expected insights of a nuclear-attuned cultural criticism were never fully realized. Paul Brians, for instance, announced in 1992 that he would be stepping down as editor of the short-lived *Nuclear Texts and Contexts*—a newsletter clearinghouse for critics working on the nuclear age—now that the pressures of the first atomic age had evaporated.[54] Yet the highly public debacle associated with the Smithsonian's 1995 retrospective exhibit on the atomic age suggested that though the era was history, the time was not yet right for it to be publicly discussed as such.[55]

Perhaps needless to say in 2011, the end of the Cold War scarcely resolved the ethical, political, and aesthetic problems raised by the nuclear age. Daily headlines announce the growing threats of proliferation, while intermittent tensions with a resurgent Russia have led some to talk of a new Cold War. But for the most part, the particular nuclear anxieties of the post–Cold War era don't take the form of anticipating planetary death; hence the terminology of a first and second nuclear age to distinguish our contemporary fear of nuclear terrorism from the fear of total thermonuclear war.[56] Likewise, Samuel Cohen has recently charted the historicist bent of much cultural production of the 1990s in relation not simply to millennial questions of retrospection but also to a lifting of the Cold War's distinctive form of nuclear threat; in his account, the gradual, though not total, disappearance of that state of emergency helped to produce a sustained interest in historical fiction.[57] We now have enough distance from the Cold War and its uniquely total threat of violence to begin to see its shaping cultural force; as Paul Boyer, the foremost cultural historian of the nuclear age, puts it, "As the Cold War recedes further into the past, the moment is opportune for those who lived through all or part of that stressful time to begin seriously the process of historical assessment—not just of the diplomacy of the Cold War, but of its social and cultural ramifications as well."[58]

On Endings demonstrates that the history of a tradition of self-reflexive postmodern fiction is intimately bound up with the Cold War's apprehension of global fragility, and that this fiction actively participates in the largest policy questions raised by the nuclear age. This is not a comprehensive study of the cultural effects of the nuclear age; rather, it is a history of a body of literature whose historical investigations remain in need of full historicization. Our distance on these texts, with our contemporary sense that the era of high postmodernism is now over, presents the opportunity to interrogate their historicity, and to begin to see how their commitment to new forms of time and narrative constitute responses to the history and politics of the Cold War.[59]

How this unrepresentable event produced the earliest visible examples of an American postmodern turn is the subject of the next chapter, which makes John Barth's career the test case for the emergence of metafiction. Barth argued forcefully across the 1960s for a model of fiction that downgraded topical reference and history in favor of aesthetic play, but in this chapter I turn to the later nonfiction in which he significantly revised his earlier statements; here I aim to reveal the enduring links between finitude and literary form across his career. The self-consciousness of his fiction is a result of an increasing uncertainty about the survival of authors, readers, and texts in the twentieth century. His evolution as an author is a response to global war in the century, and, tellingly, his emergence as a "fully" metafictional writer occurs in his novel most explicitly about the Cold War, *Giles Goat-Boy* (1966). We can explain that turn, however, by noting the extent to which Barth's earlier novels had already been concerned with the links between self-consciousness and twentieth-century warfare; this chapter reconstructs the complex dialogue between fictionality and finitude in Barth's *The Floating Opera* (1956) so as to show how we can contextualize postmodernism in relation to World War Three. Indeed, what is striking about Barth's early career is how tightly he linked questions of narrative style to global war.

Thomas Pynchon is perhaps the exemplary American postmodern author, and in chapter 2, I discuss his anomalously short novel *The Crying of Lot 49*, which was published the same year as *Giles Goat-Boy*. The year 1966 remains a plausible contender (though by no means an undisputed one!) for the moment in which postmodernism emerged as a recognizable cultural form, and these two novels were on its vanguard; understanding their nuclear referents helps to explain why that year might have been so important. *The Crying of Lot 49* has always posed a challenge for critics who are interested in Pynchon's larger interest in how history gets recorded, but I argue that the novel's less obviously historiographic interests are best read as a test of Pynchon's model of literary historiography in the face of world war in the missile age. The novel's famously frustrating denial of revelation should be read as a representation of an event that can never be viewed retrospectively, and the novel thus emerges as the text where Pynchon comes closest to writing a novel about an unnarratable future war, despite that his *Gravity's Rainbow* (1973) is far more explicit in its representation of the bomb.

The Crying of Lot 49 is a novel about the appeal and limits of the social: Oedipa Maas leaves the suburbs for the city, and over the course of the novel she realizes that the legacy bequeathed to her by Pierce Inverarity is America itself, an America with a diversity never visible from her former suburban vantage point. This Cold War public sphere, and its haunting by the possibility of total nuclear war, is the subject of chapter 3, in which I read Robert Coover's *The Public Burning* (1977) as an anatomy of the contradictions inherent in dominant versions of American national identity during the nuclear age. Long regarded as a postmodern classic for its carnivalesque, heavily metafictionalized, and encyclopedic account of the three days leading up to the execution of the Rosenbergs for pro-Soviet espionage in 1953, the novel would seem to engage politics and history only to render them thoroughly fictional: a befuddled Richard Nixon narrates much of the novel, which includes Uncle Sam as a principal character, and the novel's understanding of the violence done to the Rosenbergs comes dangerously close to being repeated rather than critiqued by the novel's metahistorical play. Through an examination of the novel's filmic intertext—the 1952 western *High Noon*—I argue that the novel represents a confrontation between a model of political community that makes future perfection central and an imagination of violence that makes such community impossible. The novel's status as an eminent example of historiographic metafiction is the result of this incoherence: at once committed to the concrete reality of historical experience and aware that our very model of historical time needed to be rethought, the novel uses metahistorical play to record this tension.

The next chapter looks at a series of works that literalize the frequently repeated charge that the most radical forms of metafiction are at best an elaborate game played at the expense of the reader. Here I turn to a series of texts—Donald Barthelme's "Game"; Robert Coover's *The Universal Baseball Association, Inc., J. Henry Waugh, Prop.*; and David Foster Wallace's *Infinite Jest*—that actively thematize the creation of parallel worlds through their stress on the self-constructed world of game playing. Rather than celebrate the world-making imagination, however, these texts all expose the limits of such self-constructed environments. "Game" and *The Universal Baseball Association* emerge in tandem, and, I argue, in dialogue with a new strategic culture of war-gaming in the 1960s that emphasized simulation and game playing as a means of understanding what might happen in a nuclear conflict. Since defense intellectuals had no history of nuclear conflict with a nuclear-armed enemy to draw on, war-gaming became an art form as committed to world-making as even the most experimental of fictions; the interplay of policy and fiction-making helps to make visible the political critique at the heart of fiction so often thought of as if it were as hermetically sealed off as the game spaces it supposedly celebrates. This chapter demonstrates that by the mid-1960s, nuclear strategy had itself entered the world of the truly fictional, and to engage it would require the resources of imaginative fiction.

No novelist is as committed to representing the overlaps between sport and nuclear war as Don DeLillo, and the perspective that his 1972 novel *End Zone* offers on his longer career is the subject of chapter 5. The story of a nuclear-war-obsessed football player, *End Zone* initially resembles an investigation of the overlaps in vocabulary between any two professional discourses; in this novel, the languages of nuclear strategy and football constitute elaborate and almost indistinguishable systems of professional jargon. Most readings have taken the novel's interest in the peculiar vocabulary of nuclear strategy as incidental to larger points the novel raises about reference and language in a hypermediated environment, and most readings bypass any extended analysis of the particularities of the analogy with which DeLillo is working. A close examination of the text, however, reveals DeLillo's interest in a very particular vision of football as a purely offensive game, and a parallel interest in a version of nuclear war in which defense is indefensible. These peculiarities help to position the novel in relation to the larger policy debates about the paradoxically destabilizing nature of defensive preparation that culminated in the "breakthrough" of the SALT 1 (Strategic Arms Limitation Talks) negotiations, the signing of the ABM (Anti-Ballistic Missile) treaty in 1972 (the year the novel was published), which made the world supposedly safer by limiting defensive antimissile missile shields. In other words, what at first seems the most ludicrously absurdist feature of DeLillo's novel may in fact be a nuanced interrogation of contemporary strategy and global politics.

Along with David Foster Wallace, Richard Powers is usually regarded as among the most significant heirs to the tradition I have been discussing, and my final chapter takes up the distinctive features of Powers's vision of late postmodernism, and reveals its links to the history of the nuclear age. Powers's *Prisoner's Dilemma* reveals that his distinctive aesthetic is an attempt to offer a therapeutic alternative to the realities of the nuclear age, and lets us see that Powers's longer career might be thought of as an attempt to produce alternatives to our dangerous propensity to accept too easily the world we live in. Sharply aware of the fact that literature makes nothing happen, Powers is equally aware that not telling stories means that we have given up hope in the future.

1 / Institutionalizing Postmodernism: John Barth and Modern War

Holding distinctly antagonistic visions of the nature of fiction during the different phases of his career, John Barth exemplifies the metafictional turn in American writing during the 1960s, and provides a perfect case study for understanding some of the social and political pressures that contributed to the emergence of this new aesthetic. Furthermore, Barth was the great institutionalizer of metafiction both within the American university (first at Buffalo, and then at Johns Hopkins) and for a larger reading audience, providing a public face— in lectures, journalism, and reviews—for what we would come to call the postmodern canon.[1] Yet, while Barth came to define a moment and a method, his critical statements have perhaps obscured some of the most interesting features of his fiction: his copious nonfiction has given his critics little room to maneuver with his novels and stories because it exhaustively explained and defended his work in ways that made contextual and referential readings difficult (even perverse); his reputation, as Amy Hungerford has noted, has suffered as a result, since in highlighting his own "creative" exploration of novelistic form he implicitly—and in some cases explicitly—downplayed the importance and achievement of writers committed to representing the social world.[2] It is the contention of this chapter, however, that we should understand Barth's career, and the larger question of the emergence of metafiction, in the light of the Cold War: that we can, in fact, read the history back into a movement that seemed—through spokespeople like Barth—to flaunt its purely formal and linguistic interests. As we shall see, even

Barth himself came retrospectively to realize how problematic some of his statements from the 1960s and 1970s can look.

Before he became the unofficial public advocate of postmodern fiction, Barth was the author of more traditional "serious" novels in the 1950s, and it is essential to return to this "apprentice" work if we seek to historicize the turn to metafiction. Self-conscious narratives though these early novels are, they are hardly the elaborate imaginative exercises that have come to define Barth as an exemplary metafictionist. *The Floating Opera* (1956), Barth's first novel, is heavily influenced by the existential mood of the 1950s, and I want to show in this chapter how highlighting the relationship it posits between finitude and literary form makes it possible to historicize and politicize Barth's more playful later fiction. Barth is interested in periodizing the twentieth century in relation to global conflict, and his early work reveals the links between history and narrative self-consciousness in ways that help to indicate the Cold War content of his later metafictional forms.

In a political reading of Barth's later *Sabbatical*, Allan Hepburn notes that "most critics read Barth's fiction for its formal high jinks at the expense of reading its political subtexts";[3] and this tendency has had especially pronounced effects on how the early fiction is understood. Barth's first two novels—*The Floating Opera* and *The End of the Road* (1958)—tend to get isolated as early efforts of interest only to the extent that they anticipate formally the later novels usually considered Barth's most distinctive and distinguished work (and even this is debatable; for some critics and reviewers they are simply apprentice pieces, not even worthy of such qualified interest). In his recovery of the social vision of the early novels, Thomas Hill Schaub suggests that the dominant critical trend has been to read Barth backward, and in so doing erase the political even in those novels that retain or display a commitment to relatively straightforward reference: "In fact, since the publication of the experimental stories in *Lost in the Funhouse* (1968) and *Chimera* (1972), critics have tended to read Barth's first novels entirely outside of or disentangled from their social and historical moment, and find in them the origins of his later 'metafiction' and postmodern experimentation."[4] Schaub presents two options: either we read the early texts as the origin of the later metafiction, or we read them inside their social and historical moment; a third possibility, though, would be to combine the two, reading them within their historical moment in order to find in that historical moment the origins of Barth's move to metafiction.[5] In so doing, I engage what I take to be the implicit claim made in Schaub's account of the critical history: that readings of the early texts through the perspective offered by the metafictional "achievements" of the later ones erase the political precisely because those later texts don't seem to have a political or social point; the early novels "produce" the later ones in that they prefigure the interest in pure fiction-making, displaying in miniature some of the features of Barth's later work even though they seem on the surface to be largely realist texts. At the risk of sounding perverse, I would entirely reverse Schaub's equation: by understanding the metafictional qualities of the early novels—especially the ways in which they link history and fiction—and in seeing how they anticipate the later work, we can begin to see the political vision at the heart of the more explicitly metafictional novels. Only by seeing the metafictional impulses in his more realistic work can we see the burden of history in Barth's metafictions.

On with the Story

Part of the problem is that Barth has been so forcefully schematic in establishing binaries that divide his early fiction from his later work, realism from metafiction, and politics from art. Perhaps the most programmatic example of this tendency is his famous essay "The Literature of Exhaustion" in which Barth argued for the refashioning of fiction as the only way to replenish the depleted form of the novel. But even a reader familiar only with Barth's fictional works would be aware of Barth's own account of his career during the 1960s. For instance, the 1967 preface to the revised and combined edition—revised to restore them to their original darker endings, after *Giles Goat-Boy* had established Barth as the foremost "fabulator" of his generation—of *The Floating Opera* and *The End of the Road*, gives us a ready-made template for understanding Barth: "Is your muse the lady with the grin or the one with the grimace? Are you a realist or a fantast? Ought you to make your art for its own sake or engage it in the service of some lofty cause? Are you more interested in the thing said than in its saying (the Windex approach to language) or vice-versa (the stained-glass approach)?"[6] Barth goes on in his foreword to suggest that his early works come down on one side of this divide and his later on the other, and his other critical writings from the mid-1960s only confirm this metafictionist conversion narrative. In his "Muse, Spare Me" (1965), for instance, Barth announces that he has now entered a new phase: "In any case, the image I'm lately fonder of—the aptest, sweetest, hauntingest, hopefullest I know for the storyteller—is Scheherazade."[7] Crucially this version of Scheherazade ignores the fact that her storytelling is primarily a way to ward off her own death, and those of her women compatriots, at the hands of a tyrant king: what Barth values in the *Arabian Nights* (even though he is clearly aware of the frame tale) is the purely artistic rather than the social or political meaning of aesthetic production: "But I say, Muse, spare me (at the desk, I mean) from social-historical responsibility, and in the last analysis from every other kind as well, except artistic."[8]

When read according to Barth's insistent prompts from the 1960s, it is quite easy to ignore the tensions in the 1987 preface to Barth's extraordinarily playful *Giles Goat-Boy* (1966), a novel that Barth designated the first of his fully fabulatory projects. This is how he narrates his revolution/conversion: "By 1960 I had completed what I regarded as a loose trilogy of novels—*The Floating Opera*, *The End of the Road*, and *The Sot-Weed Factor*—and I felt, particularly in course of writing that extravagant third item, that I had put something behind me and moved into new narrative country. Just what that movement was, I couldn't quite have said; today it might be described as the passage made by a number of American writers from the Black Humor of the Fifties to the Fabulism of the Sixties." This story of an escape from parodic reference into "fabulism" accompanies, however, Barth's interest in the most pressing features of contemporary experience, since *Giles Goat-Boy* is so obviously an allegory of the Cold War. Even as Barth seemed to be disavowing the "Windex" approach to language, he was producing the novel that most directly engaged the history of its present. Indeed, alongside his much longer accounts of the aesthetic and personal origins of the novel, Barth offered the following in his new 1987 introduction, where, if only in retrospect, his plea to his muse seems somewhat more complicated than the earlier disavowal of social responsibility in favor of aesthetic bliss: "At the end of 'the Fifties' the Cold War was chilly indeed: Both the U.S. and U.S.S.R. by then had operational hydrogen bombs, intercontinental ballistic missiles, and nuclear submarines. The successful Sputnik launch of 1957 had triggered both the 'space race' and an epidemic of academic gigantism in the U.S.: a massive effort to 'catch up,' fueled by an inpouring of federal money that would fertilize the groves of Academe right through the Sixties. And the Cuban missile crisis of 1962—another reasonable benchmark for the change of decades—had brought home to many, as the atmospheric testing of thermonuclear weapons had not, the specter of apocalypse."[9] Paradoxically, the rejection of topical reference accompanies a deep interest in it. These passages from Barth's 1987 preface imagine two paradigm shifts—one is aesthetic, the other military—separating *Giles Goat-Boy* from Barth's earlier novels. In what follows I explicate the relationship between these two shifts.

"More Than a Little Overwrought, and Too-Clever by Half"

The massive influence of Barth's own critical statements from the 1960s about the primacy of aesthetic production for its own sake can be felt in the extraordinary critical obliviousness to the central conceit of *Giles Goat-Boy*: that it is an unmistakable, albeit comedic, allegorical portrayal of the Cold War.[10] George Giles, who has been raised as a goat by a disgraced, and now pacifist former weapons scientist named Max Spielman (a Robert Oppenheimer clone) comes to learn that he is human, and quite possibly the child of WESCAC, the massive computer system that keeps in operation the west campus of a university that stands in for the universe. Giles understands that in a world where no one can graduate anymore (that is, no one can move on to a new future, or even really escape campus), he must end the border dispute between west and east campus fueling the post–Campus Riot II era of "Quiet Riot," and prevent the computers that now run the campus/world from EATing (annihilating) everyone. Many key 1960s American politicians and defense intellectuals are represented in the text; an electric boundary fence between campuses mimics the Berlin Wall; and proxy wars and spheres of influence are represented when New Tammany College (the America of west campus) worries about the reactions of T'ang College (Asia) and Frumentia College (Africa).

However, critics have represented this aspect of the novel as at best incidental, or subservient to the "real" point of the book. The historical allusion is "quite superficial," Robert Scholes wrote in 1967: "It functions merely to remind us that this is *not* a literal transcript of Reality."[11] Thus Scholes transforms the novel's referential content into a kind of radical antireferentiality: the historical allegory works, in his account, to remind us that this isn't in fact history—an odd argument in itself, and strikingly odd in view of the elaborate lengths to which Barth goes in order to establish and maintain that Cold War allegory over the course of the novel. Readings of the novel have conventionally emphasized its use of archetypes of the hero and the quest narrative; somewhat inevitably these also tend to treat the allegorized 1960s setting as irrelevant.[12]

To point out that the novel allegorizes its immediate present is not to minimize its exuberant fabulation: The central character thinks he is a goat, after all; the novel is built on the exorbitant conceit of a university as the universe; and the novel is encountered through an elaborate series of prefaces that call into question the authorship and ontological status of the text we are about to read. In short, the novel is a textbook example of what Brian McHale has called the "dominant" of the postmodern, namely the ontological questions raised by a novel that actively asks us to consider its own status as text. And reading the novel alongside Barth's contemporary nonfiction, it is certainly tempting to follow Scholes in seeing the real-world content of the novel as beside the point. But what if we take Barth's 1987 preface seriously? What if literary transformations are, as Barth came to suspect, related to military ones?

In a new (1984) preface to that old classic "The Literature of Exhaustion" in *The Friday Book*, Barth wrote that he could now smell the tear gas of campus unrest in the margins of the essay. This acknowledgment clearly anticipates the 1987 preface to *Giles Goat-Boy*, where he linked the intensification of the Cold War, and especially the arrival of new weapon delivery systems with another way of seeing the division between his early and later work. I've quoted Barth's "Muse, Spare Me" already, but it is worth returning to this 1965 essay, because his revisions to it reveal a growing self-consciousness about the historicity of metafiction. Barth had been commissioned to write a short piece on the black humorists of the 1950s and 1960s, and he began by condescendingly distancing himself from their interest in contemporary life: "I beseech the Muse to keep me from ever becoming a Black Humorist. Mind, I don't object to Black Humorists, in their place; but to be numbered with them inspires me to a kind of spiritual White Backlash. For one thing, they are in their way *responsible*, like more conventional social satirists: They dramatize— and good for them!—the Madness of Contemporary Society, of Modern Warfare, of Life With the Bomb, of What We Have Nowadays.... I'm not impressed by the apocalyptic character of the present age."[13] When Barth returned to the essay in *The Friday Book* nineteen years later, it was with embarrassment: "For the posturing in my first paragraph—'I'm not impressed by the apocalyptic character of the present age . . .'—I apologize. If I ever wasn't, I have certainly become so."[14] What Barth sees when he revisits his 1960s writing is the connection between the then-trumpeted aesthetic break with contemporary politics and the specific problems caused by the Cold War, perhaps now highlighted for him by the visibility of nuclear threat in the Reagan era. Barth can now see something resembling an unconscious in those texts; symptoms of an age he had yet to fully integrate into his conscious writing mind can now be seen as such.

Fiction and the Figures of Death

To say that Barth's fiction flirts with destruction is to state the obvious: the title of his second novel, is, of all things *The End of the Road*; *The Floating Opera* ends with a narrowly avoided explosion that would have killed several hundred; the threat of total annihilation hangs over the university in *Giles Goat-Boy*; and his later Chesapeake Bay fictions are set against a backdrop of Cold War espionage and the national security state. For most readers of Barth, however, the horizon of apocalypse in Barth's world has seemed primarily an aesthetic matter: how, in the face of the used-up quality of traditional fictions, do we invent the novel anew? What forms of ending are appropriate to this new aesthetic? How do we avoid the sedative traps of closure?[15] Such questions have tended to erase the specificity and historicity of his novels' treatment of endings. Yet *The Floating Opera* is nothing less than an accelerated *history* of finitude in the twentieth century: its narrator and protagonist, Todd Andrews, is born in 1900, and his life is in many ways an allegory of twentieth-century life (and death). And this history of the possibility of death is also a history of the literary techniques appropriate to the forms that death has taken in the century of world wars.

Todd Andrews's virtuoso experiments in genre and form engage the problems of communication and audience raised by modern mass death. World War One makes visible the contingency of modern life, and World War Two a new indistinction of civilian and soldier that requires a new critical relationship to narrativity and to audience. In this representation of the changes in literary technique caused by modern war, *The Floating Opera* contains within itself a miniature version of the split in Barth's career that I outlined at the beginning of this chapter. The difference in kind between Barth's early fiction and his metafiction is already registered as a difference of degree in his first novel, and this difference helps us read Barth's longer career; this first novel suggests how we might align the story of Barth's aesthetic transformation from black humorist to fabulist with the story of how modern war was transformed in the nuclear age.

As critics who have linked this novel to Barth's later fiction have pointed out, *The Floating Opera* has a fairly complex structure. It is narrated by Todd Andrews in 1954, and describes a day (either June 21 or 22) in 1937 on which Andrews decides to kill himself and then changes his mind. Since 1938, Andrews has been determined to recount the events of that day, but has managed to do so only now in 1954. In a further temporal deferral, the 1937 decision is the direct result of his learning in 1919 that he could die at any moment of a heart attack. The result, as Charles B. Harris argues, is that properly there are two Todd Andrews in the novel: "Todd the *character*, the 'pre-1937' Todd, whose various masks and activities are directed 'inward' toward the other characters and incidents in the novel; and Todd the *author*, the post-1937 Todd whose activities as narrator are directed 'outward' toward his audience."[16] The Todd Andrews who narrates the novel is radically different from the 1937 Todd Andrews about whom he writes.

Brian McHale has suggestively described *The Floating Opera* as a late-modernist text, by which he means that it combines epistemological and ontological concerns.[17] This understanding of the text as formally at the crossroads of modernist and postmodernist aesthetics can be usefully combined with Harris's understandings of two Todds: to combine them we might say that the "pre-1937" Todd Andrews is primarily concerned with epistemological questions, while the post-1937 Todd Andrews, the Todd who narrates the novel, has seen the limits of epistemology as a means for understanding experience, and as he tries to narrate his own story he increasingly turns toward those questions of ontology associated with the nature of textuality and fiction.

As we shall see, these two version of Todd Andrews have very different relationships to death, and thus to writing. In both cases, death is central, and centrally connected to issues of narrative self-consciousness: early in the novel the narrator explains that he is living on borrowed time because of his "subacute bacteriological endocarditis," which leads to a high risk of heart attack: "any day I may fall quickly dead, without warning—perhaps before I complete this sentence, perhaps twenty years from now. I've known this since 1919: thirty-five years (5). Hence his elaborately stylized relationship to finitude; for instance, he pays his hotel bill daily rather than weekly or monthly, as a way of dramatizing his mortality, and makes much of the fact that any sentence or sip of water might be his last. Indeed, it would seem that mortality is central to his very being, though in ways that suggest there are yet another two Tod/d/s:

> So. Todd Andrews is my name. You can spell it with one or two *d*'s; I get letters addressed either way. I almost warned you against the single-*d* spelling, for fear you'd say, "*Tod* is German for death: perhaps the name is symbolic." I myself use two *d*'s, partly in order to avoid that symbolism. But you see, I ended by not warning you at

all, and that's because it just occurred to me that the double-*d Todd* is symbolic, too, and accurately so. *Tod* is death, and this book hasn't much to do with death; *Todd* is almost *Tod*—that is, almost death—and this book, if it gets written, has very much to do with almost-death. (3, italics in original)

While Todd Andrews has known for thirty-five years that he might drop dead at any moment, and death's proximity is built into his very name, the fact of death has had vastly different implications for him in his two (pre- and post-1937) periods. The distinction between these two Todds is at least obliquely a distinction between two larger cultural imaginations of death, and in charting this distinction interior to *The Floating Opera*, we begin to see why the emergence of new delivery technologies for nuclear weapons might make such a difference, and why they might act as a dividing line between Barth's early fiction and his more "mature" metafiction.

Andrews comes of age in the First World War. He enlists in 1917, and figuratively enters adulthood in the service: the one battle he fights in is the Argonne offensive of 1918, the year he turns eighteen. And while we might expect that his attitude toward death is fundamentally shaped by that engagement, at first it seems only incidental. Although it is an army doctor who examines him after he passes out on a parade ground, his peculiar problem—the fact that at any moment he might drop dead—seems ironically divorced from conflict, even as the peculiar temporality he continues to live under is that of a combatant.

Intriguingly, Lois Parkinson Zamora has argued that Andrews's supposed illness is an elaborate self-fashioning, a fiction, and that he is at once "a paradigm of the apocalyptic situation of the storyteller and a parody of it."[18] Zamora cites the fact that he has never bothered, in the intervening thirty-five years, to have the diagnosis confirmed (indeed, he has avoided doctors), and suggests that he has built an elaborate system in which he can enjoy his supposed imminent death, because it "justifies his good-humored solipsism and allows him his detached perspective."[19] Though Zamora makes the point only as an aside, there is substantial textual evidence to support her claim. The Missouri-born doctor who diagnoses Andrews is marked as a simpleton, as the phonetic rendering of "his very words" makes clear: "Ah sweah, Cawpr'l, if that isn't endocahditis yew got! How in the heyell did yew git in the Ahmy, boy? Yew too young to have a haht attack, now ahn't yew?" (126). Despite that the diagnosis appears to call into question the quality of army medical care, given that this supposedly obvious diagnosis was missed at enlistment, Andrews makes it the central fact of his life. One reason why he might do this is that it helps him to deal with his traumatic relationship to the war.

Although Andrews claims that his "Army career was largely without influence on the rest of my life" except for "a single incident," his account of that single incident clearly invites psychological diagnosis (61). He enters the Argonne battle when it is in full swing, and his outfit is sent in to replace an annihilated rifle company. Thirty-six years later, his account of a day and night spent in battle is a coherent narrative of a fundamentally incoherent event, and is punctuated with gaps of time and space. At one point he finds himself alone in a foxhole, where he first experiences "real fear": "It swept over me in shuddering waves from my thighs and buttocks to my shoulders and jaws and back again, one shock after another, exactly as though rolls of flesh were undulating. There was no cowardice involved; in fact, my mind wasn't engaged at all—either I was thinking of something else or, more probably, I was just stupefied. Cowardice involves choice, but fear is independent of choice" (62–63). In this moment, Andrews is reduced to a singularly physical presence devoid of cognitive and motor function. As he comes out of this state he realizes he is in the middle of a hellacious battle, and will surely die. Only one thing offers him some solace: "There was no question in my mind but that I'd be killed; what I feared was the knowledge that my dying could very well be protracted and painful, and that it must be suffered alone. The only thing I was able to wish for was someone to keep me company while I went through with it" (64). Andrews gets his wish when a German soldier jumps into his foxhole. After some brief tussling he pins the German, and nicks his neck with a bayonet, before convincing him that he bears him no ill will, and they become momentary friends. As Tom Engelhardt has noted, this scene is a recurrent feature of cinematic treatments of World War One, a way of asserting both the moral superiority of American forces as well as the universal humanism that might link allies and enemies.[20]

But Andrews is plagued by doubt as to the trustworthiness of his former enemy, and offers an early account of the cracks in what Engelhardt has called America's "Victory Culture." After spending the night in the foxhole, he kills the German soldier in the morning by bayoneting him in the neck, and his (non)-memory of the event suggests how profoundly the war may have affected him: "Of the noises in my life, one of the loudest in my memory is the tiny popping puncture of my bayonet in the German sergeant's neck—that sergeant with whom I choose to think my soul had lain for a while. Were I ever so foolish as to try, I'm sure I could close my eyes and hear that puncture as distinctly now as I heard it then, and the soft slide of my metal into his throat" (126). The distinction between the noise of the memory and the actual ("tiny popping puncture") suggests a process of traumatic amplification. And this helps to explain his own commitment to his purported illness; this is his reaction to the diagnosis: "Can you understand at once—I neither can nor will explain it—that I was relieved? To say that the puncture had deranged me would be too crude, but—well, I was relieved, that's all, to learn that every minute I lived might be my last" (127). The suggestion that the diagnosis is less a disaster and more what Andrews needs contextualizes both the form of his self-fashioning between 1919 and 1937 and his imagination of writing during the period. If at its most surreal his killing of the German soldier is represented as a union ("the soft slide of my metal into his throat") between Andrews and the German soldier, in which Andrews kills the German only as he is joined with him in a sexualized encounter, in the wake of the war Andrews imagines he can become a witness to his own death-in-life. Above all else, his attitude toward himself from 1919 to 1937 is theatrical:

> I had been a not-very-extraordinary boy; then one day in 1919 while standing retreat I collapsed on the parade grounds at Fort Meade, Dr. Frisbee looked up from his stethoscope, and I began to eat, drink, and be merry at Johns Hopkins—my first mask. In 1924 Betty June Gunter slashed me with a broken bottle, a man named Cozy rabbit-punched me and threw me out of a Calvert Street brothel, Marvin Rose found a wicked infection in my prostate, and I became a saint—my second mask. In 1930 my father, with whom (thinking my saintliness was bringing on maturity) I had thought I was beginning to communicate, *inexplicably* hanged himself; I took the belt from his neck, mailed my legacy to Col. Morton, and became a cynic—my third mask. And each time, it did not take me long to come to believe that my current attitude was not only best for me, because it put me on some kind of terms with my heart, but best in itself, absolutely. (223–24, italics in original)

While this account suggests that Andrews understands selfhood as performance (his "masks"), it also suggests that Andrews can imagine himself as an observer of his own performances, and that this observational distance on himself can help him deal with his own finitude (since the masks help him to relate to his heart). His relationship to his own death is as close as he can get to witnessing what is unwitnessable. Furthermore he can avoid coming to terms with what he has done to the German soldier by replacing that German soldier with himself; in a sense, he stands as a witness not to an act he has committed but to an act done to him. In short, his primary psychological issues here are epistemological: Is the mask or persona I've crafted adequate? Will someone survive me, and witness my suffering? What are the terms on which I can achieve some form of psychological distance on myself?

Not surprisingly, the writing project with which this younger Todd Andrews is engaged before 1937 is one that foregrounds epistemological questions about our knowledge of each other. Todd's father loses nearly everything in the stock market crash of 1929, and on February 2, 1930, Todd returns from the office to find that his father has hanged himself in the basement. This is the event that makes Todd a writer. The telling title of his work (*Inquiry*) makes clear its epistemological concerns: "The full title of the *Inquiry*, if it ever should reach the stage of completion where a title would be appropriate, will be *An Inquiry into the Circumstances Surrounding the Self-Destruction of Thomas T. Andrews, of Cambridge, Maryland, on Ground-Hog Day, 1930 (More Especially into the Causes Therefor)*, or something of the sort. It is an attempt to learn why my father hanged himself, no more" (217–18). While Todd knows from his reading of David Hume (and his project clearly echoes Hume's *An Enquiry Concerning Human Understanding*) that at best he can posit only conjunction rather than strict causation, his understanding of his project still makes knowledge central, even as it understands that causation will be impossible to prove: "It's the purpose of my *Inquiry* to shorten as much as is humanly possible the distance over which I must leap; to gather every scrap of information that a human being might gather concerning the circumstances of my father's suicide" (218). Andrews becomes the consummate researcher: he reads books his father has read; scrutinizes economic theory, contemporary newspaper articles, and bank statements; interviews friends of his deceased father; and fills boxes with notes. And while this project really has no end, the measure of its success will be how plausibly it turns facts into explanation.

1937

Andrews changes dramatically in 1937. We learn early in the novel that the system of masks he has used to distance himself from himself since 1919 has become increasingly inadequate:

> Be content, if you please, with understanding that during several years prior to 1937 I had employed a stance that, I thought, represented a real and permanent solution to my problem; that during the first half of 1937 that stance had been losing its effectiveness; that during the night of June 20, the night before the day of my story, I became totally and forcibly aware of its inadequacy—I was, in fact, back where I'd started in 1919; and that, finally and miraculously, after no more than an hour's predawn sleep, I awoke, splashed cold water on my face, and realized that I had the real, the final, the unassailable answer; the last possible word; the stance to end all stances.... *Suicide!* (16, italics in original)

The novel thus recounts the day on which Andrews has determined to kill himself and subsequently decides that death has no more meaning than life, and thus is no better a solution than continuing to live.

But why 1937? What is it about a summer day in that year that leads Todd Andrews to embrace and then almost immediately reject the existentialist position that death, and especially the individual's control over his or her own death, might make life meaningful again? In fact, it was in that very year that Andrews's carefully crafted exceptional relationship to death could become something like the rule, and the fantasy of death as a theatrical event witnessed by others began to unravel in the face of the realization of what future wars would be like. At the heart of the novel is an elaborate legal case (there are seventeen distinct wills in question) concerning the estate of Harrison Mack Senior, and Todd Andrews has been retained by his friend Harrison Mack Junior to argue that he, rather than his mother, deserves to be the sole inheritor of the Mack pickle fortune. The case has much to tell us about the novel, as it has everything to do with the ability of one's writing, in this case a will, to survive one's own death and have an impact on the world, and about how complex and digressive forms of textuality might intersect with political history. But, most importantly, the case is an examination of the legacy of leftist sympathy and the unfortunate consequences of youthful idealism.

Previously a communist, Harrison Mack Junior finds that his entire future hinges on his ability to distance himself from his former beliefs: his father has specified (in most of the wills) that his son must have displayed no such sympathy between 1932 and 1937 in order to inherit anything (his widow's potential claim is also conditional: absurdly, she must have consumed no sparkling burgundy since 1920). After an elaborate series of parries and motions a judge is set to assert that will #8, which gives everything to Harrison Mack Junior provided he has done no fellow-travelling since 1932, shall be the binding will and testament. In the closing moments of the hearing his mother's attorney produces "evidence" against him when he reveals that Harrison Mack Junior has been a regular contributor to the Spanish Loyalist cause in its fight against Fascism; he is "a blue blood with a Red heart" (94).

The rise of Fascism is mentioned repeatedly over the course of the novel, principally with regard to the Mack family's plan to spend a year in Mussolini's Italy. And while the novel never directly represents the coming world war, Andrews finds himself curiously gripped by what is occurring in Spain, as when he listens raptly to a local shop owner's account of the future of Europe: "'Well, I doubt it'll go good for the Loyalists,' he declared. 'They've been holding their own lately, but it can't keep up. They've got the Russians, but Mr. Franco, he's got the Germans, and like it or not, the German's a better soldier than the Russian is'" (150). Asked if he thinks that Franco has the battle won, the shop owner suggests that the crucial question is really only whether Franco can wind up the Civil War before global war itself descends on everyone ("By that time the whole shebang might blow") (151). And it is just such a fear that recurs in the novel, a feeling that total war is about to arrive in Europe; Harrison Mack Junior, for instance, wants to live in Italy for a year "while there's still time" since he suspects "things are going to blow up over there sooner or later" (208).

I'd suggest that what interests Andrews in the "whole shebang" blowing up is how he might imagine this coming war in relation to the war through which he has already lived, and which has structured his life from 1919 to 1937. For what 1937 had demonstrated in Spain was that the carefully contrived distance that Andrews has maintained both on his own death and the death that he has caused will necessarily fall apart, and that future wars will not be describable in theatrical metaphors. Destroying an admittedly fragile, given previous conflicts, dividing line between soldier and civilian, the bombing of Guernica inaugurated a new culture of aerial warfare. The fact with which Todd Andrews has lived for so long, and which has supplied, in its lack of meaning, a paradoxical meaning for his life, is no longer the exception but the rule. It would be hyperbolic indeed to suggest that World War Two made everyone into Tod(d)s, but by 1937 it was common knowledge that the "theater" of war would now include the home front, at least in Europe and Asia, and that the convention of a demarcated battlefield or "front" would no longer separate audience from action.

Although it had famously been conceded as early as 1932 that the bombers would always get through in a future war, the destruction of the Basque town of Guernica by the German Condor Legion was the first large-scale demonstration of the terrifying new vulnerability of the civilian in the era of air power.[21] In his seminal *The Great War and Modern Memory*, Paul Fussell argues that one of the features that gave the Great War its "special freight of irony" was the "ridiculous proximity of the trenches to home," and he cites the example of an officer who breakfasted in the trenches yet had dinner in his private club in London.[22] The "absurdly near" quality of England wouldn't look so much absurd as tragic after 1937, when it became obvious to the public that the private club—and, indeed, the public itself—could in fact become a target. As Ian Patterson has argued in his chilling *Guernica and Total War*: "One of the most fearsome ideas to emerge in the course of the twentieth century was the idea of total war—the belief that the most effective way of winning wars was by the obliteration, or the threat of obliteration, of the civilian population of the enemy's town and cities by means of an annihilating attack from the air. The first, and still in some ways the most striking, demonstration that this could be done came in April 1937, when the ancient Basque town of Guernica was almost completely destroyed by the blast and incendiary bombs of the German Condor Legion."[23] Thus it makes sense that in 1937, or at least a 1937 as viewed from 1954, Todd might embrace and then reject an existential relationship to his own death. I say 1937 as seen from 1954, of course, because the critiques of existentialism that were mounted in the wake of the Second World War typically imagined that it was the Holocaust and the atomic bomb that had called into question the meaning-giving quality of finitude. But for Barth's protagonist, it would seem that 1937 marked the arrival of a different relationship to death than the one he had inherited from World War One. If an existential bearing of death in one's very being was a "solution" to World War One, 1937 was the year when such a position would start to seem hopelessly inadequate.

Notwithstanding the resilience of the phrase "theater of war," the imagination of a dividing line between audience and action was to be forever different; the "ironic" closeness of the war to civilian life would now be an unironic indistinction. And in the light of this it is instructive that Andrews's theoretical relationship to himself changes after 1937. If he could imagine personality as a mask, and could imagine himself as a character of sorts from 1919 to 1937, he now becomes a thoroughly self-conscious "biographer," and the 1954 Andrews is well on his way to becoming the metafictionist that Barth became in the early 1960s. And if between 1919 and 1937 he could imagine himself as a character wearing a mask, with a still-clear distinction between himself and that role, after 1937 he no longer can. As the next chapter on Pynchon demonstrates, writers interested in periodizing the century shared the sense that one dispensation gave way to another in 1937. We might say that it was then that the post–World War One era definitively came to a close as the next war—and the next system of warfare—became visible. This is not, of course, to say that writers yet imagined the destructive force of nuclear weapons (though, to be sure, science fiction had been imagining them for years) but only to suggest that the nature of what would come to be called "conventional" war was visibly evolving.

In the aftermath of his decision to kill himself and his subsequent change of heart, Andrews decides that he must narrate that decision. And while it might appear at least initially that this project wouldn't confront him with the impossible epistemological gap driving his *Inquiry* into his father's death, the reality is far odder, and takes us away from the problems of biography and into questions of the ontology of textuality itself. In trying to tell his own story, Andrews turns to the resources of fiction, rather than those of journalism or history.

The Floating Opera opens with Andrews claiming that the novel we are about to read bears little resemblance to the writing he has been doing between 1930 and 1937: "To someone like myself, whose literary activities have been confined since 1920 mainly to legal briefs and *Inquiry*-writing, the hardest thing about the task at hand—*viz.*, the explanation of a day in 1937 when I changed my mind—is getting into it" (1). Even as Andrews recounts his research and writing projects, he admits that they have left him ill-prepared to deal with the job ahead. More telling, however, is Andrews's sense that he is driven to fiction by the inability to write within the confines of a previously used form the story of the day he changed his mind. His account of the origins of the novel we are reading exemplifies the idea of a change of dominant from the epistemological to the ontological: "Now then, the title, and then we'll see whether we can't start the story. When I decided, sixteen years ago, to write about how I changed my mind one night in June of 1937, I had no title in mind. Indeed, it wasn't until an hour or so ago, when I began writing, that I realized the story would be at least novel-length and resolved therefore to give it a novel title. In 1938, when I determined to set the story down, it was intended only as an aspect of the preliminary study for one chapter of my *Inquiry*, the notes and data for which fill most of my room. I'm thorough" (5–6). What had started as a "thorough" work of investigation here turns into a work of fiction. After telling us that the text we are about to read is of an entirely different kind than the *Inquiry*, Andrews begins a self-conscious meditation on the nature of fiction: "To carry the 'meandering stream' conceit a bit further, if I may: it has always seemed to me, in the novels that I've read now and then, that those authors are asking a great deal of their readers who start their stories furiously, in the middle of things, rather than backing or sidling slowly into them. Such a plunge into someone else's life and world, like a plunge into the Choptank River in mid-March, has, it seems to me, little of pleasure in it" (2). Needless to say, these arguments with, and reflections on, fiction occupy long sections of the novel, and almost immediately we realize that, despite the narrator's stated ambition simply to describe a single day, the novel is at least as much interested in describing *how* that day might be narrated. By the second page, we are being treated to elaboration such as "Where were we? I was going to comment on the significance of the *viz.* I used earlier, was I? Or explain my 'piano-tuning' metaphor? Or my weak heart? Good heavens, how does one write a novel!" (2). The answer, increasingly, is to fictionalize and metafictionalize. Read in the light of his later, more radical metafiction, then, these moments read as a kind of self-conscious precursor—but one that could emerge only when Andrews finally decided to account for 1937.

Early in *The Great War and Modern Memory*, Fussell claims that "the Great War was perhaps the last to be conceived as taking place within a seamless, purposeful 'history' involving a coherent stream of time running from past through present to future. The shrewd recruiting poster depicting a worried father of the future being asked by his children, 'Daddy, what did *you* do in the Great War?' assumes a future whose moral and social pressures are identical with those of the past."[24] Read in these terms, Barth's account of the origin of *Giles Goat-Boy* as a moment in the history of the Cold War strikes me as especially insightful. Much as Andrews turns from realism to self-conscious fiction as he loses his spectatorial relationship to death, Barth turns from self-consciousness to metafiction because of a changing relationship to ending, moving from the forms of finitude that the end of the First World War made visible for Todd Andrews to the forms of violence and destruction made visible by the end of "Campus Riot II" in *Giles Goat-Boy*.

What these various works trace, then, is an evolving relationship to narrativity itself: for Andrews, the replacement of epistemological questions (the kinds of questions central to his *Inquiry*) with ontological questions (his self-representation in the novel we have been reading) is a response to the changing cultures of war and mass death, and by *Giles Goat-Boy*, the residual epistemological concerns that still occupy *The Floating Opera* will have disappeared, or, more properly speaking, been supplanted: Andrews's self-conscious meditations on just what a novel is will be replaced by a far more pronounced debate about the nature of textuality itself, since questions of audience and survival have changed yet again.

McHale has made the case that we might consider 1966, the year of *Giles Goat-Boy*'s publication, as postmodernism's "year one." Writing in response to Andreas Killen's claim that the epochal events of 1973 (*Roe v. Wade*, the Paris peace accords, the oil embargo, the meltdown of the Nixon presidency) when read alongside the appearance of texts such as *Gravity's Rainbow* and *Learning from Las Vegas* mean that 1973 should be read as the year when everything changed and postmodernism began, McHale provocatively suggests that 1973 is actually born in 1966, a year that rivals its harvest of groundbreaking texts.[25] And if we accept McHale's account of what defines the postmodern—ontological plurality takes priority over modernism's epistemological concerns—then his origin story for the postmodern makes perfect sense. McHale adduces the influential compositions or publications of that year—*In Cold Blood*, *Wide Sargasso Sea*, *The Crystal World*, the revised "cut-up" version of *The Soft Machine*, *Babel-17*, *Do Androids Dream of Electric Sheep?* and *Ubik*, for instance—as evidence of the arrival of a definitively new aesthetic.

Giles Goat-Boy and *The Crying of Lot 49*, however, are both central to his argument, and both novels implicitly present their techniques and revisions as motivated by the new nuclear realities of a Cold War that finally had in place all the technologies required for total thermonuclear war. Nineteen sixty-six was also the year that both structuralism and poststructuralism arrived on American soil, and McHale notes as well that "1966 is a year of *self-reflection* and *recursiveness*, when the prefix *meta-*, with which we have become so familiar, begins insistently to attach itself to various substantives, as in *metalanguage* and *metafiction*."[26] It is also the year that narratology appears as a discipline. While these changes are surely overdetermined, Barth (along with Pynchon, as discussed in the next chapter) reveals how narrative was an issue precisely because ending had new cultural meanings. And while it might seem that *Giles Goat-Boy* is above all else a campus novel, and perhaps designed to be read only on campus, the university in which Barth writes is one that was, as McGurl has noted, fundamentally reorganized by the Cold War.[27] After all, the institutional setting of the production of metafiction meant that writers were the beneficiaries of the massive expansion of the American university system in the Cold War, an expansion fueled in no small part by the role those universities played in the research and development of the nuclear national security state.

2 / *The Crying of Lot 49*, circa 1642; or, Pynchon, Periodicity, and Total War

A third of the way through Thomas Pynchon's *The Crying of Lot 49* (1966), the mystery deepens. Oedipa Maas's quest to untangle the confusion surrounding a dead lover's estate has sent her to see *The Courier's Tragedy*, a barely known (and in reality nonexistent) Jacobean revenge tragedy. The play initially sounds exactly as you would expect if Pynchon decided to do revenge tragedy: absurd, unbelievably complex, over-the-top, a "Road Runner cartoon in blank verse."[1] There are land mines, a falcon with envenomed talons, an exploding goat, a lye pit, and a scene in which a character's tongue is ripped out with pincers before being impaled on a rapier, lit on fire, and waved across the stage by a madman reciting an almost unreadable send-up of apocalyptic rhetoric. So the play reads much like a Pynchon novel as a whole, pushing the limits of good taste and generic form, and the audience's reaction to the play within the novel echoes the frustration and anger many readers have experienced upon finishing the novel itself.

However, in spite of the play's relentless escalation of revenge tragedy's famous intensity, and for all its unbelievably complex plotting, Pynchon, through Oedipa's viewing experience, offers a crystalline vision of the play's significance: "though the words were all spoken in Transplanted Middle Western Stage British, Oedipa found herself after five minutes sucked utterly into the landscape of evil Richard Wharfinger had fashioned for his 17th-century audiences, so preapocalyptic, death-wishful, sensually fatigued, unprepared, a little poignantly, for that abyss of civil war that had been waiting, cold and deep, only a few years ahead of them"

(49). In an instant, the seemingly pastiche-driven and metageneric play becomes proleptically representational: the play's power comes into being only when it is viewed from a certain historical distance, and what seems at first the over-the-top satirizing of a genre can look—from the right distance—like the beginning of a historical chain that links the aesthetic with the political. It is the contention of this chapter that the novel rewards a reading that remembers this account of the play, and that asks us to consider what future event might stabilize, as anticipatory symptom, the novel's famous indeterminacy.

Pynchon's crucial gesture toward the play's imaginative power suggests a certain talent for literary history. Jonathan Dollimore has written extensively about how Jacobean revenge tragedy was transformed across the twentieth century: a genre that was all about the limits of humanist self-knowledge in 1961 was politicized by the 1970s, and in 1982 seen by Franco Moretti as a possible cause of the English Civil War.[2] So Pynchon's sense of the genre's forward-looking importance itself looks forward, coming as it does in a novel published in 1966. I'm not out to establish the political significance of revenge tragedy, though, or to describe the ability of texts to generate real-world events (Moretti's reading of revenge tragedy).[3] Rather, the understanding of the play's historical imagination that Pynchon offers is at once deeply familiar and oddly unsettling, and suggests one way in which the novel's own historical imagination might be rethought. The historicizing gesture is familiar to the extent that many readers of Pynchon's expansive career will recall that his novels are filled with amateur historians (Stencil and Fallopian come immediately to mind) who reveal how the passage of time allows us retrospectively to understand the spectral foreshadowings of the future in various past events. So, for instance, Pynchon's novels often return to how the grisly events of colonialism forecast the inevitable slide into the total wars of the twentieth century. Pynchon's novels often look backward like this in order to imagine the links between the narrative's present setting and an expansive past; though they certainly flirt with—and even at times embrace—paranoia and conspiracy, their historiographic negotiations are never entirely reducible to either.

But the novels also frequently cut in another direction, exploiting the distinction between their historical setting and the time of their publication and reading. Just as Pynchon's characters use their knowledge of the past to recognize the significance of events in ways unavailable to any contemporary observer of them, so too is the reader able to grasp realities unavailable to any character. Thus *Gravity's Rainbow* derives its power from its prophetic imagination of the emergence of the Cold War, globalization, and information economies in the waning days of World War Two; *Mason & Dixon* from the reader's awareness that the Mason-Dixon Line's horrific future is already spectrally apparent; and *Against the Day* from the visibility of the looming catastrophes that will come to define retroactively the seemingly innocent days of the early twentieth century. Pynchon's particular version of what Hutcheon calls historiographic metafiction[4] places his texts at the intersection of two diverging historical trajectories, one into the past, and one into the future, and he takes advantage of the differences between the time of setting and the time of reading.[5] Depending on how one glosses these historiographic negotiations, one gets either a sharply deterministic and teleological Pynchon who sees history as a process of entropic slide into greater and greater states of disarray, or the antithetical Pynchon of potentiality, whose historiographic investigations continually gesture toward lost possibilities and alternative paths not taken.[6]

Despite the familiarity of these historiographic maneuvers for readers of Pynchon, Oedipa's historicist reaction to *The Courier's Tragedy* remains unsettling. While the novel has its amateur historian in Mike Fallopian (whose last name suggests a regress beyond obvious moments of conception), and through him offers alternative histories of the Civil War (finding its origins in postal reform movements that began in 1845) and the Cold War (finding its origins in a naval encounter between the Confederacy and Russia in 1864), the second aspect of Pynchon's historiographic method is necessarily absent. Unlike Pynchon's big historical novels, *The Crying of Lot 49* offers almost no disjunction between the time of initial publication and the time of setting. While the narrator occasionally distances the reader from Oedipa's perceptions, we are never in a noticeably more privileged position with regard to knowledge.[7] Within the novel, Oedipa's attempts to connect her present with the past are also frustrated, because the narrative never resolves the principal mystery of whether or not a long history of alternative postal delivery actually exists. These points help to explain why the novel is usually sidelined in discussions of Pynchon's historiographic interests, and perhaps even why Pynchon once claimed that the novel was a failure, somewhere he forgot almost everything he had learned.[8] Instead of foregrounding the novel's metahistorical continuity with the bigger novels, most readings follow Tony Tanner in seeing the novel as primarily metafictional, an "inverted detective novel" that continually solicits an expectation of revelation and then denies it, and so the novel has a predictably central place in discussions of Pynchon's ambiguity or difficulty.[9] Thus, for instance, in his *Pynchon and History*, Shawn Smith devotes full chapters to Pynchon's big novels—*V.*, *Gravity's Rainbow*, *Vineland*, and *Mason & Dixon*, while devoting comparatively little attention to *The Crying of Lot 49*, while Alan Wilde has noted how, despite that Pynchon's reputation as the quintessential American postmodernist depends primarily on other novels, *The Crying of Lot 49* is actually his most postmodern work.[10] The novel's last scene is usually central to such discussions, as N. Katherine Hayles has noted, with its insistently apocalyptic tone and subsequent denial of any kind of revelation.[11] So Pynchon's familiar gesture about his invented revenge tragedy feels strangely out of place in a novel that would seem to deny the possibility of reading the novel in the same way: Oedipa's historical distance from the play is not available to any contemporary reader of the novel in 1966, and the novel's postmodern difficulty seems to mock the kind of instantaneous revelation of historical importance that Pynchon offers us about the play.[12] Instead, and as Tanner has noted, the novel moves from "a state of degree-zero mystery" to ever-increasing confusion.[13]

I want to suggest, however, that *The Crying of Lot 49* should be read according to Pynchon's historiographic vision even as it exposes the limits of that very method. Much as the textual zaniness of *The Courier's Tragedy* emerges as a harbinger of a future war, the particular difficulties of *The Crying of Lot 49* expose the limits of Pynchon's proleptic imagination when the war foreshadowed is not the English Civil War, nor the American Civil War, nor even one of the two world wars, but the not-yet-arrived-at horror of a fully thermonuclear war. It isn't simply that occluded references to the bomb exist in the text—although they certainly do—but that the novel's particular structure and its insistent failure to reward the apocalyptic desires it inculcates suggest the limits of Pynchon's method when confronted by new forms of warfare that differ in kind, and not simply in degree, from previous conflicts. Looked at from a distance, and after the fact, Richard Wharfinger's *The Courier's Tragedy* becomes the precursor to a future war. Likewise, *The Crying of Lot 49* is just as "preapocalyptic, death-wishful, sensually fatigued" as the play within it, and when we reread its famous difficulty in the light of an imaginary future, it looks very different (49). Indeed, the difficulties of supplying a definitively revelatory reading of the novel's unanswered questions are precisely what marks it as both a radical intervention into the literature of World War Three and a testing of the limits of Pynchon's literary historiography; the war that the novel prefigures is one that no reader could ever live through, and the novel's failure to provide its own meaning marks the impossibility of that meaning ever arriving for a surviving audience.[14] Part of the play's extremity lies in its depiction of "every mode of violent death available to Renaissance man" (58), a standard impossible to update when forms of violence now include the sixty-foot-long missiles that flank the Yoyodyne headquarters.

Before turning to *The Crying of Lot 49*, however, I'll place Pynchon's historicization of *The Courier's Tragedy* in dialogue with another of his acknowledgments of the relationship between difficult textuality and proleptic historical understanding by turning to his first novel, *V.* (1963), which implicitly aligns his understanding of literary history with one of the definitive statements about the relationship between modernism and World War One. Recognizing how consistently Pynchon investigates the connections between difficult textuality and war helps to bring the specificity of *The Crying of Lot 49* into focus, and makes apparent the larger patterns of literary history that interest Pynchon. Like Barth, Pynchon understands the shaping power of the century's conflicts on literary periodization, with important implications for how we might imagine the textual production of the nuclear age.

The Leading Edge

The clearest example of retrospective periodization comes in *V.* when Stencil reads the "Confessions of Fausto Maijstral": justifying the importance of his confession, Maijstral identifies himself as a member of the "Generation of '37," an invented group of Anglo-Maltese poets. In Maijstral's sense of his literary relationships, we see the same set of concerns that Pynchon will raise in *The Crying of Lot 49* about textuality and the foreshadowing of war because, by identifying himself as a member of the "Generation of '37," Maijstral makes us think more broadly about the ways in which the twentieth century has been periodized in relation to world war. After all, it was in 1937 that 1914 was enshrined as a watershed literary moment, joining 1910 (when human character changed, according to Virginia Woolf) and 1922 (the year in which *The Waste Land* and *Ulysses* were both published) as a definitive reference point for dating modernism. It was in 1937 that Wyndham Lewis coined the phrase "the men of 1914" to define the modernist project, in an interim memoir that is centrally interested in periodizing modernism and that begins by making the same overture to the limits of autobiographical thinking as Maijstral's confessions. What is particularly striking is that the problem facing Maijstral in his confession and Lewis in *Blasting and Bombardiering* is the same: How do we collate autobiography, aesthetic periods, and world history? Both men account for themselves as members of an artistic generation defined by a year (1914 for Lewis, 1937 for Maijstral) even as they insist on the multiplicity of ways in which the century and their own careers might be subdivided. The influence of Lewis's formulation in *Blasting and Bombardiering* (both a soldier memoir and an account of his friendships with Pound, Eliot, Joyce, Gaudier-Brzeska, and Hulme) still reverberates in modernist studies, where World War One retains the definitional hold given it by Lewis, whose interest lay in how the passing of the war into historical memory had made the war visible even in texts that predated it. Crucially, Lewis's valuation of "the men of 1914" lies along the same lines as Pynchon's valuation of *The Courier's Tragedy*: "You will be astonished to find how like art is to war, I mean 'modernist' art. They talk a lot about how a war just-finished effects art. But you will learn here how a war *about to start* can do the same thing. I have set out to show how war, art, civil war, strikes and coup d'états dovetail into each other."[15] By making 1937 the year that defines the Maltese generation, then, Pynchon invites us to read this extended chapter of *V.* as an intervention into the various attempts to periodize the century, in such a way as to recall Lewis's account of the importance of 1914.

Maijstral's generation of 1937 only publicly emerges as such long afterward, just as Lewis's men of 1914 can only be seen as such in 1937 (after all, Eliot, Pound, and Joyce hadn't yet produced their major work in 1914).[16] In fact, the distance between Lewis's 1937 and the men of 1914 is almost identical to the difference between Maijstral's generation of '37 and the year (1956) in which Maijstral supposedly writes his confessions (and is strikingly similar to Todd Andrews's sense, in Barth's *The Floating Opera*, of the temporal gap he has experienced in trying to narrate his 1937 decision). As with Joyce, Eliot, and the other men of 1914, the bulk of the work that would come to define Maijstral as the most important voice of his generation was only produced some time during and after the war—in this case, World War Two—that came to define the generation retroactively: "Somehow there had accumulated a number of poems (at least one sonnet-cycle the present Fausto is still happy with); monographs on religion, language, history; critical essays (Hopkins, T. S. Eliot, di Chirico's novel *Hebdomeros*). Fausto IV was the 'man of letters' and only survivor of the Generation of '37, for Dnubietna is building roads in America, and Maratt is somewhere south of Mount Ruwenzori, organizing riots among our linguistic brothers the Bantu."¹⁷ As with "the men of 1914," this generation is only publicly visible as a group defined by a war *after* the full impact of the war they supposedly "anticipated" has been recorded. Pynchon's point is that legitimacy is only retrospectively conferred on generations or schools: like Lewis's men of 1914/1937, the men of 1937 can only publicly emerge as a generation some time in the mid-1950s, even though they were sure of their greatness at an earlier date. History is always retrospective, but the paradigmatic change in the possibilities of global war after 1945 will put into question the possibility of retrospective history itself. Born in 1937, and publishing his first novel in 1963, Pynchon is two generations later than the "men of 1914" and a generation younger than the "Generation of '37." His model of literary historiography suggests that we should be thinking of his texts from the 1960s in relation to World War Three. But what kind of text could predict that conflict?

Pynchon's Bombs

Much Pynchon scholarship acknowledges that the rocket at the end of *Gravity's Rainbow* hurtling toward a California theater is a nuclear-armed intercontinental ballistic missile (ICBM), and that the novel is, among other things, about the emergence of the bomb and the Cold War out of the ashes of World War Two. This is the arc that connects the V-2 rocket of the novel's opening with the 1970s of the novel's last section, and the links between the German rocket program and American missile and space technology are well known. The novel's epigraph from Wernher von Braun and the tattered newsprint that announces the Hiroshima explosion further underscore the novel's nuclear subtext.¹⁸ Although most critics note the ICBM at the end of the novel, far fewer have made the case that the novel's nuclear content should significantly shape our critical readings of it, and fewer still have made the bomb central to their analysis of Pynchon's longer career.¹⁹ John Dugdale makes the most sustained effort to locate the veiled historical references of Pynchon's pre–*Gravity's Rainbow* fiction, and he reads it in light of the suggestion in *The Crying of Lot 49* that *The Courier's Tragedy* manifests a ritual reluctance to articulate its "real" content. For Dugdale, allusion is Pynchon's mode, and his nuanced readings identify the intertextuality and historical reference at the heart of Pynchon's early work. In his reading of *The Crying of Lot 49*, Dugdale finds the bomb in recurrent shapes that suggest mushroom clouds and missiles; in the small locked room at the end that suggests the "war room" of *Dr. Strangelove*; in the negative associations of the number three, which he links to Trinity (the site of the first atomic test); and in a play written by "war-finger" rather than Wharfinger, which of course recalls fears of a new culture of push-button or turn-key nuclear warfare.[20] But for Dugdale these allusions join a host of other possible referents for the novel: race, class, and power in Los Angeles; the assassination and legacies of JFK; Vietnam and the Gulf of Tonkin episode. All of these add up to his remarkably understated claim that readers could learn much about mid-1960s American culture from the novel. Nowhere does he suggest why any of this latent content must be buried in the first place, or why the novel solicits only to mock the reader's desire for revelation.

That desire for revelation finds its most powerful denial at the end of the novel. The endlessly confusing possible intersections between the (non)existence of the Tristero postal conspiracy and everyday life have finally left Oedipa at her breaking point, tottering between the horror of coincidence and the horror of conspiracy, between the threat of meaning's absence and the equally threatening possibility that meaning is present in every aspect of her life. The only thing that might rescue both Oedipa and the reader from such a perplexing choice between meaning and meaninglessness would presumably be the identity of the buyer of the mysterious stamps—Lot 49—which have attracted such interest from the auction's attendees. As the auctioneer begins, and the novel ends, we get no such help:

> Loren Passerine, on his podium, hovered like a puppet-master, his eyes bright, his smile practiced and relentless. He stared at her, smiling, as if saying, I'm surprised you actually came. Oedipa sat alone, toward the back of the room, looking at the napes of necks, trying to guess which one was her target, her enemy, perhaps her proof. An assistant closed the heavy door on the lobby windows and the sun. She heard a lock snap shut; the sound echoed a moment. Passerine spread his arms in a gesture that seemed to belong to the priesthood of some remote culture; perhaps to a descending angel. The auctioneer cleared his throat. Oedipa settled back, to await the crying of lot 49. (152)

A language of religious revelation here encounters the distinctly anti-revelatory nature of the words running out.[21] The perfect postmodern masterpiece, no?

In the 1984 article I quoted in the introduction, Jacques Derrida asserted that a truly nuclear war, a war which in its severity "conditions every discourse and all strategies" could never be fought in any manner that would allow us to understand it as having occurred.[22] Total nuclear war would be one in which no actors, witnesses, or archives survived; it would be anti-apocalyptic altogether, without the time even to understand the end as an end. His title "No Apocalypse, Not Now" could just as easily be the title of Pynchon's novel, so long as one remembers the definitional relationship between apocalypse and revelation; as Derrida reminds us, the origins of "apocalypse" lie in unveiling and retrospective judgment rather than in simple conclusion, even as common usage has tended to assign the term to any particularly nasty form of ending. Richard Klein's extension of Derrida's thought into the paradoxical temporality of a future without a future suggests the event that might stabilize Pynchon's novel as its forerunner. Paradoxically, however, that same move helps to explain why *The Crying of Lot 49* can never announce itself as such a text: the war that would show the novel to be essentially anticipatory could never come to pass within the confines of narrative or memory. The novel's denial of closure doesn't in itself make the novel about World War Three, but the interpretive problem of the inconclusive ending, when read through Pynchon's association of difficult textuality and the foreshadowing of coming conflict, perhaps does. This ending is the textual equivalent of the "absolute self-destructibility without apocalypse, without revelation of its own truth" that Derrida identifies as the particular problem of nuclear ending.[23]

Working backward from the ending, it becomes clear that the particular interpretive difficulties of the text have been implicitly identified with the bomb all along. Consider, for instance, the pun in Oedipa's puzzling first discovery of a contemporary postal problem. Oedipa has just received a letter from her husband, Mucho, and the blurb next to the cancellation mark includes a telling mistake: "REPORT ALL OBSCENE MAIL TO YOUR POTSMASTER" (33). When Oedipa asks Metzger what a "potsmaster" is, he replies with a list of important dishwashing duties before wondering whether the mistake matters: "'So they make misprints,' Metzger said, 'let them. As long as they're careful about not pressing the wrong button, you know?'" (33). This is one of the few moments in which the novel acknowledges its nuclear present, and it initially seems as though the point might be one of cruel understatement: why care about the mail when the potential for global destruction should concern anyone interested in conspiracy? But the pun relies on more than simply the reversal of the first "s" and "t" in postmaster: a potsmaster, especially given the implied nuclear threat of Metzger's argument, might just as easily be one of the three world leaders (Stalin, Truman, and Churchill) who effectively began the Cold War by dividing up Europe at the Potsdam Conference (which built on the agreements already reached at Yalta) in the last days of World War Two. But Potsdam was also where atomic diplomacy began: Truman was at the conference already when the Trinity test proved a success, and he received word of the outcome at 7:30 p.m. on July 16, the day before his first meeting with Stalin.[24] A message containing more extensive details of the weapon's power arrived on July 21, and Truman immediately began asserting himself in meetings, thanks to the confidence the news gave him.[25] And it was at Potsdam that Truman, Churchill, and Chiang Kai-shek offered Japan the choice between surrender and total ("prompt and utter") destruction; in other words, and in retrospect, Potsdam is where the bomb, the instrument that would come to define the new global order, was first "mentioned" without being explicitly revealed or named—an emblematic text for Pynchon's amateur historians, who are obsessed by moments such as this. That Pynchon was aware of the significance of Potsdam seems obvious given that Slothrop wanders into the conference in *Gravity's Rainbow*, and Pynchon's interest in and use of puns (postmaster/potsmaster) is of course a signature device.[26]

The point might then be that there is no real difference between the novel's postal conspiracy and the psychopathology of everyday life during the Cold War. Lurking behind the "failure" of meaning—and what could better illustrate the poststructuralist view of language than an unmastered postal service?—is the bomb. The crisis of meaning within the novel leads us in search of those who would stabilize it, those who would make sure that messages get from sender to recipient; what we find instead of that postmaster is the misprint that isn't a misprint at all. The obscene truth of the novel might be hidden in plain sight: the crisis of the post (in the sense of the postal) is the crisis of the post- (as in postwar), which is to say the bomb first alluded to at Potsdam.[27] The novel's own postal failure, then—its failure to arrive at a destination from which could be communicated the solution to its mystery—is the denial of apocalyptic revelation in favor of the sudden ending that allows no revelation at all. Tobin Siebers, writing about the history of literary criticism, urges us to think in just these ways when he proposes that "the link between our postsomething schools of thought—the poststructuralists and postmoderns—and the postwar era has been concealed by creating a more visible link between the postromantic and the postmodern, as any good students of postmodernism will immediately understand."²⁸ Pynchon provides, in an oblique and postmodern way, the history behind Siebers's point that the postmodern needs to be thought of as conditioned by the emergent political realities of the postwar era, and here tantalizingly hints that during the Potsdam Conference the world, and the nature of communication and meaning, changed almost literally overnight.

The scene early in the novel when Oedipa first sees San Narciso is often cited in discussions of the novel's insistent inculcation of revelatory expectations. As Oedipa drives into town, she suddenly perceives San Narciso as the remembered circuit card of a radio: "Though she knew even less about radios than about Southern Californians, there were to both outward patterns a hieroglyphic sense of concealed meaning, of an intent to communicate. There'd seemed no limit to what the printed circuit could have told her (if she had tried to find out); so in her first minute of San Narciso, a revelation also trembled just past the threshold of her understanding" (14). Southern California's links to the defense industry help to explain Oedipa's comparison of San Narciso to a circuit.²⁹ Indeed, we might go so far as to claim that the secret of San Narciso *is* the printed circuit: the economic engines driving Southern California in the Cold War were the defense and aerospace industries, literally circuit-based. The reader learns soon after that Yoyodyne, "one of the giants of the aerospace industry," is the town's largest employer and was lured there by Pierce Inverarity (15). In his 1966 essay "A Journey into the Mind of Watts," Pynchon notes that much of the wealth of Southern California is built on "systematized folly," reliant as it is in part on huge aerospace contractors that rise and fall according to the whims of the secretary of defense.³⁰

It is hard not to think of Pynchon's San Narciso as something like the postmodern city par excellence. As opposed to a densely packed city built around an identifiable center, "like many named places in California it was less an identifiable city than a grouping of concepts—census tracts, special purpose bond-issue districts, shopping nuclei, all overlaid with access roads to its own freeway" (13). The point is brought home absurdly when Oedipa finds herself in a "neighborhood that was little more than the road's skinny right-of-way, lined by auto lots, escrow services, drive-ins, small office buildings, and factories whose address numbers were in the 70 and then 80,000's. She had never known numbers to run so high" (15). But perhaps this is not absurd at all. While these clichés about the decentered, primarily postindustrial city (after all, the factories here seem almost an afterthought) are familiar to any reader of postmodern theory, offering as they do an account of what Peter Galison calls "an urban geography of Deleuzian rhizomes burrowing every which way without beginning or end," there are other, and more directly historical, ways of understanding this cityscape.[31] Oedipa finds the city at once familiar and strange, puzzled by this new experience of addresses running into the 80,000s. As Galison points out, however, the cityscape that found one explanation in the postmodern theorizing of the 1980s was in fact a material product of the Cold War. Rather than accounting for the decentered city by "a generalized zeitgeist, by a shift in an economic base 'reflected' in the cultural superstructure, by an epochal postwar taste change toward suburban life, or by an entropic flow away from an ordered city core," Galison describes how the Allied procedures of carpet bombing and the development of atomic weapons led to a "moral-cartographic vision" of dispersing national industry, modeled on the largely successful German effort to avoid concentrating industrial production in nodal points.[32] By 1951, the encouragement of industrial dispersal was official American federal policy, and by 1956, the federal highway system had $25 billion in funding.[33] We can see precisely what changes if, for instance, we compare the Southern California of Raymond Chandler and Pynchon; though separated by little over a decade, the landscapes of *The Long Goodbye* (1953) and *The Crying of Lot 49* couldn't be more different.

Near the end of the novel Oedipa's aerial purview of San Narciso is echoed in a passage that has to be read alongside this original failed revelation. Oedipa has just telephoned The Greek Way (a bar) to ask a man she met there if he is part of a conspiracy to confuse her in her quest. When he refuses to answer her question and hangs up the phone, a panicked Oedipa tries to orient herself in space: "She stood between the public booth and the rented car, in the night, her isolation complete, and tried to face toward the sea. But she'd lost her bearings. She turned, pivoting on one stacked heel, could find no mountains either. As if there could be no barriers between herself and the rest of the land. San Narciso at that moment lost (the loss pure, instant, spherical, the sound of a stainless orchestral chime held among the stars and struck lightly), gave up its residue of uniqueness for her; became a name again, was assumed back into the American continuity of crust and mantle. Pierce Inverarity was really dead" (146–47). The instantaneous revelation that the earlier view of San Narciso promised, and which is echoed in other moments when Oedipa feels herself in the presence of revelation, is here reversed: this is a moment of pure loss in the instantaneous disappearance of the text, the image of the city, that had initially promised epiphanic knowledge. But the language points toward a reason for the lack of revelation here: the one thing that can make a city the size of San Narciso disappear instantly is the hydrogen bomb—and "city-killing" is a key term in the contemporary discourse of thermonuclear strategy.[34] A hydrogen bomb has not actually been dropped at this point in the novel, obviously, but the language describing the loss of the city is strikingly suggestive of one. The "spherical" vision only underscores this suggestion, recalling as it does the blast in its pre-mushroom-cloud shape, and the assumption of San Narciso back into the "crust and mantle" of America suggests that the city has been swallowed by a massive crater in the punctured outer layers of the planet. And while the reference to the noise of a single orchestral chime as a marker of this disappearance might seem less "nuclear," it takes us back to an earlier moment in the text, if only as the muted inverse of that earlier scene's extended aural marker of closure. This is when *Cashiered*, the movie starring the young Metzger in his child career as the actor Baby Igor, is finally coming to a close, and we realize that Baby Igor, his father, and their Saint Bernard won't make it back from their heroic submarine journey. After the dog drowns and Baby Igor gets electrocuted, the film escalates once again: "Through one of those Hollywood distortions in probability, the father was spared electrocution so he could make a farewell speech, apologizing to Baby Igor and the dog for getting them into this and regretting that they wouldn't be meeting in heaven: 'Your little eyes have seen your daddy for the last time. You are for salvation; I am for the Pit.' At the end his suffering eyes filled the screen, the sound of incoming water grew deafening, up swelled that strange '30's movie music with the massive sax section, in faded the legend THE END" (30). The scene inverts the novel's ending. Here we have every generic marker—aural, visual, technical, formal—of closure, right down to a speech that assigns divine judgment. The single orchestral chime that marks the city's disappearance, in contrast, is a noise as far as possible from the film's almost literally overblown sax section. The deflation is doubled when we realize that orchestral chimes are never singular; the instrument is typically composed of multiple chimes, and they are struck together. In contrast to the film, this solitary and nearly silent gesture stands as the aural marker of the antithesis of closure. And we should remember, of course, that *Cashiered* is a *war* film; just as in *The Floating Opera*, World War One is imagined in terms of our own witnessing of the deaths of others.

I take it as especially significant that the moment of its instantaneous loss is what converts the city back into its name again for Oedipa, and causes it to lose its uniqueness. Oedipa's realization that the city has no secret to be cracked is produced out of a vision of the city's obliteration, and her position at this point is strikingly similar to the reader's at the end of the novel. For both, what has seemed a hermeneutically rich text disappears too quickly, and every attempt at self-orientation fails; Oedipa is left unable to find a point in space with which to connect and the reader with no more words that could promise revelation. Just as Oedipa notes that at this moment of disappearance San Narciso "became a name again," this novel's closing five words are its title, and the first time we learn what the title refers to. In its ending, the text is perfectly analogous to San Narciso at its moment of disappearance.

Speculations on the novel's enigmatic title (why 49?) have been central to the novel's critical history, but I would like to propose one more by extending Dugdale's.[35] Dugdale catalogues a variety of potential meanings, among them the idea that there are 49 continental states, and that the 49th parallel is a significant national border. In light of this, he glosses "lot" as a "unit of real estate" and lot 49, accordingly, as the nation. Oedipa's transformation of the absolute singularity of San Narciso into just another piece of the "American continuity of crust and mantle" enacts the same dynamic of national union. That this transformation happens at the moment the city instantaneously disappears suggests the communal vulnerability of a Cold War population. The "crying" of the title, then, would signify the lament of a population assigned a common lot, a common destiny as the target of a total war that would instantaneously destroy them all. Pynchon's point is that San Narciso's uniqueness is exactly what makes it nonunique, since the particular weapons developed by Southern California's defense industry make every city a potential (and, indeed, likely) target. At the moment San Narciso disappears, it becomes paradoxically typical because its particular legacy is that all cities can now disappear: an ironic gloss on the narcissism implicit in its name. This is a far more radical notion of the impact of the bomb than merely a missile falling on the Orpheus Theatre at the end of *Gravity's Rainbow*, and so it might be said that *The Crying of Lot 49* is a more thoroughly "nuclear" novel than Pynchon's later work, despite that the later novel is more explicit in its references to the bomb.

Much has been made of the fact that sound connects the end of *The Crying of Lot 49* with the beginning of Pynchon's next novel, *Gravity's Rainbow*.[36] The final sentence of the former—"Oedipa settled back, to await the crying of lot 49"—perhaps finds continuation in the famous opening of the latter: "A screaming comes across the sky." But this falsely collates the development of Pynchon's career with the development of the Cold War, and argues that the assuredly more explicit place of the bomb in *Gravity's Rainbow* makes the novel "about" the bomb to an extent that the earlier novel is not. As I show in chapters 4 and 5, the world of defense strategy was certainly a complex one during the late 1960s and early 1970s, but these readings of Pynchon's career ignore the fact that by the 1970s total nuclear war was far less likely than it had been in the mid-1960s: while the weapons were still an essential part of defense strategy in the 1970s, the likelihood of an all-out exchange had declined significantly thanks to the thaw in international relations after 1963 (though, as I describe in chapter 4, the increase in stockpiles meant that the possibility of limited use if war broke out was also disappearing). To read a link between the last sentence of *The Crying of Lot 49* and the first sentence of *Gravity's Rainbow* is to miss the central insight of the earlier novel. It isn't that apocalyptic revelation has merely been suspended in the earlier novel for a later date, but rather that such revelation can *never* arrive; we can only wait for it in the knowledge that the end offered by total nuclear war will be one we can't even experience as an end. There will be no time to cry, either in a scream of collective pain or a scream of collective mourning, since no one will survive long enough to do either, and there certainly won't be enough time to do to *The Crying of Lot 49* what Oedipa does to *The Courier's Tragedy* when she unpacks its historical importance. In short, one can only wait for that crying in the knowledge that it will never arrive because it cannot.[37] If the particular problem of *Gravity's Rainbow* is that you hear the supersonic rocket only if you have survived it, then it might be said that this is a "luxury" that the earlier novel does not offer.

This is not of course a competition between the two novels where *The Crying of Lot 49* becomes more important by virtue of having a more radical notion of finitude than *Gravity's Rainbow*. Rather, the projects of the two novels are related, though by no means identical, and to call them both Cold War novels—of course they are—risks obscuring their differences.[38] The Cold War was no monotone conflict, and the degree to which it was defined by the threat of total nuclear war ebbed and flowed considerably. *The Crying of Lot 49* was written in the aftermath of arguably the most dangerous moment of the conflict up to that point, the Cuban Missile Crisis, an event that marked one of the most pronounced periods of American nuclear anxiety. This was also the era of Tsar Bomba, the 1961 test by the Soviet Union of the world's largest hydrogen bomb, a weapon approximately three thousand times more powerful than the weapon that destroyed Hiroshima. We should also note that Pynchon had spent 1960–62 working for Boeing on the BOMARC and Minuteman missile projects.[39] The 1964 setting of *The Crying of Lot 49* places us in the immediate aftermath of arguably the most dangerous period of the conflict prior to the Reagan years, and thus it makes sense that 1966 would be the year that Barth and Pynchon both addressed the paradigm-changing nature of nuclear weapons, and did so in texts that might be said to inaugurate a definitively "postmodern" fiction.

Historians of the period have even suggested that the conflict be viewed as two distinct wars, the first lasting from the escalation of rhetoric in the period immediately after the Second World War through to the signing of the Limited Test Ban Treaty in 1963, and the second coinciding with the inflammatory rhetoric and military buildup of the Reagan years. Indeed, these moments produced the central canon of nuclear fiction and film. The crisis point of the first period (the late 1950s and early 1960s) saw *On the Beach* (1957 novel, 1959 film), *Red Alert* (1958), *A Canticle for Leibowitz* (1959), *Level 7* (1959), *Alas, Babylon* (1959), *Fail-Safe* (1962 novel, 1964 film), *Dr. Strangelove* (1964), and *The War Game* (1965), among others. The 1980s brought *God's Grace* (1982), *The Day After* (1983), *Testament* (1983), *Threads* (1984), *Fiskadoro* (1985), and *The Postman* (1985).[40] But these texts are about nuclear war in a way that total nuclear war could never allow, since so many of them are survivor narratives of an event that in its most extreme form would leave no survivors.[41] This is why Derrida claimed that fiction mimetically about nuclear war was useless in guiding our thinking about this ultimate event: the reality of finitude at work in nuclear war was so radical that it was best dealt with, perversely, in a group of prenuclear modernist writers (Mallarmé, Kafka, and Joyce) whose work tested the limits of narrativity.

In an essay from the same year as Derrida's, Pynchon implicitly agreed, arguing in his "Is it O.K. to Be a Luddite?" that a significant strand of American science fiction had been unable to truly conceptualize nuclear war, and adding that the "modern Luddite imaginations have yet to come up with any countercritter Bad and Big enough, even in the most irresponsible of fictions, to begin to compare with what would happen in a nuclear war."[42] For Pynchon as for Derrida, nuclear war is, it would seem, less something to be represented than a challenge to representation itself. More recently Tony Jackson has offered a provocative account of the rise of narrative theory during the postwar period as a symptom of anxieties that the atomic age produced, and reads Frank

Kermode's *The Sense of an Ending*, delivered as lectures in 1965 and then published in 1967, as an exemplary text.[43] For Jackson, Kermode's disavowal of a difference between an end brought about by angels and one brought about by nuclear weapons is part of a systematic repression of the facts of contemporary conflict, even as Kermode's book is already symptomatic of that conflict. Published contemporaneously, Pynchon's novel might ultimately be said to play Hyde to Kermode's Jekyll, and is perhaps the representative text for what Jackson calls "the Cold War sense of an ending" given its denial of any form of revelatory ending for the reader. Perhaps then, pace Derrida, we don't need Kafka for this so much as we need an expansive vision of what nuclear (non)-reference might look like. In a way, then, Tanner was right all along: the novel *is* an inverted detective novel, but it is also a historicizing of its own form, the symptom of a crime that a detective can never reconstruct after the fact. And while the postapocalyptic novel is always a kind of detective novel, as survivors try to reconstruct the disaster that has happened, and to reassemble civil society out of its ruins, Pynchon reveals that the novel of World War Three can never offer revelation.

3 / The Time of the Nation, the Time of the State

Early in Robert Coover's *The Public Burning* (1977) the reader gets another shock. We've already had to process that Richard Nixon narrates much of the novel, that the Rosenbergs are going to be executed in Times Square during a giant public party, and that Uncle Sam is a "real" person rather than a mythic hero. Now, during a particularly loaded golf game between Richard Nixon and Uncle Sam, the intimacy of Nixon's contact with the national symbolic turns into pure absurdity. The urgency with which Sam has been forcing Nixon to pursue the execution of the Rosenbergs becomes newly marked by an unexpected affective dimension: the outcome of the Rosenberg case could determine not just the score in a particular encounter with the Soviet threat but the outcome of the entire Cold War now that the very existence of Uncle Sam is at stake: "Oh, I ain't immortal, son. I'd hate to think I was. Nothin' goes on forever, Amber, not even History itself, so why should I?"[1]

I begin with this passage because it so elegantly condenses some of Coover's major concerns in the novel, which is itself a kind of conversation between "real" history and extravagant fabulation, here represented in a conversation between Nixon and Uncle Sam. As critics have pointed out, this is perhaps the central problem the novel poses for readers: to call it autotelic metafiction respects its extravagant fabulation, but ignores the scrupulous historical research that went into it; to call it a historical novel misses its frankly bizarre unreality, and its commitment to representing history as almost purely discursive.[2] Set in the three days leading up to the execution of Ethel and Julius Rosenberg in 1953, its cast includes the notable American political personae of the time: Nixon, Eisenhower, Hugo Black, Joe McCarthy, and William Douglas are but a few of the characters. The executions take place in Times Square, on the night of the Rosenbergs' fourteenth anniversary, at an event organized by a virtual who's who of America: Cecil B. DeMille, Bernard Baruch, Betty Crocker, Conrad Hilton, Sam Goldwyn, Walt Disney, Ed Sullivan, the director of the Mormon Tabernacle Choir, the chiefs of staff, and the Holy Six are among the members of a vast organizing committee. As I show in the next few pages, this exchange between Nixon and Uncle Sam also raises some of the key issues that have largely been ignored in scholarship on the novel, which has failed to grasp fully the novel's complex argument about the relationship between state power and national iconography. For in addition to being a conversation between "real" history and fabulous invention, this scene is also a moment in which the executive branch of the government is talking to the national symbolic itself.[3]

Whatever the reader's reaction to the golf scene might be, for Nixon this encounter is devastating. Uncle Sam is offering a new understanding of the stakes of the Cold War: it isn't simply that the United States might lose but that, in losing, the very idea of America, an idea usually abstracted into the symbolic dimension yet here incarnated in a living, and potentially mortal being, might perish as well. The stakes of war are now such that losing means more than occupation, collaboration, or colonization, events that would hold out hope for the reestablishment of America, and American ideals, in some imaginable future. In contrast, if the Cold War goes hot, America might cease to exist as both a living reality and an abstract ideal, as both contemporary avatar and future dream. A mortal Uncle Sam is able to make the nation both incredibly powerful and hauntingly ephemeral, a live presence in the everyday experience of the citizenry and yet threatened with destruction at any moment. Nixon becomes the perfectly interpellated national subject in his imagination of the nation as both strong and directly interested in him, while being simultaneously vulnerable enough that his own actions matter. The rhetoric of national strength and national vulnerability that underwrote the ideas of civil defense, McCarthyism, and domestic containment could find no fitter send-up than this preposterous encounter.[4] And while this may seem merely emblematic of early Cold War fears of national destruction, it is important to note that this is an idiosyncratic imagining of that destruction: the typical postapocalyptic text witnesses the destruction of the government and the state while holding on to some residual belief in a nation that might one day rise again, a belief emblematized in some artifact that reminds us that although the United States has disappeared, "America" might yet be reborn.

Attempting to wring historical and cultural context out of such relentlessly antimimetic fiction (after all, I've begun with a scene where Nixon is playing golf with *Uncle Sam*!) might seem misguided, but in Coover's thoroughly absurd representation of national citizenship, he offers a cogent analysis of some of the pressures that the Cold War brought to bear on the concept of the nation, and of the historical character of the American metafictional writing that emerged across the second half of the century. Coover's relentless anatomizing of national fantasy has American nationality emerge as a temporal as well as a spatial category, and his destruction of the imagined coherence of the nation is the result of a temporal problem of historicity, and specifically the possibility of imaginatively locating oneself within the richness of historical time in a culture increasingly defined by the possibilities of nuclear exchange. Coover's alternate world offers a vision of what happens when national myth and Cold War reality collide: the collapse of any possible distinction between imaginary ideals of the nation and the actuality of state power in political circumstances that threaten the destruction of both.

The Rosenbergs are, of course, familiar figures of national allegory, figures for the moment at which the supposedly triumphant moral purpose of World War Two degenerated into the security state of the postwar, a point made by texts as separate in time and diverse in content as Sylvia Plath's *The Bell Jar* and Tony Kushner's *Angels in America*.[5] Coover's use of the Rosenbergs is radically stranger, however, than a straightforward critique of their execution. Most noticeable of all is that the portrayal of the Rosenbergs is, in Richard Walsh's words, "surprisingly unsympathetic."[6] In addition to its invention of a public execution attended by Gene Autry and the Mormon Tabernacle Choir, the novel asks us to imagine much more than simply a counterhistory still recognizable as a possible world that might mesh with what we take to be the basic conditions of reality. Coover goes well beyond hyperbolic satire when he rethinks the ontological altogether: Uncle Sam is a real character, a demon who flies through open windows to catch Nixon masturbating at his desk; the battle between Western capitalism and Soviet communism becomes combat between Uncle Sam and his archnemesis the Phantom; *Time* magazine routinely breaks out into verse to commemorate these momentous days, and is worried about his younger brother *Life*; here the reimagining of the concrete and the historical confronts a destruction of the line between history and the utterly fictional.

Coover's desire to foreground the violence of the executions is understandable. However, deconstructing history as a means to critique the execution of the Rosenbergs perhaps too quickly turns into deconstructing the Rosenbergs as a means to critique the very idea of history proper. Particularly at the moments of greatest narrative play, one wonders if Coover needs the Rosenbergs more than the Rosenbergs need him. My own response to the ethics of the novel's historical and metaphysical revision will be to offer a third path, asking whether the view of history that the novel professes, a view that leads into the aporia of history's textuality that I have just described, might itself be seen as a very specific historical response to a crisis of temporality. In short, the destruction of realist historical reference is here cast in sharply historicized terms, a paradox I unpack by paying attention to the temporality of nation in Coover's novel. In the section that follows, I play devil's advocate by revealing and then critiquing how the novel invites a straightforward political interpretation that would assimilate it into a condemnation of the state policies associated with the McCarthy period and "containment culture." By understanding the ways in which *The Public Burning* can't quite be understood through this paradigm, I hope to show how Coover turns a story of the physical intimacy between Nixon and Uncle Sam into a larger critique of the supposed temporality and historicity of American citizenship. This is a novel, after all, in which *Time* is the national poet laureate.

Hot Times for the Cold War

Recent work on the literary production of the Cold War has done much to complicate our sense of how the investment in "containing" Soviet communism reshaped both domestic life and literary production. Deborah Nelson's *Pursuing Privacy in Cold War America* (2002), for example, reads the emergence of confessional poetry alongside the contemporary Supreme Court cases that redefined notions of privacy. A key insight of Nelson's book is how both domains emerge as symptomatic responses to the paradoxes of containment during the Cold War. Far from being a stable term with fixed Cold War limits, "privacy" emerges as a central metaphor that is continually contested, and presents the most focused site for understanding the nexus of personal autonomy, the state, and the body.

Nelson's work extends the recent reassessments of the paradoxes that link the official account of containment as the attempt to ensure the continued viability and expansion of democracy with the undeniable fact that the antidote was often no better than the poison. The central paradox that emerges around privacy in the work of Nelson and other critics such as Timothy Melley is that to be ensured it must be unceasingly violated; the patriotic commitment to privacy and its concomitant freedoms requires the citizen to constantly forgo it, to open up the realm of the private to the state surveillance that might "protect" it.[7] Such a paradox renders the idea(l) impossible; the very thing that might define the value of the public culture of Cold War America—the ability to retreat from it—becomes precisely what you must renounce in order to join that culture at all.

In the figure of narrator Richard Nixon, Coover voices the centrality of privacy to American experience, painting a picture of a long-suffering Nixon who casts aside his own personal modesty for the good of the state. Just a few pages from the end of the novel, after Nixon has been publicly humiliated by appearing bare-assed on the stage on which the Rosenbergs are to be executed in front of millions, and after Ethel Rosenberg has written "I am a scamp" across his backside with lipstick, he offers the following personal narrative:

> Maybe, I'd thought, this is what hell will be like for me: endless self-exposure. This was a Self that was not in my mother's lexicon. It was the toughest part about being a politician, the one thing I personally hated the most. I'm no shrinking violet, I'm not unduly shy or modest, but I'm a private man and always have been. Formal. When I have sex I like to do it between the sheets in a dark room. When I take a shit I lock the door. My chest is hairy but I don't show it off. I don't even like to *eat* in public and just *talking* about one's personal life embarrasses me. And now all this today—Christ, I believed in touching the pulse of the nation, but this was going too fucking far! (526–27, italics in original)

The very public unveiling of the dangers of privacy—the trial and execution of the Rosenbergs, "private" citizens whose private actions threaten the public that maintains the possibility of privacy—is supposed to underwrite the possibility of privacy, though in Nixon's case it threatens it.

The real destruction of Nixon's privacy, however, has just begun. Rivaling the description of the execution of the Rosenbergs, in which Ethel requires so much electricity to kill her that she finally catches fire and is whipped about the stage like a puppet, is the real last scene of the novel: evidently Coover feels (to borrow Nixon's language) that things haven't gone fucking far enough. At the very moment when things seem to have returned to "normal"—Nixon has returned home to the domestic realm of his wife and children—we learn the true cost of election, when Uncle Sam arrives and rapes Nixon to incarnate him as a future president. Nixon's description is telling: "And in he came, filling me with a ripping all-rupturing force so fierce I thought I'd die! This . . . this is not happening to me alone, I thought desperately, or tried to think, as he pounded deeper and deeper, destroying everything, even my senses, my consciousness—but to the nation as well!" (532). Here an act of physical and sexual violence destroys not just the body but also the mind, reshaping Nixon in ways he can hardly understand. But, more importantly, when Nixon tries to think the experience figuratively, the effect is just plain creepy: "it felt like he was trying to shove the whole goddamn Washington Monument up my ass!" (532). Nixon is not, after all, simply a figure of national allegory in the scene. He is, in a sense, being raped by the Washington Monument, as well as by every other iconic figure or symbol of America, since the rapist in this case is Uncle Sam.

So just when the United States has been "saved" by the executions, we learn that the cost of becoming American, by becoming the representation of the will of the people, is the destruction of all that "America" is supposed to stand for. Bodily and psychic borders are both shattered as the price of becoming coextensive with the nation; and national allegiance becomes the ultimate form of false consciousness: "Of course, he was an incorrigible huckster, a sweet-talking con artist, you couldn't trust him, I knew that—but what did it matter? Whatever else he was, he was beautiful (how had I ever thought him ugly?), the most beautiful thing in all the world. I was ready at last to do what I had never done before. '*I . . . I love you, Uncle Sam!*' I confessed" (534, italics in original). The last word is telling, since confession is the one action that might have saved the Rosenbergs.

What Coover is trying to do here seems so patently obvious that it requires almost no explication. But, of course, you could do this in any number of ways that deflect the charge of ridiculous pastiche elicited by Coover's novel; registering the price of national identity during the Cold War doesn't require you to make Uncle Sam a real entity, much less a rapist, nor does it require you to instrumentalize the real death of the Rosenbergs into a fantastical public extravaganza. The danger of Coover's maneuver is that in making even the future president the victim of Sam's violation, Coover makes state power into a kind of absolute experience, in which even its future executive undergoes violation at its hands; even Nixon is a victim here.[8]

The problem with such a reading, however, is that it forgets the paradoxical quality of this national sex crime. Within a conventional language for thinking about American political experience, and for critiquing Cold War politics, we would likely reverse this scene. Throughout the novel, Nixon has been represented as above all else an agent of the state, the hands-on dirty operative who insulates Eisenhower from charges of corruption by doing the backroom deals necessary to maintain the administration's hold on power. Uncle Sam's position has been somewhat more nebulous. While clearly an ally of the administration, he is also a figure for a national belonging beyond the particularities of any single administration; instead of being the representation of a particular arrangement of state power, he is the embodiment of a far more abstract and imaginary ideal, that of the nation. Uncle Sam is Uncle Sam, a symbol of the nation in excess of any unique configuration of state power.

So in a "conventional" form of political critique, *Nixon* should be the rapist here, symptom of the administration's failure to live up to the promise of America announced through a national symbolic that guarantees freedom, protection, and privacy. Nixon's backroom dealings might be read as a way of revealing how the veneer of democracy is always maintained by democracy's suspension. But a conventional language for describing the anticommunist hysteria of the 1950s turns McCarthyism into an aberration, a moment when a particular arrangement of state power forgot the national ideals it was supposed to protect because of the threat communism posed to those ideals (as well as to the power of the state). And this, of course, is precisely what *isn't* happening in Coover's novel. It is the abstract ideal—rather than the concrete institutions or elected officials of the state—in which the suspension of the ideal originates. Needless to say, it is easier to imagine the executive branch doing violence to the nation than to imagine a national symbol doing violence to the executive branch, and it would make far more sense to write the scene in those terms if Coover aimed simply to offer a conventional critique of state excess during the Cold War.

The scene would also make sense as allegory if the abstract America were punishing a failure on the part of a particular arrangement of political power to live up to its promise. But again this doesn't work to explain the scene; this violent meeting with Uncle Sam is Nixon's reward rather than his punishment. Not only does the encounter with the nation violate psychic, sexual, and physical boundaries in *The Public Burning*, but the violation cannot be said to end—to the extent that Nixon remains alive, he remains American and violated, American as violated: "He [Sam] was buttoning up his striped pantaloons, which were now stained with the lipstick off my ass. Or maybe this time it *was* blood. I fell back, curled up around my pain. Oh my God, so this was what it was like! I felt like a woman in hard labor, bloated, sewn up, stuffed with some enormous bag of gas I couldn't release" (533, italics in original). Here the peculiar intimacy of the nation is predicated on violation, and is no longer an intimacy that guarantees personal autonomy as the reward for national consciousness. If the reading of the novel I have just offered suggests a poor fit between conventional accounts of 1950s paranoia and what the novel does with the story of the Rosenbergs and Nixon, the next section suggests what Coover offers in place of that reading, and how we might explain the novel's reversal of state and nation.

Cold Noons

High Noon (1952), a film all about the relationship between community and temporality, is a consistent intertext in the novel. Of course *High Noon* has long been read as an allegorical account of the domestic Cold War, and especially of McCarthyism: Stephen Whitfield notes, for instance, that scenarist Carl Foreman intended its story of a sheriff abandoned by his town in the face of an arriving threat to be taken as a story not of the small town of Hadleyville, but of Hollywood itself during the HUAC (House Un-American Activities Committee) era.[9] But Richard Slotkin has noted that such a leftist allegorical reading "does not exhaust the film's ideological utility" since the film is so ambiguous about the values the sheriff ultimately defends.[10] I would like to propose that the film is ultimately a revelation of the new forms of violence brought into being in the nuclear age, and of how those understandings of violence complicate received ideas of community.

The film first emerges in Coover's opening chapter, when we learn that a Texas high school marching band has been hired to perform the movie's theme song at the execution; it then reemerges as both Eisenhower's favorite movie and the title of the novel's fourteenth chapter. It is also structurally very similar to the novel since both take the form of a countdown to an act of violence (the film abandons the traditional episodic structure of violence characteristic of the western, when it defers the revelatory act of violence until the end of the film).[11] *High Noon* should be read as an extended meditation on the effects of a new generic understanding of violence, a violence that can only come at the end since that violence is total. Of course, *High Noon* can never represent the ultimately unrepresentable act of total violence shadowing its Cold War moment, but its break with the tradition of the western asks to be read as a perhaps inadequate response to a new understanding of the relationship between violence and ending. The film's choice of a black-and-white palette only tempts us further, asking us to see the world in sharply Manichean terms: this is a world of two political orders, and a world sharply divided between the promise of future perfection and the immanence of ending.

Coover's extended use of the film offers an allegory of reading as well, suggesting in the fictional Eisenhower's uncomprehending obsession with the film how we might in turn become better readers of this novel. Coover, I argue, agrees with the points made in alternate forms by Derrida and other critics about the fabulously textual nature of nuclear conflict, but in his use of the film as an allegory of current events, he shows us just how slippery such a textuality can be, suggesting that to acknowledge the textuality of the event is to take only a very small step toward understanding it, and that the imagined security provided by this allegory can actually lead us into, rather than away from, danger.

It is essential to remember that by 1952, the year of the film's release, the Korean conflict had focalized the threat of Communist expansion. While nuclear stockpiles had yet to reach the staggering size that would make the possibility of total destruction a reality—a possibility that had been nearly instantly imagined after the weapon's development—this potential was clearly on the horizon. The Soviet tests of 1949 and 1951 suggested unambiguously how terrifyingly out of control a war might get, and the 1952 American development of the hydrogen bomb fulfilled the deepest postwar fears of weapons many orders of magnitude greater than those used in the final days of World War Two.[12] Coover's novel characterizes 1953 as, in the words of Atomic Energy Commissioner Gordon Dean, the year that would see atomic power "come of age" (10). The novel is thus self-consciously set at a watershed moment, the point at which widespread nuclear destruction was finally being realized—rather than simply imagined—as a possibility.

A brief summary of *High Noon*: The film is set on a single morning of a single day, a day in which Will Kane, the long-serving sheriff of a small town has married Amy. As part of their new life together—Amy is a pacifist Quaker—Will has agreed to step down from his post, though his replacement sheriff is twenty-four hours away from arriving. After the wedding and retirement ceremony, but before leaving town, Will gets the ominous news that a murderer—Frank Miller—whom he captured some years ago has been pardoned, though he had been sentenced to death. Three members of Miller's old gang are at the train station waiting for the noon train on which Miller is presumed to be returning. Though Will and Amy briefly leave town, Will quickly returns and reassumes the job of sheriff, despite Amy's threat that she will leave him if he does so. As Will prepares for the noon encounter, which we expect will be violent—Miller had threatened to kill him rather than hang—the town gradually abandons Will, leaving him to face Miller alone. Townspeople who had fallen over themselves to praise Will just a few hours earlier, and who owe their livelihood and security to him, offer a range of weak reasons why they won't join him in defeating an obvious evil. Very quickly the viewer realizes that no matter what happens at the train station, damage has already been done: the latent divisions within the town have ossified into factionalization, and there is a very real possibility that the town may cease to exist as any kind of recognizable community or public regardless of whether Miller arrives or not.

The film, then, is structured around a threat of final violence that will usher in a nightmarish new era in the town's history whether or not it actually happens. The potential for this violent confrontation is the result of political "failure" since Miller has been pardoned by a weak northern jury, a model of the enduringly familiar argument about how quickly political softness can lead to a terrible threat, and a model of the way in which a factionalized America supposedly threatens itself with internal weakness. The threat of that violence restructures the domestic in any number of ways: Will's wife leaves him; the judge packs up all the symbols of the rule of law—his legal codes and the scales of justice—and flees; and one of the few ethnically marked characters in the film sells her business at a clear loss to get out of town. In short, the mere threat of violence reshapes both the juridical and domestic spheres: Will even breaks the barriers between church and state when he makes a rare appearance at a church in order to recruit potential deputies. With the townspeople debating possible strategies in the church, the film goes so far as to offer a debate on the logic and ethics of the first strike, a tactic ultimately rejected because it destroys the very law it was designed to protect.[13] The film condenses the domestic reshaping of the Cold War into a single town, and its ominous last moments before the final encounter record the destruction of anything like a public sphere: everyone goes indoors, and even the bar, a hotbed of Miller loyalists, falls silent.

Though Will survives, and the gang is killed off, the obvious implication is that a certain amount of damage has been done, damage represented in the final image of Will throwing his badge onto the dirt before he rides off wounded, although reunited with his wife. Indeed, the damage would have been done even if Miller hadn't arrived since what reshapes the town is less violence than its threat.

If the overall thematic of the film is not quite enough to convince one that this is a thinly veiled allegory of Cold War (and especially nuclear) life in America, then the film's recurrent visual motif, the various clocks that record the agonizing real-time countdown to the moment of the train's arrival, might tip the scale. Margot Henriksen offers a nuclear-historicized account of the film's terrors when she explains the particular significance the clocks might have held for a contemporary viewer: "The film's obsessive attention to and compression of time—the very notion of an impending crisis culminating at 'high noon' and the sense of time running out for civilization—emphasized the atmosphere of suspicion, urgency, and insecurity that accompanied life under the threat of atomic annihilation. The film's attention to the clock also provided a daytime equivalent to the scientists' atomic age symbol of crisis: the 'doomsday clock' included in each issue of the *Bulletin of Atomic Scientists* (beginning with the June 1947 issue), where the hands of the clock moved closer to midnight as the world moved closer to the probability of annihilation."[14]

In this context, the film's ultimate message is clear: the absolute evil of Frank Miller and his gang is matched by the absolute cowardice of a populace that refuses to confront it, leaving the resolute morality of one man to save the day. Such a reading goes a long way toward explicating just why Coover's Eisenhower finds the film so attractive. We know he has seen the film multiple times, and, as I have mentioned, the film's theme song becomes an unofficial prelude to the execution. Here we can stop and read Eisenhower's obsession in multiple ways. We might wonder at how pathetic is his focus on a film that, for all its possibility as allegory, fails to adequately, or even partly, come close to a representation of the actual world situation that Eisenhower faces. Or we might follow John Wayne's suggestion that the film is the most unpatriotic, communist film he had ever seen, since in the end Will Kane drops his badge.[15] In this case, we might imagine that Eisenhower's obsession is Coover's attempt to craft a more conflicted Eisenhower out of the ashes of history, an Eisenhower who emerges in tandem with Coover's evil but ultimately human Richard Nixon.

But all these options for understanding Eisenhower's obsession imagine that in his multiple viewings he has actually managed to *watch* the film. In reality, the president's interest in the film renders farcical the tragedy of his need for film as a means to comprehend the contemporary political situation: "The only TV program he was known to watch was 'The Fred Waring Show,' which he took to be a classical-music program. He sometimes liked to take in a movie in the White House basement, but generally snored through them, *High Noon* being one of the few that seemed to keep him awake. More or less awake: he tended to doze off during the kissing scenes (did he resent it that the wife was a Quaker?), then would wake up snorting: 'What time is it?'—meaning, Is it noon yet?" (31). The president's question is, quite frankly, stupid; even a first-time viewer could almost instantly figure out if it was noon yet. For one thing, the music changes to a track of ominous intensity, and the visual texture of the film changes as well, to one that makes it quite clear that we have moved into the final moments of the film. But Ike is hardly a first-time viewer; we know he has seen the film multiple times, and his initially laughable question now seems painful in its inappropriateness. If we take his obsession with the film as a result of his very real need to ensure that we never reach noon, then one would at least hope that he might be able to read the textual markers of impending crisis. But Eisenhower can't even remember the text, much less use it as a guide to a proleptic understanding of the world. Furthermore, the one thing that might wake up a sleeping viewer is the whistle of the train's arrival at noon, the one loud noise that punctuates the film until the fighting and gunshots commence. Eisenhower, then, in an important sense always wakes up too late: he is one of the townspeople rather than the sheriff. It isn't simply that the fictional Ike looks for textual analogues, no matter how inadequate, to help him understand the unthinkable event that structures political life: He cannot even bring these textual examples into focus. The idea of a president being fascinated by world politics allegorized in a movie is scary enough. This Eisenhower, however, is doubly nightmarish, since he misreads even this readerly text.

Through Ike, Coover offers an account of reading that suggests we might pay particular attention to the novel's arguments about time, particularly since it, too, is structured by the countdown to an event that might purify or destroy. Like the film, the novel is so centrally concerned with the idea of a countdown that its narrative temporality seems self-evident. And like the film's, the self-evident political critique of the novel starts to get progressively more complicated, and even contradictory, when you start testing its supposed obviousness. But in Eisenhower's misreading of the film, Coover shows just how wrong the interpretation of even the most self-evident temporal qualities of a text can go, and suggests one possible route for thinking through the ways in which conventional understandings of Cold War culture don't really account for Coover's paradoxical treatment of the relationship between state power and national embodiment. Like *High Noon*, *The Public Burning* contains a complex account of the implications of changes in structures of temporality. When we follow this suggestion, we open up a new way of reading the novel, in which its relentless metafictional play emerges not as the denial of historical reference, but as the emergence of a model of history shorn from the fullness of time. In short, the fabulation of the novel is an attempt to render the idea of America without a future tense, to represent American national identity when the very structure it requires is modified. The film offers a model of how one might "read" a structure of time not as a thing in itself, but as the cause of any number of symptomatic reactions; it is the film's link between temporality and the social that proves so useful in tracing out a more complex reading of Coover.

Hallucinating the Nation

Uncle Sam initially seems a straightforward spin doctor, intent on imagining politics as an endless PR game, and always privileging the present and future over the past: "Hell, *all* courtroom testimony about the past is ipso facto and teetotaciously a baldface lie, ain't that so? Moonshine! Chicanery! The ole gum game! Like history itself—all more or less bunk, as Henry Ford liked to say" (86). The reason for such a lack of concern for the past is that Sam's America resides within an entirely different temporal register, and in a culture that registers time in a somewhat counterintuitive way, as we see when he lectures Nixon:

> "... Ya know, people useter think of time like some kinda movin' knife edge cuttin' acrost the entire universe, but that was on accounta they was locked up in a room in Europe somewhere and not heedin' what was roarin' up over here! America was on the go—not only on horses, but on wheels, on trains, on steamships and automobiles, even into the air. Einstein seen this. And while he was skinnin' his eyes for what this signified, it suddenly come to his attention that a movin' clock appears to run slow set off agin an identical clock sittin' still and the—hope I'm not too fast for you, son ...?"

"No! No, I . . ."

"Bodies in motion just don't age as fast, that's what it boils down to. America, by stayin' off its ass, was stayin' young! No surprise Albert come to live here when he got his chance! This here's a country of beginnin's, of projects, of vast designs and expectations! It's got no past; all has an onward and prospective look! The fountain of youth!" (205, ellipses in original)

Though his language is a bit over-the-top, Uncle Sam speaks in a familiar American idiom of futurity: he is but one more critic in the lineage of the frontier thesis, the romance thesis, or the jeremiad, who identifies the particular tense of American identity as futural: America is that ideal that is yet to come (for Sam, a "closed frontier was like a hardened artery" [205]). One thinks here of the last scene in *The Great Gatsby*, with its imagination of an "orgastic future" that continually escapes us even as we keep trying to achieve it.

The bizarre temporal paradox to which Uncle Sam's notions lead is easy to imagine. The future emerges out of a present that is never allowed to become history, and thus the present can only emerge out of the future in a circularity that leads to formulations such as this one: "This is to be a consecration, a new charter of the moral and social order of the Western World, the precedint on which the future is to be carn-structed to ensure peace in our time" (91). The present speaks forward to the future only to ensure its own status. If Uncle Sam offers us a vision of America that depends entirely on the future to understand the present, what happens when the present can lead to futures that are simply incapable of existing? This is a point raised ironically when we realize that even as Sam is making this case for the future, he is crafting a "miniature mushroom cloud" with pipe smoke (91). The danger to which the jeremiad or errand speaks is that we might fail in our mission, that the future which might come about will retroactively assign a failure to the present from which it emerged. But what happens when the actions of the present potentially leave no future that we can imagine retroactively engaging our present, and indeed leave no position from which to understand that now there is no future, nor present, nor past?

The answer is that this novel is what happens. The novel's metafictional account of American history is an attempt to render the paradox of a nation that depends on a now-nonexistent notion of temporality, a temporality rendered untenable by historical change. The destruction of national history in the novel is a historically specific account of an epochal shift in notions of temporality. We need to remember just how problematic the structure of the jeremiad looks in this world, since the future that emerges from the concrete engagements of the present is not guaranteed; the particular technology defining the Cold War leads to the impossibility of a model of present consecration built around the future, since the present is defined by a technology that can destroy the future so completely that no witnesses and no archives survive. A novel in which Uncle Sam is a real character is absurd fabulation, no doubt; but that absurdity is also a way of unpacking the paradoxes of a national imaginary that is continually located in a tense no longer available to it. Coover's sense of the violent intimacy of contact with the national symbolic registers the compression of futurity by making "America" uncomfortably close, both physically and temporally. The incoherence of the scene where Nixon is raped by Sam thus records the incompatibility of a futural national imaginary and a world that may have no future.

Now would be a useful time to remember the unique temporality of the nuclear, and its concomitant criticism, a temporality nicely summarized by Richard Klein as "a futureless future, a time in which it may no longer be possible collectively to mourn the past, a future in which there will not have been a posthumous perspective."[16] Klein's formulation of a future without future shows up in Nixon's ephemeral grasp, near the end of the novel, of the problems inherent in Uncle Sam's formulation of a national future tense: "I was hanging on then by the grace of one thought only: that the day had to end, it would all be got past. Had to. Time marches on. Shakespeare said that in some play, I believe. Some tomorrow would inevitably become today and we could start forgetting, that was the main thing. I'd never doubted this until that moment the doctors said she was still alive: then suddenly I'd felt like we were teetering on the brink of infinity. Scared the hell out of me" (524). Nixon is suddenly able to grasp, if only for a single terrifying moment, the distinction between a normal clock and the Doomsday Clock, the distinction between the inevitable arrival of the future and the fragile future tense of the nuclear age.

In the figure of Uncle Sam we have the most overt reference to the idea of the immediacy of the nation, a vision of what it means when you can't place national fantasy either in a distant past or in the revelatory promise of future consecration. Instead, the abstraction of America must become present in a way that foregrounds just how imaginary and incoherent the very idea of nation has become in the Cold War as Coover sees it. Uncle Sam is the incarnation of the nation without time other than the moment, a vision of what "America" might mean if we take away the future in which it "should" be located, and make the present tense the only place where America can be experienced.

When Nixon experiences the terror of the failed execution as a temporal crisis, he imagines it as a challenge to a model of temporality based around forgetting: we take solace in the fact that no matter how terrible a particular moment might be, it will recede into a past that we might then transcend. But in Uncle Sam we have a vision of the radical simultaneity of American identity, in a figure assembled out of bits and pieces of former presidents. Though Uncle Sam continually speaks to the future realization of America, he roams a world haunted by the idea that any belief in futurity may be impossible to maintain. And if we don't have a future, we also don't have a past; what we have instead is the radical simultaneity of an all-too-present "America." It is here, finally, that I see Coover's central point: The public burning of the Rosenbergs is also the burning of the very idea of a public, the result of the destruction of the models of time that are required for community to come into being as anything other than pathological intimacy.[17]

Uncle Sam is certainly all too present in the novel, most notably in his forced violation of Nixon's body. Yet this violation is only the most brutal manifestation of a novelistic world that is everywhere spatially claustrophobic, culminating in the packed crowds of Times Square at the end of the novel. And that pouring of bodies into New York City certainly reverses a grand narrative of westward progression, in which national identity is dependent on a rugged individualism tested in exploration and wilderness. But spatial claustrophobia is, in this novel, precisely analogous to a temporal claustrophobia and compression. The relentless countdown to the execution is the textual manifestation of the fact that notwithstanding Sam's belief in the future as the place where "America" might be realized, Sam is both spatially and temporally stuck in the present, and thus violates classic accounts of American culture that locate America elsewhere. As Mitchell Breitwieser points out, the two classic formulations are ultimately the same, locating as they do "America" in either a place or time that isn't coextensive with where one currently is ("present" in both senses of that term). And while the subject of Breitwieser's *National Melancholy* is primarily that identification of America with a "particular permanent futurity," he finds that sense of Nation as a not-yet-arrived-at potentiality disappearing in the middle of the twentieth century, coming to "final expression" in the work of, among others, Allen Ginsberg, Jack Kerouac, and possibly John Updike and Pynchon.[18] Though Breitwieser doesn't discuss Coover, we might say that *The Public Burning* is ultimately the novel that historicizes—as a result of the nuclear age—this disappearance of a particular form of national feeling.

In 1951, Perry Miller asked his readers what the invention of nuclear weapons might mean for a religious tradition centrally defined by eschatology; with the end of the world now imaginable as purely secular antirevelatory nuclear exchange, how might American thought adapt?[19] Some twenty years later, a near-perfect coincidence: Sacvan Bercovitch bypassed Miller's question when he identified the jeremiad as the central trope for American literature just one year after Coover had announced the death of the future that its model of errand required.[20] And so the jeremiad was enshrined as the definitive rhetorical structure for American literature around the very moment when Coover was putting it to rest by revealing it as a distinctly historical imagination of the shape of American history.

4 / Unthinking the Thinkability of the Unthinkable

In Tim O'Brien's 1985 novel *The Nuclear Age*, the increasingly hysterical protagonist has only one "practical" response to his fear of imminent thermonuclear war: he digs a big hole in his backyard in the hope of completing a fallout shelter for himself, his wife, and his daughter before the missiles fly.[1] A pure product of the Cold War, and a disenchanted veteran of one of the New Left's aggressive subfactions, William Cowling's dreams are haunted by destruction.[2] O'Brien's novel reminds us of just how intractable the Cold War seemed to be in 1985; no one could have foreseen that the conflict would end only a few years later.[3] However, the punch line that accompanies his decision in the first chapter to start digging complicates the picture: "No metaphor, the bombs are real."[4] In contrast to those who would regard him as crazy, Cowling here claims special insight, and suggests the form of action appropriate to that knowledge. In view of the threat that everywhere surrounds him, his family, his nation, and his planet, Cowling wants to focus on the truth that figurative language works to conceal. Cowling thus insists on a form of pure reference: tellingly, Cowling's wife is a poet, and Cowling's argument with her about the appropriateness of metaphor is an argument with any form of linguistic mediation of the bomb—the threat is so huge that it must be approached without any intervening aesthetic or anesthetic.[5]

In a critical reading of arms proliferation discourse, and especially of the West's tendency to imagine Third World nations' nuclear ambitions as motivated principally by religious extremism, Hugh Gusterson surveys some of the reactions to Pakistani and Indian nuclear proliferation.

After noting that Western commentators mistranslate weapons' names in order to claim that the developing world names its weapons after instruments of divine violence and retribution (and thus can't be trusted to have them), Gusterson points out that "if Western commentators were looking for a country that names its nuclear weapons after ancient gods and dead warriors, they need have looked no further than the United States, with its Jupiter, Thor, Poseidon, Atlas, Minuteman, and Pershing missiles."[6] O'Brien clearly has something similar in mind when he has Cowling describe his marital troubles in these terms: "Bobbi doesn't understand. She's a poet, she can't help it. I've tried to talk things out. I've presented the facts. I've named names: Poseidon, Trident, Cruise, Stealth, Minuteman, Lance, Pershing—the indisputable realities. Trouble is, Bobbi can't process hard data. The artistic temperament. Too romantic, too sublime" (58). While there is no evidence that Cowling is being ironic, O'Brien certainly is: the distinction between fact and art collapses in the face of the narrative baggage that those facts carry, and the implicitly gendered opposition between "rational" thinking and poetic "intuition" falls apart when facts are named for myths. So it would seem that Cowling's initially laudable quest to access the reality of the bomb is actually impossible, and when reread the full passage deconstructs itself under the weight of its desire: "I'm a man of my age, and it's an age of extraordinary jeopardy. So who's crazy? Me? Or is it you? You poor, pitiful sheep. Listen—Kansas is on fire. What choice do I have? Just dig and dig. Find the rhythm. Think about those silos deep in fields of winter wheat. *Five, four, slam the door.* No metaphor, the bombs are real" (4, italics in original). As the "rhythm" of digging becomes the "rhythm" of thinking, we realize Cowling is closer to his poet wife than he knows.

While it is tempting to continue to trace the ways in which O'Brien complicates the distinction between fact and metaphor, what I would like to note at this point is that part of Cowling's resistance to metaphor might lie in how comprehensively he was once seduced by a very common and instructive rhetoric: the comparison of nuclear war with sport. Paul Boyer has noted with some frustration that the public has had only episodic outbreaks of nuclear fear despite the continual presence and near-constant expansion of the weapons since 1945.[7] While Cowling's own periods of nuclear fear don't map perfectly onto Boyer's account, they do reveal something important about the relative dangers of nuclear war, and about that danger's intermittent hold on the American imagination. What mutes Cowling's first outburst of nuclear dread in 1958 as he enters his teen years is a game. A child who has never known a non-nuclear reality, Cowling begins to have dreams of destruction but finds his parents and community oddly complacent about the nuclear threat under which they live; he concludes that in the face of their obliviousness he must act alone.[8] Cowling, then, is an adolescent whose time is out of joint with that of his community, and he frantically builds a blast and fallout shelter in the family basement, heaping lumber and charcoal on top of a Ping-Pong table, and creating walls out of newspaper-stuffed cardboard boxes, in something like the nuclear version of the familiar childhood fort-building game.[9] He goes so far as to line the walls with pencils, mistakenly believing that their graphite cores contain lead that might shield him from radiation. He stocks the shelter with food and medicine, and makes a fallout mask out of a paper bag. Young enough never to have known a nuclear-free world, Cowling has grown up with a nuclear unconscious, and childhood dreams of "whole continents on fire, oceans boiling, cities in ash" (12). His limited agency means that his ersatz fallout shelter is the best he can do by way of preparation.

When Cowling's father discovers his son huddled for a second night in his basement shelter, O'Brien brilliantly represents one of the ways in which nuclear war was displaced in the American imagination. In an effort to cheer him up, Cowling's father suggests they clear the top of the shelter and play a game of Ping-Pong. Even though Cowling knows what his father is up to, they end up playing several tough games, and the games affect Cowling to an extent that seems disproportionate to such a minor display of parental interest: "And for the next decade my dreams were clean and flashless. The world was stable. The balance of power held" (32). Cowling survives the Cuban Missile Crisis without any terrifying return of his symptoms, and when they do return, they come back strangely unmoored from any of the key crisis events of the Cold War.

Though the Ping-Pong game initially seems a minor episode, what O'Brien has done is to condense one of the dominant ways of imagining nuclear war into a single scene, transforming a child's fear of unwinnable total destruction into a violent but ultimately rational game of skill that could be prepared for, lived through, and even won. By turning the makeshift shelter back into a Ping-Pong table, Cowling's father converts nuclear war into a governed exchange, and the game convinces Cowling that, even in the face of a strong opponent, skill and hard work are all that is needed: "And they were good, tough games. My dad had a wicked backhand, quick and accurate, but I gradually wore him down with my forehand slams. Boom, point. Boom, point. A couple of times it almost seemed that he was setting me up, lobbing those high easy ones for me to smash back at him. But it felt good. I couldn't miss" (32). While Cowling has the sneaking suspicion that his father isn't playing up to his full ability, the games work: Cowling remains nightmare-free for a decade after these nighttime contests. Such a transformation of nuclear war into a rule-governed exchange (almost, in the end, a conversation) rather than the catastrophe that Cowling dreads is one of the most frequently recurring features of late 1950s and 1960s nuclear rhetoric, and a transformation taken up with suggestive regularity by the core writers of American postmodernism.

It is the contention of this chapter that recovering the modes of thinking that guided military strategy during this period offers a crucial means by which to contextualize metafiction: a discourse of simulation and of the need to create worlds parallel to our own runs through both, and the ten years between 1958 and 1968, the years in which Cowling remains free of dread, prove crucial to the development of both disciplines. The ultimate claim that *The Nuclear Age* makes about the politics of nuclear discourse is quite vexed: the text demonstrates that the desire to contemplate the bomb as a thing-in-itself is doomed to failure, but it also insinuates that such a desire may be just as problematic as the recourse to metaphor.

Possible Worlds: Strategic Culture after Hiroshima

In the wake of World War Two, the military, and a parallel civilian defense establishment located primarily in the new think tanks that arose after the war, planned future wars simultaneously. Though all wars generate new technologies, a hitherto unknown pace of technological development characterized World War Two: "It was a war in which the talents of scientists were exploited to an unprecedented, almost extravagant degree. First, there were all the new inventions of warfare—radar, infrared detection devices, bomber aircraft, long-range rockets, torpedoes with depth charges, as well as the atomic bomb. Second, the military had only the vaguest of ideas about how to use these inventions; thinking about new problems was not an integral feature of the military profession."[10] After the end of the war, the need for civilian help in understanding these new weapons grew rapidly: for one thing, postwar demobilization made civilian help a logistical necessity; for another, it quickly grew apparent that a future war with another global power might well be a nuclear exchange, and would likely be so short that the chance to mobilize the industrial resources of the country to match an enemy aggressor would be lost.[11] In elaborate and ever-more-sophisticated projections of future technologies and political realities at the RAND Corporation and Hudson Institute, men and women who had never seen combat imagined what future wars would be like. Strategy became metastrategy, imagining the future wars of future worlds.

War-gaming has always been a part of military strategy, but what distinguished this new imagination of war-gaming was precisely the *imagination*.[12] One couldn't, after all, stage live-fire exercises with nuclear weapons against a nuclear opponent, and the fact that there would be no time in which to develop counterweapons to the enemy's new weapons meant that one had to imagine the possibilities years into the future. The result, as Sharon Ghamari-Tabrizi has pointed out, was an elaborate world of simulated reality that spun out multiple future possibilities. At its heart was one of the twentieth century's most original and most striking intellectuals, Herman Kahn.[13] While game theory could help us imagine how two rational opponents might respond to each other in a simulated exchange, the initial situation that could provoke the exchange had to be endlessly reimagined, since no one was sure what the key variables would be in nuclear conflict, and because the technologies were evolving at such a rapid pace.[14] As Ghamari-Tabrizi has revealed, this was Kahn's special contribution to the art of war-gaming, since he was the consummate imaginative author of the situation(s) that could trigger future nuclear wars. This tension between the rationality of game theory and the imaginatively constructed scenario in which it could be used is nicely summarized in the fears of one member of the joint chiefs of staff: In a public discussion of war-gaming, he mentioned that he was afraid that the audience would "associate our efforts more with those of Cecil B. DeMille" than with the mathematician and exemplary game-theorist John von Neumann.[15]

This tension between rationality and creativity was basically impossible to resolve. As Kahn pointed out when generals objected to the fact that this borderline-narcoleptic civilian defense intellectual was lecturing them on how to fight a war (or, in some cases, how to fight the next several wars), none of them had fought a nuclear conflict either. He proposed that imagined scenarios were more helpful in preparing for nuclear war than even the most distinguished records of military service in previous conflicts. Bernard Brodie was even more explicit. A darling of the navy during World War Two thanks to his history of naval warfare, Brodie's response to the news of Hiroshima was that everything he had published up to that point was now obsolete.[16] It wasn't simply that history would offer no guide to the future, but that thinking guided by experience, history, or the fact of having seen combat close-up could be downright dangerous, since it would imagine the bomb on a continuum with previous weapons. For the defense intellectuals, the notorious military habit of planning for the last war it had fought would be especially dangerous when the weapons were this powerful; the infamous error of generals in 1914 imagining the cavalry as the appropriate response to the imminent cataclysm of World War One, however unbelievable it was, would be a minor strategic blunder compared to thinking about nuclear weapons via the history of conventional arms, especially because the pace of technological development was now so fast that one had to imagine wars that would be fought with technology yet to be invented.

The reaction in the 1960s to Kahn and his work was—understandably—quite mixed, with some readers diagnosing him as insane while others found in him a prime example of humanist thinking.[17] But for Kahn, the elaborate scenarios he offered were ways of making "thinkable" the unthinkably horrific, and in making them into thinkable games, he was trying to do exactly what Cowling's father does in *The Nuclear Age* when he reclaims the Ping-Pong table as a Ping-Pong table: to make nuclear fear into a rational, rather than an overwhelmingly emotional, zone of political affairs. Kahn's utter disregard for social nicety, economic reality, or the emotional impact of thinking about 50 million deaths often rendered him a sinister figure in popular discourse, but his writings appear to have been motivated by a strongly felt desire not to fall into the trap of unspeakability; to Kahn's mind, a nuclear war in which 10 million Americans died was preferable to one in which 20 million did, and was preferable enough that one was duty bound to think about how to save those "extra" 10 million lives.[18] The chart that recurs in *On Thermonuclear War* (1960) suggests his thinking: titled "Tragic But Distinguishable Postwar States," it collates the number of dead with the years it would take for economic recuperation; while 160 million dead would mean a hundred-year waiting period until the economy recovered, 40 million might result "only" in a twenty-year difficulty.[19] Looking back from the twenty-first century, we may well find such strategizing stunningly naïve; if recent military action has taught us anything, it is that simulation is only as good as the intelligence that produces it, and as we uncover the wealth of declassified intelligence that has emerged in the wake of the Cold War, we realize just how oblivious even the supposed commanders and defense intellectuals could be[20]—witness Lynn Eden's astonishing revelation of the fact that U.S. nuclear war planning never seriously considered the fires that would be caused by the use of nuclear weapons, and hence *vastly* underestimated the damage it would entail.

A short history: the air force had almost total control over the targeting decisions for its weapons from the late 1940s until the Kennedy administration. The Air Target Division was filled with specialists busy planning the use of the new weapon under the rubrics inherited from World War Two, and the Strategic Air Command (SAC) was led by veterans—first Curtis LeMay, then Tommy Power—who had earned their command on the basis of city-busting sorties over Japan.[21]

The strategy that emerged through the 1950s consequently emphasized the destruction of cities, and the notion of "killing a nation." If the goal was the total destruction of an enemy nation, rather than simply the enemy nation's ability to destroy you, there was no reason not to launch every weapon you had all at once. This was at the heart of the argument advanced by both the SAC and Secretary of State John Foster Dulles when he called for a doctrine of "massive retaliation" against any Soviet aggression.[22] And when the new Kennedy administration was briefed by the military on their targeting plans, it was revealed that the default (plan 1-A) was to launch an all-out strike, using much of the American nuclear arsenal.[23] The 1950s combination of a military nuclear establishment comprised almost exclusively of air force commanders trained in and by the history of the Dresden and the Japanese air campaigns, and an Eisenhower and Dulles looking for the cheapest possible military match for Soviet forces (despite their expense, nuclear weapons were still cheaper than keeping a war-ready conventional force deployed in both western Europe and Asia) meant that nuclear weapons were considered a key part of any future war.

The limits of this approach were obvious to defense intellectuals (especially William Kaufmann and Bernard Brodie), who quickly criticized the doctrine of massive retaliation Dulles articulated in his 1954 speech at the Council on Foreign Relations.[24] Once the Soviets came close to strategic parity in nuclear weapons, an American or NATO threat to respond to any conventional Soviet aggression with nuclear weapons began to look meaningless because it would inevitably lead to massive retaliation from the other side, and ultimately, perhaps, to the end of life on the planet. As Kaufmann and Brodie saw it, reliance on a nuclear deterrent practically guaranteed the limited wars of communist aggression it was designed to prevent, since as soon as it had approximately matched America's arsenal, the Soviet Union would feel free to call its bluff. While such theoretical thinking found a ready ear in the army (which was facing cuts to its own budget and strength, by virtue of being the force for conventional combat; Eisenhower had told the army that its critical role in a future conflict would be maintaining order in the United States after an attack), it fell on deaf ears within the corridors of true power, since Eisenhower and his cabinet were determined to imagine nuclear weapons, and a related doctrine of massive retaliation, as central to their war planning and especially to their cost control.[25]

A growing concern about the rigidity of military thinking about the bomb, as well as Kennedy's faith in civilian opinion, finally brought the defense intellectuals into the government in full force. Whereas Eisenhower had little use for civilian opinion, Kennedy's love of the "whiz kids," the group of academics and industry leaders led by Robert McNamara that defined the cabinet of the Kennedy and Johnson years, is well known.[26] McNamara was eager to explore the possibilities of nuclear weapons outside of doctrines of massive retaliation; the question that came to occupy much of his thinking was how to imagine the use of nuclear weapons on a sliding scale that began with very controlled and limited use.[27] Central to such a model of nuclear war was the strategy of "counterforce" rather than the targeting of cities.

The idea of counterforce was intended to make nuclear war appear rational and winnable, building on the elaborate escalation ladders and games that were so essential to the thinking of civilian defense intellectuals. The strategy went by a variety of other names—"war fighting" and "No Cities"—and central to it was the idea that a first-round strike would take out the enemy's offensive and defensive capabilities, destroying a large percentage of the enemy's weapons systems while holding a substantial amount of one's own weaponry in reserve. While it would perhaps not be possible to destroy all the enemy's weaponry, the hope was that enough of it would be destroyed to cause them to sue for peace, since their cities could be held hostage. If the enemy responded by launching their remaining nuclear weapons, their country could be wiped out in (nearly) its entirety, and if they delayed surrendering, their cities could be taken out one by one as a means of hastening "peace." The thought was that a rational enemy would understand a counterforce attack for what it was, and would only respond in kind rather than with total retaliation; the entire strategy was predicated on an enemy who could be relied upon to be rational even in the event of nuclear war, and who could "read" one's own strikes as rational: in this strategic culture, war becomes a form of conversation. McNamara worked very hard to ensure that if nuclear weapons were used, they would be used in a controlled fashion rather than in an all-out strike that would kill several hundred million people at minimum. Throughout the 1960s, McNamara continued to try to find ways of imagining limited nuclear war, and U.S. nuclear strategy emphasized flexibility and controlled escalation; as a result, the elaborate attempts to think through all the permutations of war fighting that simulation and thought experiment allowed became ever more important, since the possible permutations of targeting were so complex, and the resulting strategic moves so numerous.[28]

The possibility of limited nuclear war was rapidly disappearing by the late 1960s as the plausibility of McNamara's counterforce strategy was increasingly eroded by the dispersal and hardening of the Soviet arsenal, and by the potential emergence of defensive screens of antiballistic-missile missiles (ABMs).[29] Both developments meant that launching a limited number of weapons might not ensure the destruction of the enemy's military targets: the dispersal meant that one would have to launch an unacceptably large number of weapons, and if an ABM system went online, one would need to assume that many of the weapons launched would not get through. Given that mid-1960s targeting plans already called for a level of redundancy in weapons targeting (for instance, in order to "ensure" a level of destruction equal to Hiroshima, targeting plans called for a total yield roughly eighteen times the size of the Hiroshima bomb), you would now need to launch multiple weapons even at the smallest target, and the enemy might be unable to distinguish between a limited and an all-out nuclear attack.[30] In short, the very faith you put in your enemy's warning systems in a counterforce situation—that they would "read" your attack as a limited one, and respond in kind—now meant you would have to launch a total attack, since even a counterforce attack would look overwhelming, and if you knew they would respond as if you were launching a total attack, then you would have to launch that total attack preemptively since you needed to do as much damage as possible up front.

American nuclear strategy thus helps to contextualize Cowling's ten-year reprieve from nuclear fear after his Ping-Pong game. The years between 1958 and 1968 would have been the period when metaphors of gaming could most adequately reassure American citizens into believing that nuclear war wasn't worth irrational worry or preparation on their own part; the ten years between the doctrine of massive retaliation and one of assured destruction facilitated imaginations of nuclear war as a strategic exchange between two rational powers that could find analogies with games of skill. By the late 1960s, the limited use of the weapons was an increasing impossibility, and McNamara's new doctrine of assured destruction was, in the face of a Soviet stockpile that had achieved rough parity, looking more and more like a philosophy of mutually assured destruction. This history does more than simply contextualize the appeal and the limits of a game of Ping-Pong in O'Brien's novel; it also helps to explicate a series of works in which the criticism of metafiction was indirectly engaged, and enables us to see the metafictional generation of American writers in a new light.

Just Gaming

While Mark McGurl's work on the relationship between postwar American fiction and the university writing program has usefully attuned us to the fact that nearly all postwar American fiction displays a degree of self consciousness—evidence, for McGurl, of what Ulrich Beck and Anthony Giddens would call our reflexive modernity—we can still see a range of fictional self-consciousness in the period.[31] While all postwar fiction may be reflexive to some degree, metafiction remains a useful term for designating those works that emerged in the 1960s that make their own fictionality a central issue, and have thus largely been relegated to the status of mere period pieces. As I noted in the introduction, even a critic as attentive to the historiographic interests of so much postmodern fiction as Linda Hutcheon has separated historiographic metafiction (her preferred term for postmodern fiction that still reflects on the writing of history) from the less obviously referential forms of metafiction (which she sees as the endgame of autotelic modernism).[32] While recent years have given us carefully historicized readings of the historiographic impulses of Thomas Pynchon and Don DeLillo, writers such as Donald Barthelme have received substantially less attention (and to the extent that they remain part of literary history, they do so primarily as examples of fiction about fiction-making).[33]

There are good reasons for such decisions, of course. Though these writers at times contextualized their own work as a response to the enormous burden of imagining the fate of fiction after the achievements of modernism (and Barthelme's 1964 essay on his vision of fiction bears the telling title "After Joyce"), their own practice and statements often provided plenty of ammunition for critics.[34] As McGurl has noted, one of Barthelme's best-known stories, "The Balloon," is emblematic of a form of aesthetic production in which meaning and reference are, at best, only secondary to artistic achievement,[35] and, as we have seen, despite his later recantations, Barth's nonfictional writing from the 1960s (often taken as a kind of key to this generation of writers) foregrounds the purely aesthetic character of his writing. So while these writers offered spirited defenses of their aesthetic practices, accounts such as Barth's have made it easy enough to write off much of this fiction as an elaborate onanistic game, further symptoms of what Christopher Lasch has called the culture of narcissism.[36] In an era defined by Vietnam, the various social movements of the 1960s that exposed the reality of unequally distributed violence, oppression, and social injustice, and the threat of total nuclear war, metafiction and fabulation, with their celebration of aesthetic creation, could at their worst look much more like ivory tower escapism than anything resembling political engagement. And even when critics have been sympathetic to this fiction, they have rarely pursued political readings; the recent turn, for instance, to Cold War–inflected readings of Nabokov (famous for his own prompts about how to read his books in aesthetic terms) almost always begins by noting the paucity of contextual readings of his novels.[37]

Patricia Waugh, however, has noted that metafiction about gaming is a particularly fruitful archive for thinking about metafiction in general, as it is in these works that the idea of a self-constructed world is most fully developed as a thematic, given the concern within these texts with describing the "rules" governing the reality of the game-space.[38] So it is both surprising and instructive that those writers most committed to metafiction would, in their 1960s fiction about gaming, develop devastating critiques of this culture of simulation and self-constructed worlds. Coover and Barthelme suggest some of the ways in which postmodern fiction might prove a plausible—and indeed even necessary—form in which to critique defense policy.

Just as when Cowling plays the nightmare-erasing game of Ping-Pong with his father he has the sneaking suspicion that his father is going easy on him, the question of one's opponent's commitment, and one's knowledge of it, would come to haunt the work of Barthelme and Coover even in texts that seemed to revel in game-playing. "Game" (1965) is collected in Barthelme's 1968 *Unspeakable Practices, Unnatural Acts*, a collection of stories that is central to arguments about postmodernism that privilege Barthelme's interest in the purely aesthetic concerns of metafiction.[39] But "Game" tells another story too, one that dovetails with the fear that haunts Cowling about exactly how hard his father is trying, and which evidences the surprising possibilities of metafiction for pointed political critique.[40]

"Game" is about two missile officers a hundred or more feet underground in their silo who are charged with the task of turning their launch keys in sync should the order come to launch the missile. They are thus the necessarily human link in the launch chain, redundant duplicates of each other that prevent either from launching the missile on his own. Obviously such figures were under immense pressure during the Cold War, and much psychological speculation focused on whether or not governments could trust humans to function in effect as automata, without giving thought to what they will be doing when they turn the key: a sane person might well refuse; an insane person might well try.[41] And "Game" certainly performs some of the metaphorical substitutions by which nuclear officers were disconnected from actually understanding what they were doing: "Shotwell has a key and I have a key. If we turn our keys simultaneously the bird flies, certain switches are activated and the bird flies. But the bird never flies."[42] The act of launching a missile is here akin to liberating a caged animal, though the description of what exactly happens is so abstract and passively constructed ("certain switches are activated") that it becomes hard to imagine precisely where agency lies, and who (or what) might finally be responsible for massive destruction.[43]

Barthelme's story, however, shies away from familiar psychological narratives in favor of a creepier vision of what goes on in missile silos, as it tells the story of what happens when these two men are forgotten by their relief crew (or are, perhaps, the subjects of a psychological experiment), and end up spending 133 days together, instead of a single twelve-hour shift: "Each of us wears a .45 and each of us is supposed to shoot the other if the other is behaving strangely. How strangely is strangely? I do not know. In addition to the .45 I have a .38 which Shotwell does not know about concealed in my attaché case, and Shotwell has a .25 caliber Beretta which I do not know about strapped to his right calf. Sometimes instead of watching the console I pointedly watch Shotwell's .45, but this is simply a ruse, simply a maneuver, in reality I am watching his hand when it dangles in the vicinity of his right calf."[44] The story reveals how a culture of skepticism, secrecy, surveillance, and hair-trigger aggression plays out at a nearly infinite number of levels. It is difficult to imagine one or both of these characters *not* behaving "strangely" when the order comes to turn their keys simultaneously to launch the missile; the result might be done on film with a split screen: as Soviet and American missiles leave their silos or submarines and guarantee the death of both nations and the planet, in each silo missile officers pull the trigger on their handguns simultaneously, thereby repeating the problem of assured collective death *within* the sealed environment of the silo.

So one meaning of the story's title, "Game," becomes clearer: maps are not the territories they hope to represent, and no matter how rigorously one tries to imagine a war-gaming environment incorporating every contingency, the finite number of players in the game has to represent a much larger community of actors, each of whom adds the considerable complexity of the human factor into the equation of simulation. The damning question at the heart of the quoted passage—"How strangely is strangely?"—suggests the impossible-to-quantify element of judgment that would finally have to go into every decision made under the pressure of actual or potential conflict. The fact that our narrator doesn't know suggests the difficulty of trying to imagine how we might simulate a conflict with these kinds of stakes when the most basic features of the military chain of command rely on judgments that can't be schematized or modeled, dependent as they are on unique judgments which can never be factored into the constricted economy of simulation.

The story represents this problem of judgment on multiple levels. On the one hand, the two characters are identical: their job is to do the exact same thing at the exact same time, without any individual thoughts intruding. On the other hand, the two are radically unknowable to each other: the narrator has no access to the thoughts of Shotwell, and they would seem to disagree even on the most basic features of enjoyment. This blending of absolute similarity and unbridgeable difference grows more acute. As the unnamed narrator loses his mind over the course of the story, he repeatedly asserts that he is "not well." So at this stage we have two characters: Shotwell and Notwell. The interlinking of their two identities becomes more intricate still when the narrator tells us, "Shotwell is not himself." So now an escalation of the relationship: Shotwell and Notwell become Not-Shotwell and Notwell.

This sense of simultaneous similarity and absolute difference is the paradox at the heart of Cold War strategy. One must prepare to fight a nuclear war because the enemy is so different from us that they will stop at nothing to destroy us. But in order to prepare to fight that war, one must assume that the enemy is *just* like us; war-gaming and simulation only work if one assumes a rational enemy (for instance, the enemy who recognizes counterforce as counterforce), and this is why the problem of how to imagine a rational but fundamentally different enemy was at the heart of much strategic debate.[45] In his work on the origins of cybernetics during World War Two, Peter Galison has shown how early military applications consistently offered a radically different understanding of the enemy from those that typically circulated in wartime propaganda.[46] Instead of presenting enemies as caricatures of evil, Norbert Wiener's work on antiaircraft weapons control ended up analogizing enemy and friend, turning the enemy into people just like ourselves, because this was the only way to predict what they would do.[47] For Galison, this is part of a larger problem of what he calls the "Manichean sciences," which include operations research, cybernetics, and game theory: these three disciplines central to nuclear war planning are all theoretical representations "in which information, statistics, and strategies are applied to moves and countermoves in a world of opposing but fundamentally like forces."[48] Barthelme's presentation of these two missile officers echoes such an understanding, even as his account of a radically unknowable distance between them opens up a space for critiquing precisely these assumptions of strategic culture. For Paul N. Edwards, this problem of analogizing friend and foe is part of a larger problem surrounding Cold War nuclear strategizing. In *The Closed World* (and the similarity between his title and Barthelme's setting is telling), Edwards outlines in chilling detail the fundamentally self-referential nature of nuclear strategy as analogies between enemy and friend, economics and politics, model and reality, and command and control were spun out to such great lengths that, in an ever-increasing set of substitutions, they no longer referred to anything but themselves.[49]

Despite the immense pressure of being locked down in the silo, the reason the narrator seems to be losing his mind over the course of the five-page story is simple, and it provides the most telling gloss on both the story's title and on Barthelme's implicit pathologization of the culture of war-gaming and simulated worlds. The story opens with a description of *literal* game playing, as the narrator describes the activity of his silo partner:

> Shotwell keeps the jacks and the rubber ball in his attaché case and will not allow me to play with them. He plays with them, alone, sitting on the floor near the console hour after hour, chanting "onesies, twosies, threesies, foursies" in a precise, well-modulated voice, not so loud as to be annoying, not so soft as to allow me to forget. I point out to Shotwell that two can derive more enjoyment from playing jacks than one, but he is not interested. I have asked repeatedly to be allowed to play by myself, but he simply shakes his head. "Why?" I ask. "They're mine," he says. And when he has finished, when he has sated himself, back they go into the attaché case.[50]

One need not be a committed Freudian to imagine that Shotwell keeps his game solitary out of some repetitive compulsion to master potential loss, and the idea that he plays until he is "sated" certainly suggests an undefined hunger that motivates his repetitive behavior, but Barthelme's indictment goes a step further. The character's name—Shotwell—suggests how: the implication seems to be that he shoots well precisely because he only plays a single-player game, and that his skill might not be so evident if he let another player into the game space, or even if he let another player mess with the equipment. So Barthelme here indicts any strategic simulation that is self-contained; mastery is possible only if you don't allow another player or players to join in, and when you have total control over the apparatus, space, and pace of the game. The implication is that it is only possible to imagine that you shoot well when you shoot alone.

But Barthelme does more than merely point out the problems with the "reassurance" offered by repetitive loss and mastery. For Barthelme, this culture of onanistic simulation isn't simply blind to the actual reality of conflict; it may actually itself cause violence to erupt. Over the course of the story, the narrator becomes progressively more upset about a game he can't access, "aching" to get his hands on it. Indeed, the narrator even ponders whether or not Shotwell's behavior with the jacks constitutes the kind of strange behavior that should lead to a judgment of "behaving strangely" and a preemptive shooting of Shotwell, as if to say that Shotwell's solipsistic assurance that he has total control over the game might be enough to convince the narrator to "prove" to him that he has control over nothing.

When the two characters realize that they aren't going to be replaced by a new crew, the narrator understands that, in the absence of access to the jacks, he had better come up with a "recreational" activity to keep himself sane. His solution:

> I write descriptions of natural forms on the walls, scratching them on the tile surface with a diamond.... The south wall of the room containing the console is already covered. I have described a shell, a leaf, a stone, animals, a baseball bat. I am aware that the baseball bat is not a natural form. Yet I described it. "The baseball bat," I said, "is typically made of wood. It is typically one meter in length or a little longer, fat at one end, tapering to afford a comfortable grip at the other. The end with the handhold typically offers a slight rim, or lip, at the nether extremity, to prevent slippage." My

description of the baseball bat ran to 4500 words, all scratched with a diamond on the south wall.[51]

This is, of course, patently absurd. But its absurdity shouldn't mask the fact, that, in the end, it is much the same gesture as Shotwell's obsessive game playing, but with a subtle twist. Faced with a potential life imprisonment in the silo, the narrator sets out to re-create the world through his descriptions of its natural forms, to create a perfect representation of the world's perfection. But such an attempt at representation is doomed to failure: describing five things fills the entire south wall, and he will fill the walls long before he can describe even a tiny percentage of natural forms. The confusion of boundaries between natural and man-made forms also suggests a problem of scope and range: when would one's description be complete enough, and what categories need to be in place for it to work? And the description of the bat, running as it does to 4,500 words, suggests the problem of ever fully describing something even as "simple" as a baseball bat; the holism of the world means that the only proper description of the world in its totality is the world in its totality, and any attempt to schematize that world is doomed to failure.[52] In other words, simulation is doomed.

The narrator's activity also inevitably raises a question of audience, and his encyclopedic project in the silo control room starts to look more and more like a time capsule. But to whom is it addressed? For if anyone remains on the earth's surface, then a stone, leaf, or shell also remains; the descriptions seem directed to the future, but if the future survives, it doesn't need the descriptions. While no reason is provided for why these two characters have been left down in their silo for 133 days instead of a twelve-hour shift, the narrator offers two possible options: either they have been forgotten or they are the subjects of a psychological study designed to test humans' long-term resilience during underground military service. But another answer might be that no one has come to relieve them because no one is left to relieve them: the obvious reason why two missile officers are still in their silo is that World War Three has taken place, and, ironically, an underground missile control room could be one of the few relatively safe spaces left. The narrator's continual description of his own sense of not feeling well, and his surrealist descriptions of the sweating green walls of the silo control room, also suggest a postapocalyptic landscape. While it would be impossible to "prove" that World War Three has taken place in this story, it certainly could have, and could have without the characters noticing, blinded as they are by the games—both literal and figurative—that they play.

Barthelme's conclusion would thus seem to be that simulation is both the effect and cause of potential nuclear conflict: the effect because one must necessarily turn to simulation because of the impossibility of repeating the event as an actual live-fire exercise. And effect as well because in light of the immense psychological pressures brought to bear by the nuclear age, gaming provides the illusion of mastery that helps restore psychic health in the face of the threat of total destruction. But that illusory mastery can come to be a cause of conflict, too, suggesting perhaps facilely that because one can win a game, one can win a war, even as the game offers control over parameters that the war never will. Indeed, this danger seems to be almost inevitable, as the historian and theorist of technology Manuel De Landa notes: "Besides the blurring of the limits between make-believe and reality created by computer displays and the direct introduction of unreality by military bureaucrats, there is the danger of war games evolving from their 'insight-producing' role into a 'crystal ball' role, where they are used to derive predictions about the future."[53] Barthelme's literally closed world thus reflects on the problems of more figurative enclosures within the world of simulation.

The American Pastime

The narrator's realization in "Game" that the baseball bat isn't a natural form and that you can't totally describe it is echoed in Robert Coover's nearly exactly contemporary novel, *The Universal Baseball Association, Inc., J. Henry Waugh, Prop.* (1968). Here Coover provides an even more devastating critique than Barthelme's of the blindness that simulation produces, and in his critique of the solipsism of simulated worlds, Coover amplifies Barthelme's critique of the implicit violence to which such symbolic economies lead.

The title character—J. Henry Waugh—is a man obsessed by simulation of all sorts. He is an accountant by day (a form, itself, of abstraction), and his nights are filled with another kind of obsessive record keeping. In his apartment he has designed the ultimate game, based on dice, that simulates baseball to an exacting degree:

> When he'd finally decided to settle on his own baseball game,
> Henry had spent the better part of two months just working with
> the problem of odds and equilibrium points in an effort to approximate that complexity. Two dice had not done it. He'd tried
> three, each a different color, and the 216 different combinations had

provided the complexity, all right, but he'd nearly gone blind trying to sort the colors on each throw. Finally, he'd compromised, keeping the three dice, but all white, reducing the total number of combinations to 56, though of course the odds were still based on 216. To restore—and, in fact, to intensify—the complexity of the multicolored method, he'd allowed triple ones and sixes—1-1-1 and 6-6-6—to trigger the more spectacular events, by referring the following dice throw to what he called his Stress Chart, also a three-dice chart, but far more dramatic in nature than the basic ones. Two successive throws of triple ones and sixes were exceedingly rare—only about three times in every two entire seasons of play on the average—but when it happened, the next throw was referred, finally, to the Chart of Extraordinary Occurrences, where just about anything from fistfights to fixed ball games could happen.[54]

This passage gives some indication of the manic intensity with which Henry approaches his game. But Henry has more than just his charts and dice; he has a complex history and mythology built up around players and the game: he is a scrupulous record keeper who documents every game and every season; he has charts that indicate every contingency, from weather to injuries, and he has figured out a system of floating variables—a player who has statistically been better, based on the rolls of the dice, has modifiers added to his numbers that help to keep him better, since in real life not all players have the same ability.

As the novel opens, we are in the midst of the fifty-sixth season of play, and by this point the game has a well-established tradition. It isn't simply that Henry keeps records of each game and season—of course he does; this is baseball—but that he also has notebooks containing life histories of players, coaches, and managers, as well as scrupulously kept ledgers for each club. And if this weren't enough, Henry has forty 300-page notebooks (referred to in the novel as "the Book," of course: holy documents). In sum, twelve thousand pages of "the whole UBA, everything from statistics to journalistic dispatches, from seasonal analyses to general baseball theory. Everything, in short, worth keeping. Style varied from the extreme economy of factual data to the overblown idiom of the sportswriter, from the scientific objectivity of the theoreticians to the literary speculations of essayists and anecdotalists. There were tape-recorded dialogues, player contributions, election coverage, obituaries, satires, prophecies, scandals" (55–56). The passage goes on to record the lengths to which Henry has gone to simulate "reality," noting that he even gets a few things wrong intentionally: what could be more real than human error or bias, or the influence of moods? This description of the record keeping is thus the comically overblown version of Barthelme's 4,500-word essay describing a baseball bat, and both reveal just how time-consuming the abstractions of simulation may turn out to be.

Over the course of the novel, Henry's grasp on reality slowly starts to disappear. The language of baseball comes to describe events in the real world (sex, for instance, in one particularly notable scene), and the intensity of the prose used to describe the games being played turns the reader into just as much of an addict as Henry; the sections that describe his life away from the game are so boring (because his life away from the game is so boring, save that one erotic encounter) that they drive us to get back to the game. Simulation comes to replace reality as the original and more important text; instructively, Henry no longer attends "real" baseball games at all, finding them boring and slow.

The turning point of the novel comes when young Damon Rutherford, a rookie, emerging star pitcher, and son of a legendary player, is at bat against another young hotshot pitcher. Through a series of dice rolls, Henry ends up on his Chart of Extraordinary Occurrences, which indicates that Rutherford has been struck dead by a ball to the skull. This moment certainly suggests one of the limits of simulation: violence, loss, and suffering are here only ever statistical, but the game, and the violence in it, starts to have real-world effects. Henry becomes increasingly obsessed with finishing the season, and finally his recreational activity starts causing problems in his real life: it drives him to drink more and more, and when he goes into mourning for Damon Rutherford, he risks losing his job because he can't make it to work on time and falls asleep when he is there. When eventually Henry seems unable to distinguish between the game world and the real world, Coover's indictment of the culture of simulation is complete. Much like the narrator of "Game," Henry seems determined to re-create the world, but his re-creation (in both senses of the word) threatens to become the world, rather than merely a version of it, and finally Henry's experiences in game space threaten to script all his experiences outside of it.

Coover's apocalyptic moment in the text, however, takes the indictment a step further: much like Barthelme's narrator, Henry has often thought that another "real" player might make the game more interesting, but the introduction of another player jeopardizes the perfect economy of the game, and reveals the problematic assumptions of simulation. After the death of Damon Rutherford, Lou—Henry's one friend from work—becomes alarmed at Henry's mental and physical degeneration, and reaches out to him in an effort to save his job and his sanity. Henry reciprocates this kindness by inviting Lou to his apartment to see, and then play, the game.

From the moment Lou arrives—and nearly drops the pizza he has brought on the table containing the sacred forms and charts—his presence threatens to destroy the game by revealing all the underthought assumptions and axioms required for the illusion of simulation. Importantly, Henry's rules are anything but clear, and Lou immediately makes decisions about his lineup, and then increasingly about substitutions, that mystify Henry, and begin to drive him crazy; not only does Lou not seem to understand the "rules" of the game, but he repeatedly acts in ways that do not seem to be rational, and he can never refer to the proper chart. When he is suddenly faced with an actual opponent, Henry is forced to admit to himself that his players' names sound like names out of comic books rather than plausibly realistic identities, and the elaborate acronyms and shorthand he has come up with to describe particular outcomes of dice combinations ("*RF Inj Collision w/CF: D Adv 3, RF out 4 G,*" to quote just one example) are anything but transparent to a "real" opponent, who can't even keep clear the distinction between an imaginary player and a fictional manager (188–89).

Most importantly, however, the presence of another player finally destroys the simulation altogether. After repeatedly trying to leave, and having been cajoled back to the game, Lou accidentally knocks over a bottle of beer, which then spills over the sheets and charts on the table; this sets off a chain reaction whereby Henry loses his job and his mind in rapid succession. In order for simulation to be reassuring, one must control all the variables, but if one controls all the variables, one can't be said to simulate a reality in which one never does. Once again, playing well entails playing alone.

After Lou leaves, Henry goes mad: while he initially thinks that Lou's intrusion is the end of the game, in a fit of desperation he changes a dice roll of 2-6-6 on his Special Stress Chart to 6-6-6, thereby pushing him onto the Extraordinary Occurrences Chart, because he believes that his fictional players are asking him to intervene to "save" them. The result of Henry's desperate attempt to rescue the game by imagining that it is asking him to change a dice roll is that finally he can't keep reality and simulation separate. After setting down the final dice in their 6-6-6 pattern that guarantees the death of the player Jock Casey, representation and reality come together: Henry's projectile vomiting occurs simultaneously with the rupture of Casey's body in a momentary erasure of the difference between "real" and represented space.

So in their work that most explicitly engages the appeal of the closed worlds of simulation, Coover and Barthelme both indict it, suggesting that the compensations of control and mastery that such closed worlds offer inevitably lead to a potentially deadly confusion between the game and reality. Coming as they do in the mid- to late 1960s, these indictments invite us to read them as critiques of a culture of simulation. Instead of being thought of as work that turns its back on the possibility of reference, these texts might properly be historicized within a larger discussion of the appeal and politics of simulation, and of its centrality to the strategic discourses of the 1960s.

In *On Violence* (1970), Hannah Arendt provided the clearest description of the culture that gave rise to this fiction, in her critique of contemporary defense doctrine:

> Under these circumstances, there are, indeed, few things that are more frightening than the steadily increasing prestige of scientifically minded brain trusters in the councils of government during the last decades. The trouble is not that they are cold-blooded enough to "think the unthinkable," but that they do not *think*. Instead of indulging in such an old-fashioned, uncomputerizable activity, they reckon with the consequences of certain hypothetically assumed constellations without, however, being able to test their hypotheses against actual occurrences. The logical flaw in these hypothetical constructions of future events is always the same: what first appears as a hypothesis—with or without its implied alternatives, according to the level of sophistication—turns immediately, usually after a few paragraphs, into a "fact," which then gives birth to a whole string of similar non-facts, with the result that the purely speculative character of the whole enterprise is forgotten.[55]

Arendt's attack on simulated worlds parallels those of Barthelme and Coover. And while Arendt echoes some of the charges often leveled against metafiction—that in its hermeticism it offers no links to reality—Coover and Barthelme suggest that metafiction is less an uncritical example of those problems and more a critical examination of them. Metafiction's stress on the verbal construction of possible worlds, rather than on the verbal representation of the world we live in, makes it a particularly suitable form of fiction for critiquing the "purely speculative" character of strategic scenario-creation. And while metafiction and the postmodern turn are surely overdetermined, at least part of the story of their emergence is the arrival of a military-political culture that was itself fabulatory to the core. Arendt's realist critique of strategic culture and the fabulatory critiques of Barthelme and Coover are thus two sides of the same coin, approaches that share a horror at the blindness of the closed worlds of simulation, and at the implications of believing you can imagine a simulated world adequate to the real one.

Indeed, Ghamari-Tabrizi has characterized Kahn's version of futurology and strategy as part of a wider-reaching postwar avant-garde, and though she doesn't include metafiction in that discussion, her understanding of the appeal of Kahn's work, and of nuclear futurology more broadly, might have come out of a critical discussion of experimental fiction: "When I leaf through RAND publications from this period, I catch sight of typical shapes of problem formulation. The themes of open serial study, branching forms, the rejection of realism, untiring stress on insight, intuition, creativity, tacit knowledge—all blend into a distinct genre."[56] Committed to "world-making" and an avid reader of science fiction,[57] Kahn's literary taste is almost too fitting, given that *The Arabian Nights* has often been taken as a key precursor for the fictionalizing process of postmodernism:[58]

> Kahn's dynamism advanced from point to point on the stepping stones of epic strings of variables. With its pageantry of World Wars I through VIII, *On Thermonuclear War* had a Scheherazade-like architecture of nested stories that promised to continue indefinitely, there being no end either to the scenarios, or, seemingly, to the discussion itself. Thinking about the unthinkable seems to be related to this quality of endlessness. Kahn once mentioned to McWirther that the *Tales of the 1001 Nights* was one of his favorite stories. The reporter reflected, "Herman Kahn may feel that, by inventing one Scenario after another, he is holding back the changes that would seal our doom."[59]

But, crucially, the tales Kahn was telling didn't involve an endless forestalling of death by the telling of stories; rather, the elaborate fabulatory impulse at the core of Kahn's strategic vision was all too often concerned with making winnable war possible; if there is a strategic equivalent to Scheherazade's ongoing forestalling of individual and mass death, it isn't an equation where we win a war by losing 40 million people instead of 50 million. But Kahn's work exemplifies just what Arendt was critiquing:

when hypotheses start becoming facts, the line between fiction and history starts to blur.

Half Life

Jumping ahead some thirty years to David Foster Wallace's homage to, and critique of, self-consciousness, the enduring links between metafiction and nuclear culture seem clear enough; so clear, in fact, that Wallace could reverse the comparison, and in doing so reveal in new ways the poverty of the strategic culture I've been discussing. A comprehensive reading of Wallace's 1,079-page *Infinite Jest* (1996) is obviously beyond the scope of this chapter, but I do want to note that *Infinite Jest*, like a host of its mid-1990s contemporaries, records the enduring legacy of the Cold War even though the conflict had supposedly ended. And so the novel's representations of global politics are indebted to Cold War nuclear brinksmanship; its principal father-figure began his working life as a weapons scientist, and in a novel obsessed by drugs and drug culture, the "ultimate" drug (imagine, as one character puts it, "acid that has itself dropped acid") is called DMZ (the one place where the Cold War survives its supposed end is the demilitarized zone between North and South Korea).

But Wallace's novel is also a loving if critical look back on a prior generation of postmodern writers. The missing father at the heart of the novel is not only a former weapons scientist, but also a highly self-conscious filmmaker whose work displays all the hallmarks of metafictional self-consciousness.[60] And so one of the tasks of the novel is to move past the attachment to a father who has never been properly buried, and working through that is also an attempt to move past the Cold War.

Set in, among other places, an elite tennis academy in New England, Wallace helps us to reimagine the pressures of simulation in the 1960s by satirically hypothesizing that nuclear war-gaming could, in an imagined twenty-first century, become the psychic antidote to the pressures of sport; the analogy between the two disciplines is so ridiculous, in other words, that it can be reversed, and in his critique of the possibility of maps ever adequately representing territories, Wallace links postmodern aesthetics and nuclear strategy in particularly brilliant ways. The students at Enfield Tennis Academy are under immense pressure to perform, and part of their training involves a radical rethinking of the game they are trying to master. Coach Schtitt argues that to become a tennis star, the players must learn to regard the court as a world in itself.

UNTHINKING THE THINKABILITY OF THE UNTHINKABLE / 99

There is always an excuse for not winning: "Cold. Hot. Wet and dry. Very bright sun and you see the purple dots. Very bright hot and you have no salt. Outside is wind, the insects which like the sweat. Inside is smell of heaters, echo, being jammed in together, tarp is overclose to baseline, not enough of room, bells inside clubs which ring the hour loudly to distract, clunk of machines vomiting sweet cola for coins. Inside roof too low for lob. Bad lighting, so. Or outside: the bad surface. Oh no look no: crabgrass in cracks along baseline" (458–59). The solution to such abundant contingency is to remake yourself into a citizen of a "second world" by never imagining alternatives to the bare space of play; to be a great tennis player means fully (and only) inhabiting the court—the court is not a subset of reality, but reality is a subset of the court. Reality is simply *too* real: to deal with it you have to imagine the court as a closed system, and play "real" tennis as if it were "simulated" tennis.

The result of this immense pressure to "occur" within the closed space of the court is a series of neuroses, repetitive behaviors, and addictions, and Hal Incandenza's recurrent nightmares suggest why:

> In this dream, which every now and then still recurs, I am standing publicly at the baseline of a gargantuan tennis court. I'm in a competitive match, clearly: there are spectators, officials. The court is about the size of a football field, though, maybe, it seems. It's hard to tell. But mainly the court's complex. The lines that bound and define play are on this court as complex and convoluted as a sculpture of string. There are lines going every which way, and they run oblique or meet and form relationships and boxes and rivers and tributaries and systems inside systems: lines, corners, alleys, and angles deliquesce into a blur at the horizon of the distant net. I stand there tentatively. The whole thing is almost too involved to try to take it in all at once. (67)

Hal has recourse to a variety of self-medicating strategies to deal with these pressures, but the novel's most telling coping mechanism is Eschaton, a fantastically involved homemade game to which players often become addicted when they reach puberty and gain the capability of "really abstract-capable thought" (321).[61] As these children become capable of abstraction, they find solace for their tennis woes in a game of nuclear strategy; if in the mid-1960s gaming offered a compensatory recourse in the face of the nearly ungraspable "reality" of nuclear conflict, Wallace's encyclopedia has nuclear war-gaming as the solution to the psychic pressures brought about by trying to imagine the space of the tennis court as the space of the world. The contrast with O'Brien's novel is almost too perfect: Imagine a William Cowling unable to fully master the intricacies of Ping-Pong, but who finds relief in playing war games.

Eschaton maps the entire globe on four tennis courts, with various items of clothing marking any and all targets of strategic interest, from major metropolitan areas and military bases to important public infrastructure such as dams, bridges, and nuclear power plants. The players are then divided into groups that represent the major strategic power blocks—NATO (AMNAT), the Warsaw Pact (SOVWAR), China (REDCHI), a Middle Eastern block ("LIBSYR or more formidable IRLIBSYR"), and, if there are any extra players, the remaining powers—and assigned a number of tennis balls that correspond to the total available megatons of nuclear weaponry that complex calculations have suggested would be available on that day (322).

Although the game is played in a defined literal space just like tennis, the variables that go into a game of Eschaton are almost comically massive: "A quorum of the day's Combatants has to endorse a particular simulated World Situation as Lord's stayed up well past several bedtimes to develop it: Land-Sea-Air force distributions; ethnic, sociologic, economic, and even religious demographics for each Combatant, plus broadly sketched psych-profiles of all relevant heads of state; prevailing weather in all the map's quadrants; etc" (324). This need to capture everything from psychology to precipitation is clearly Wallace commenting on the impossibility of simulation ever helping us to make real-time decisions in the real world; the game only helps us to learn about a game scripted by *these* variables. In addition, before each match of elaborately lobbed tennis balls begins, the players gather to discuss the kinds of issues heads of state discuss, from mutual nonaggression pacts to the codes of conduct that might govern armed conflict. If that weren't enough, the whole thing needs to be justified, since war doesn't just "happen" on its own, and the particular trigger event will produce a further set of game variables:

> A Russo-Chinese border dispute goes tactical over Sinkiang. An AMNAT computracker in the Aleutians misreads a flight of geese as three SOVWAR SS10s on reentry. Israel moves armored divisions north and east through Jordan after an El Al airbus is bombed in mid-flight by a cell linked to both H'sseins. Black Albertan wackos infiltrate an isolated silo at Ft. Chimo and get two MIRVs through SOUTHHAF'S defense net. North Korea invades

South Korea. Vice versa. AMNAT is within 72 hours of putting an impregnable string of antimissile satellites on line, and the remorseless logic of game theory compels SOVWAR to go SACPOP while it still has the chance. (325)

Far from being merely a narrativized excuse for play, the triggering situation produces a unique set of constraints for each game, a constantly shifting set of rules and expectations within which the players' tennis skills can be enacted; crucially, one's skill with a racket is only part of the game; all moves have to be "allowed" by a computer that runs them through a complex flowchart of possibilities, and a lob that might kill a certain number of the enemy on one day might "only" kill a fraction of that number on another, depending on the weather conditions assigned by the game-master.

However, the holiday game of which we get an account in the novel destroys this illusion that one could ever adequately simulate reality in a game space, or use a game to predict real events. During a temporary moment of détente, when the leaders are talking among themselves about possible peace terms, and have walked to a section of the court roughly corresponding to Sierra Leone, all hell breaks loose. The arrival of snow on the actual courts (not in the "virtual" world of the game) leads to a certain conceptual confusion: "J. J. Penn of INDPAK all of a sudden gets the idea to start claiming that now that it's snowing the snow totally affects blast area and fire area and pulse-intensity and maybe also has fallout implications, and he says Lord has to now completely redo everybody's damage parameters before anyone can form realistic strategies from here on out" (333). Penn's claim produces outrage among the assembled players, and especially Pemulis, for the way in which it hopelessly confuses represented and actual game space: "It's only real-world snow if it's already in the *scenario!*" (334, italics in original). The weather situation has led to a kind of ontological crisis for the game, the destruction of the "delimiting boundaries that are Eschaton's very life-blood," as well as for the ability of the players to think through their options (335).

If the map/territory equivocation weren't bad enough, Evan Ingersoll, the leader of IRLIBSYR, takes to the next level the chaos generated by the snow. After witnessing the détente between the two superpowers, Ingersoll quickly realizes the strategic implications of such a summit for the Middle East, given the relentless logic of the game. His solution—to launch a tennis ball/five megaton warhead at the summit, such that it hits Ann Kittenplan on the back of the head—is totally unprecedented:

"No matter how frayed players' nerves, it's never made a lick of sense. A Combatant's megatonnage is too precious to waste on personal attacks outside the map. It's been like this unspoken but very basic rule" (336). The problem, though, is that the unspoken rule depends on a vision of map/territory nonequivalence that has never been explicitly stated, even though the game has seemed to depend upon a perfect equivalence of the two. Ingersoll goes on to claim that he has wiped out the entire chain of command of both the Soviet Union and NATO, and, since both sides had carried their buckets full of tennis balls with them, that he has wiped out the nuclear arsenals of the two superpowers as well. The absurdity continues with one player asserting that since the actual combatants who have been virtually annihilated were wearing multiple items of clothing and—because clothing according to a rigid system represents various kinds of strategic targets—that the actual point value of vaporizing what was Sierra Leone is much greater than "simply" wiping NATO and the Eastern Bloc off the map. Thus Pemulis's rant: "Players themselves can't be valid targets. Players aren't inside the goddamn game. Players are part of the *apparatus* of the game. They're part of the map. It's snowing on the players but not on the territory. They're part of the *map*, not the clusterfucking *territory*. You can only launch against the *territory*. Not against the *map*. It's like the one ground-rule boundary that keeps Eschaton from degenerating into chaos" (338, italics in original). The problem is that this fundamental assumption that keeps the game from degenerating into chaos, the equivalent of the bare shape of the court within tennis, is one that has never actually been specified: "Players' exemption from strikes goes without saying, Pemulis says; it's like *pre*axiomatic" (338, italics in original). The unspecified distinction between map and territory is so basic to the game that it is required for the game's axioms to work, but it is also so fundamental that it has remained an assumption rather than a declared protocol.

This section of the novel is littered with references to how completely absorbed Hal is in this problem of map/territory equivocation, though Hal can't figure out just what it is about the problem that he finds so compelling. I'd suggest that his absorption exists because this crisis in the game taps so deeply into the structure of anxiety that his nightmare made clear, that one is never able to completely map the situation within which one is forced to act. Much as the court shifts within Hal's dream from a space one can master into an unrecognizable mess, so here do the rules of Eschaton collapse into chaos: in the resulting free-for-all that begins when players become targets, the computer containing the entire "nervous system" of the game is destroyed when a player, fleeing the violence, collides with it and puts his head through the monitor. The crisis that began by calling into question the animating assumptions of the game ends up literally destroying it. Furthermore, the represented violence that is so central to the game spills over into the "real" world when multiple players end up in the hospital, and disciplinary action leads to Pemulis's expulsion and Hal's withdrawal from drugs.

With regard to postmodern fiction, perhaps no single work has had such an extraordinary run of explanatory power as Jean Baudrillard's *Simulacra and Simulation* (1981). Central to Baudrillard's theoretical claims about contemporary experience is that the map has replaced the territory; the real has been supplanted by representation. As we have seen, the desire for perfect simulation took on an especially urgent character during Cold War strategic planning, since the real was the very thing at stake. But in a body of fiction usually considered central to the high postmodern canon, we see not an unhesitating agreement with Baudrillard about the nature of contemporary experience, but more an attack on the ethical, political, and destructive implications of simulation. This fiction should properly be seen as anatomizing and critiquing the wholesale shift in the nature of experience and reference that found its prime economic and philosophical sponsor in the armed services and the Department of Defense. It is surely no accident that the last section of Baudrillard's canonical "The Precession of Simulacra" begins with "the apotheosis of simulation: the nuclear."[62] As I have already acknowledged, the emergence of metafiction is certainly overdetermined, but in the work most self-consciously about the metafictional strategy of simulation, Coover, Barthelme, and Wallace historicize the will to simulate as a direct result of the nuclear age.

5 / Trying to Understand *End Zone*

"I became fascinated by words and phrases like thermal hurricane, overkill, circular error probability, post-attack environment, stark deterrence, dose-rate contours, kill-ratio, spasm war. Pleasure in these words. They were extremely effective, I thought, whispering shyly of cycles of destruction so great that the language of past world wars became laughable, the wars themselves somewhat naive."[1] William Cowling would no doubt be furious at Don DeLillo's apparent reveling in the language of "professional" nuclear war strategy, revealing as it does the radical divide between signifier and signified at the heart of a strategic culture that could contemplate killing nations.[2] As lines embodying the seductions of nuclear language in DeLillo's second novel, *End Zone* (1972), suggest, DeLillo is keenly aware of the possibility that description can often turn into acceptance, even glee: in a novel concerned with the Wittgensteinian possibilities of description, DeLillo suggests that naming is never a neutral gesture and can help make the unthinkable perversely commonplace. In this respect, he is perhaps thematically the exemplary postmodern writer, as he repeatedly represents in his fiction the process of signification.

Throughout his forty-year career as a novelist, DeLillo has explored the landscapes of contemporary risk: his world is definitively shaped by terrorism, the bomb, environmental catastrophe, simmering conflicts, random violence, shadowy conspiracy, and the threat of global financial panic, and his fiction has often eerily prefigured emergent threats. Simultaneously, however, these novels are filled with characters who find in language a kind of solace beyond simple signification, and DeLillo's fiction has frequently returned to language as a subject rather than merely a medium, from his interest in the languages of advertising in *Americana* and pop music in *Great Jones Street* through to the ontology of proper names in *The Names*. Virtually every paragraph in DeLillo's fiction evidences a postmodern concern with the complexities of linguistic reference and the arbitrariness of signifiers.

For instance, in *White Noise*, his novel most explicitly about the public culture of disaster—an "airborne toxic event" engulfs a small American town—DeLillo explores how the media obscure rather than illuminate threat. In the face of the chemical accident that defines the world of the novel, the Gladney family spends more time dwelling on the name given to the event than on the event itself. What the media initially describe as a feathery plume becomes a black billowing cloud, before finally claiming its status as "the airborne toxic event." Whatever the thing is—a plume, a cloud, an event—it is its naming that seems most important, as we see in Jack Gladney's reaction to his son's utterance of its final designation: "He spoke these words ['airborne toxic event'] in a clipped and foreboding manner, syllable by syllable, as if he sensed the threat in state-created terminology."[3] DeLillo's representation of how the event is displaced by its various names is just a continuation of his signature interest in the massively mediated structures of everyday life in contemporary America, an interest that reaches high comedy in this novel's frequently discussed "The Most Photographed Barn in America" vignette. DeLillo's fiction seems tailor-made for readings that follow Baudrillard in interpreting the massively simulated nature of contemporary experience as our new reality, and for accounts of the postmodern as a fundamentally depthless era that endlessly confuses medium and message. Certainly the critical bibliography on his fiction has made this interpretation of his oeuvre central.[4]

As I argued in chapter 4, however, questions of simulation unite the concerns of defense strategy and American metafiction in this period. What I want to suggest here is that DeLillo's most nuclear-obsessed novel, *End Zone*, also actively contributes to a critique of the nuclear age that moves beyond merely noting and satirizing the language of defense strategy.[5] Even if the novel initially seems to make language its ultimate horizon, the novel's descriptions of the language of nuclear strategy are means to an end and not the end itself, as becomes clear when the novel is properly situated within contemporary cultures of strategy and risk. Ursula K. Heise has offered an important start to this project of contextualizing DeLillo by reclaiming *White Noise* as a powerful analysis of contemporary risk culture rather than merely a satiric portrayal of a world of mediation in which the real disappears behind and beyond layers of representation.[6] Drawing on the work of Ulrich Beck on the nature of contemporary risk assessment and distribution, she reads *White Noise* alongside Richard Powers's novel *Gain*, suggesting that both novels provide crucial insights into a culture that lives under immense environmental threat. For Heise, the point of DeLillo's interest in environmental risk in *White Noise* is not so much to suggest the ways in which threat disappears from view in a postmodern ontology that substitutes representation for reality as to actively debate the ontological uncertainty about how various risk factors relate in an ecology now so complex that it cannot be readily understood.

In my reading of DeLillo's *End Zone*, I follow Heise's lead, and offer a more complicated account of DeLillo's investment in unspeakability and simulation than Baudrillardian readings have allowed. As I've already suggested, these terms are crucial to DeLillo scholarship, which typically reads him as a novelist interested in the incessant colonizing of all forms of human communication by either the media or the state. In *End Zone*, however, DeLillo offers his most sustained deployment of two features that are crucial to such arguments: first, the idea of the untellable; and second, the intermixing of two professionalized languages in ways that initially suggest that signifier and signified are in entirely arbitrary relationships. Indeed, O'Brien's William Cowling would likely, so to speak, explode were he to read a novel that so consistently renders the bomb metaphorical by equating football and nuclear conflict.

End Zone is narrated by a college football player named Gary Harkness, a running back being given his last chance at a small Texas college after blowing his prior opportunities at several football powerhouses. Logos College has also recruited a top new coach, Emmet Creed, who has also had his share of troubles at better and bigger schools, and Harkness and Creed are now in purgatory together. Obviously DeLillo is aggressively foregrounding questions of the linguistic: *Logos* College, Gary *Hark*ness, Emmet *Creed*; the irony that the founder of *Logos* was mute; the elaborate understandings of the massively linguistic nature of football (the calling of plays being the most explicit example); and long descriptions of the etymology of a name or a word. And just as obviously DeLillo is calling attention to the laborious linguistic mediation of nuclear language and the language of sport, as over the course of the season Gary Harkness nurtures a growing obsession with nuclear war.

Harkness takes particular pleasure in the vocabulary of nuclear strategy after becoming hooked on the nuclear during a class on modes of disaster technology he took at one of his many previous colleges.

Metaphor certainly threatens to overtake language's supposedly original signifying ability: the list of nuclear terms with which I opened comes just a few pages after Gary has remembered his initial education in signification, a moment that DeLillo represents as an encounter with an actual sign hung by Gary's stern father on Gary's bedroom wall: "WHEN THE GOING GETS TOUGH / THE TOUGH GET GOING":

> I looked at this sign for three years (roughly from ages fourteen to seventeen) before I began to perceive a certain beauty in it. The sentiment of course had small appeal but it seemed that beauty flew from the words themselves, the letters, consonants swallowing vowels, aggression and tenderness, a semi-self-re-creation from line to line, word to word, letter to letter. All meaning faded. The words became pictures. It was a sinister thing to discover at such an age, that words can escape their meanings. A strange beauty that sign began to express. (17)

This passage suggests dimensions to language outside of simple referentiality that simultaneously threaten and attract us, especially given the subject matter of so much of the novel. But just as in *The Nuclear Age*, we are faced with the problem of the simultaneous necessity and danger of nuclear terminology, as we see in the conversation between Gary and Major Staley, an instructor in the campus ROTC program:

> "Major, there's no way to express thirty million dead. No words. So certain men are recruited to reinvent the language."
> "I don't make up the words, Gary."
> "They don't explain, they don't clarify, they don't express. They're painkillers. Everything becomes abstract. I admit it's fascinating in a way. I also admit the problem goes deeper than just saying some crypto-Goebbels in the Pentagon is distorting the language." (85)

Gary's claims suggest that perhaps the ultimate problem of nuclear language is less a political and ethical one than an ontological one; in suggesting that the problem runs deeper than unseen hypothetical fascists distorting the language, DeLillo may be proposing that nuclear language is merely an exceptionally fertile terrain on which one might examine larger problems related to reference.

With Gary's rapturous interest in the vocabulary of nuclear war being announced just a few pages after his lesson in semiotics, one has to wonder whether his study of nuclear war has kept the bomb real or erased it entirely; the links between the bomb and other kinds of sublimated desire is made more explicit when he falls for a female student who wears an orange sweater with a gigantic mushroom cloud appliqué on its front. More generally, however, the novel suggests that Gary's diminished sense of the bomb's reality even as he begins to understand it more clearly might be seen as the general condition of thinking about the nuclear, anticipating the claim O'Brien would subsequently make in *The Nuclear Age*: to the extent that the bomb becomes knowable, the novel seems to argue, that knowledge is ultimately false, or at least extensively qualified by the assumptions guiding it.

DeLillo's statements in interviews have tended to confirm the primacy of the linguistic for thinking about the novel. In his 1982 conversation with Thomas LeClair, DeLillo made a statement that has been cited time and time again, almost as if it provided the master key for his work: "My work also grew more precise. I began to study things more, disassemble them. Possibly what I was studying was ways to use the language. It may be the case that with *End Zone* I began to suspect that language was a subject as well as an instrument in my work, although I'd find it hard to say in what ways exactly."[7] Whatever DeLillo's own difficulty in discovering the exact ways in which language surfaces as a subject in his work, criticism obviously hasn't shared it, turning DeLillo's sense that language is *a* subject in his work into the idea that language is *the* subject of it. No doubt the combination of DeLillo's own admission, his fiction's obvious interest in exploring the full range of linguistic possibility and seduction, and the contemporaneity of DeLillo's statement with the 1980s institutionalization of deconstruction in the American academy have led to a strikingly homogeneous body of criticism on these novels—itself historically marked, even as it renders DeLillo's fiction deeply ahistorical.

One way of restoring the historicity of a novel overtly concerned with nuclear discourse is to note that the year of its publication, 1972, was a key year in the history of the nuclear era, the year in which the Strategic Arms Limitation Talks (SALT 1) between the Soviet Union and the United States led to the first major arms-control treaty signed by the two superpowers, and though it is never mentioned directly in the novel, I will argue that SALT 1 is the crucial context that makes possible the novel's elaborate comparison of football and nuclear war. *End Zone*, I suggest, is an extended meditation on the problems and paradoxes at the heart of the SALT 1 agreement and contemporary arms control, and the particular extended analogy between football and nuclear war makes full sense only when read in relation to the defense culture of the late 1960s and early 1970s.

As David Cowart has noted, critics writing on *End Zone* have generally followed the novel's own warning that to comment on the relationship between football and war is to "risk death by analogy," but in the pages that follow I want to suggest that such a "death" is worth risking, provided we first fully understand the analogy the novel is making, and allow that such an understanding requires that we listen in quite literal ways to the points the novel makes about language.[8] Late in *End Zone*, Taft Robinson, the African American running back who has been turned into a symbol by the school's administration, its marketing expert, and indeed at times by Gary himself, tells Gary that such symbolic stature isn't what he wants: "I want you to take me literally. Everything I've said is to be taken literally. I've got this room fixed up just the way I want it. It's a well-proportioned room. It has just the right number of objects. Everything is exactly where it should be" (238). This is an odd statement, and especially odd coming at the end of a novel in which literal reference has been endlessly displaced; *End Zone* seems to be a novel that above all else sees "literal" reference as an impossible desire, at least in the realm of nuclear strategy—in other words, taking the novel literally seems to require giving up on the notion of literalness. And it is odd as well since in a novel that endlessly reveals the problems of chance, contingency, and the impossibility of imposing order on the chaotic space of battlefields—both athletic and military—it makes the case for careful design.

I will argue that the seemingly obvious interest in the novel with the forms and features of linguistic mediation actually masks a complex argument about the nature of reference, and in particular the nature of analogy. What the novel is literally about, then, is football as nuclear war, and nuclear war as football, and what makes it possible to speak of one in the language of the other. And though the reading that follows moves on to allegory, it does so by first taking the novel literally at those moments of linguistic eruption that would seem to be literalness's enemy. As we shall see, the novel argues against wide-ranging analogy: instead, it asks the reader to think in very precise terms when comparing disciplines, and it does so in ways that implicitly call into question readings that would privilege the free play of signification. Most importantly, however, it argues that questions about speakability and reference are always political and ethical in nature, and asks us to remember those stakes whenever questions of referentiality emerge: not death by analogy so much as the analogies that could yet again make death possible, and make analogy valuable in strategic circles. Understanding the novel's argument about reference and analogy allows us to finally and fully read the comparison between football and nuclear war, and to see it as a historical, rather than an ontological and linguistic, problem.

"We Delve into the Untellable"

In a novel filled with active reflections on the world-making power of language, an academic course on the "untellable" is a good joke—precisely the kind of course you shouldn't be able to take at "Logos" College. The course is introduced as such, as another of the school's elegantly weird offerings: "Billy was in the process of memorizing Rilke's ninth Duino Elegy in German, a language he did not understand. It was for a course he was taking in the untellable" (64). Billy is Billy Mast, the smartest student at the school (curves are often set by him in large classes), and from the get-go, a comic reading of the course is suggested: untellability is simply literal incomprehension if you can't read German: "Billy Mast, who roomed two doors away from me, worked every night at memorizing a long poem in a language he'd never read before, never spoken, never even heard except in one or two movies.... Every night he did more work on the elegy. I'd visit him sometimes just to hear the sounds he made, his guttural struggle against those grudging consonants. He liked to hit his desk with both hands as he recited. Billy's course in the untellable was restricted to ten students. Knowledge of German was a prerequisite for being refused admission" (73). The criterion for admission is linguistic incompetence: the course works because none of the students have any German. But the course, it seems, could then be taught equally well around any text in any language that its participants cannot understand. Much is made of ignorance as the course requirement when Billy's friends quiz him on just what is going on in the class, since they know that he doesn't speak or read German, and when Billy laments his having inadvertently picked up a few words of German along the way.

But near the end of the novel, the course appears again, and the "untellable" is now suddenly reimagined in an immensely serious way: "The course is pretty experimental. It's given by a man who may or may not have spent three and a half years in one of the camps" (181). Here the politics implicit in certain kinds of belief in tellability or its opposite become far more complex, and in ways that take us away from the traditional emphasis on DeLillo's interest in linguistic play. The evocation of this paradigmatically "untellable" event newly explains why German should be the language of the course, and why the instructor, identified only as someone "who may or may not have spent" time in the camps, would choose it. "I think the theory is if any words exist beyond speech, they're probably German words, or pretty close," says Billy Mast, thus supplying the missing history (181). In other words, DeLillo suggests that untellability is neither a basic condition to be superseded by linguistic competence nor a condition of all language, but what happens in the exercise of mass violence and extermination.

Giorgio Agamben's rebuttal of one strand of contemporary ethical philosophy in his *Remnants of Auschwitz* makes clear precisely why the instructor's decision to teach a course on untellability in German might be read as a form of moral and political action:

> Years ago, a doctrine emerged that claimed to have identified a kind of transcendental condition of ethics in the form of a principle of obligatory communication. It originated in a European country that more than any other had reasons to have a guilty conscience with respect to Auschwitz, and it soon spread throughout academic circles. According to this curious doctrine, a speaking being cannot in any way avoid communication. Insofar as, unlike animals, they are gifted with language, human beings find themselves, so to speak, condemned to agree on the criteria of meaning and the validity of their actions. Whoever declares himself not wanting to communicate contradicts himself, for he has already communicated his will not to communicate.[9]

Basing ethics around this principle of obligatory communication is, for Agamben, to participate in an attempt to expunge the camps from historical memory. For Agamben what the camps make visible is precisely a subject excluded by force from such a system of communication, a subject pushed back into the "bare life" of biological existence without the ability to speak, eat, or live and die under the rubrics of "authenticity" inherited from phenomenology and existentialism.

By making Rilke the subject of the course, DeLillo is furthermore calling into doubt the entire legacy of "authentic" and "inauthentic" death that permeates German thought; as Agamben remarks, Rilke, as much as Heidegger, was at the center of Adorno's critique of authenticity after the war.[10] What initially reads as DeLillo's interest in the mystery and magic of language now looks more like an investigation into the structures of power implicit in any attempt to claim or dismiss unspeakability as an innocent object of intellectual inquiry.[11]

To turn such a course into a merely abstract discussion of a language, leaving out its obvious historical referent, misses the point: what seems at first like a clever postmodern joke about either the silliness of academia or the limits of language is in fact an invitation to investigate the ethics of language and the implicit politics that surround questions of tellability and silence. What is at stake in these two distinct readings of the untellability course are two distinct readings of the novel itself. The first reading of the course makes the ultimate horizon of the course language as such, stripped of any reference, and independent of the putative "content" of the course. This is analogous to readings of the novel that make the particularities of its comparison between nuclear war and football incidental to its implicitly "larger" points about language (and it is notable that so much of the criticism on the novel barely mentions the analogy at all, finding it so obvious as to be not worth discussing). The second reading of the course, however, makes the subject matter vitally important: Rilke and the German language are absolutely central to any attempt to discover the limits of tellability, and I would argue it is this reading of the course that should guide our interpretation of the novel as a whole, and make us conceptualize the content of the novel not as some incidental issue to pass through on the way to a larger point about linguistics, but as the central problem the novel investigates. This is especially important given its nuclear content; as Mark Osteen has noted, "*End Zone* implies a theological and linguistic relationship" between the untellability of the course and the unthinkability which is so much a part of nuclear jargon.[12] As the course makes the problem of untellability historical, so too does the novel make the unthinkability of nuclear war thinkable, in ways that we must respond to.

Analogy and Death

As I discussed in chapter 4, the possibility of the comparison between nuclear war and games of skill had come to look decidedly problematic by the late 1960s: the advances in, among other things, defensive weapons meant that the "limited" model of nuclear war that centered on exchange looked decidedly out of date. And *End Zone* would readily support the critique of nuclear simulation and war-gaming I offered in that chapter. Early in the novel, Gary visits Major Staley, the commander of the college's Air Force ROTC. After Staley offers his thoughts on the possibility of a "humane war" in which "you'd practically have a referee and a timekeeper" and things "wouldn't be nearly as bad as most people might expect," Staley admits that "this entire concept is full of flaws" (82–83). Perhaps most telling is the way that strategic calculation is always built on assumptions that are then erased when you start imagining destruction: "The nuclear nations have a stockpile of fissionable material I would estimate in the neighborhood of sixty thousand megatons in terms of explosive power. That's a personal estimate, based on whatever tech-data I've been able to accumulate in the journals and the bulletins, *accurate within a factor of maybe three of four*. But just for the heck of it, figure that out in terms of pounds of TNT. That's pounds now, not tons. I bet you can't do it without paper and pencil. The trick is to keep count of the zeros" (83, italics added). The idea that the trick is to keep track of the zeros is obviously an authorial joke, in that the entire set of calculations you are making is built on an initial figure arrived at by guesswork rather than real intelligence.

Likewise when Gary goes to see him about what nuclear war might be like, the major gives him an answer, but an answer prefaced in such a way as to make clear that the language of abstract science is based upon pure supposition, since "it all depends on the megatons, the fission yield, air or surface burst, wind velocity, mean pressure altitude, descent time, median particle size" (86). In other words, every calculation is dependent on an immense string of variables. This reaches comic heights later in the novel when they actually play a war game. While Major Staley admits that war-gaming is always problematic, given that players are aware that the game isn't "the real thing," DeLillo is after a more serious critique. Staley's claim that "the basic situation . . . is definitely in the area of what we know to be projected crisis situations" (220) is so heavily qualified as to be almost ludicrous, and the situation he describes is so highly specific in its details as to make the extraction of any general insights from it impossible; the narrative of the world-historical situation that produces the war is almost twice as long as the description of the twelve-move game that results from it. We are left wondering whether it really matters that three, rather than, say, two or four, "high-ranking agents defect to the West" or that the factory ship struck by torpedoes while being delivered to NORKOR (the name for North Korea in the game) is "Dutch-built" (221). The point here seems obvious enough: games are never adequate to reality, and the novel's interest in combining nuclear war with football underlines this point. As we will see, however, the comparison of nuclear war and football in *End Zone* indicates how that model came to have a new life through the bizarre world of international relations and arms-control treaties. Thinking about the *abstract* similarity between football and war is to miss that the novel discusses only a particular kind of football and a particular kind of war.

An account of the novel that aims to do justice to the overlap in vocabulary between nuclear strategy and football needs to remember the definition of a function proposed by Billy Mast, a perfect example of how an interest in language may indict rather than celebrate the multiplication of meaning. After losing the big game against West Centrex Biotechnical, Dennis Smee, the defensive captain, has worked out "word for word" a speech with Kimborough, the offensive captain, designed to remotivate the fallen team: "That's our function as co-captains. To work for the good of the team" (149). But the speech, even though it has been carefully crafted, isn't really the point: this speech from Smee produces a stream-of-consciousness response from Mast, which initially appears to be just another example of the proliferation of meaning, as Mast jumps off from one of the words Smee has used: "'Function,' Billy said. 'A rule of correspondence between two sets related in value and nature to the extent that there is a unique element in one set assigned to each element in the corresponding set, given the respective value differences'" (149). Obviously Mast has (seemingly) confused multiple meanings of the term under discussion, but his version of what a function is (and Mast is, after all, the philosopher of the group) should provide readers with a caution as they assume that football and war may be linked only in some very general way in the novel. This eruption of language at its most "random" suggests that we might yet map precise relationships between two separate discursive fields. And another "random" eruption of language is present early in the novel. After Terry Madden asks "What's the good word?" at dinner one night, Harkness gives us an answer, when he overhears another player reading from his "monolithic integrated circuitry" textbook; as Jessup puts it, "The pattern match begins with the search for a substring of a given string that has a specified structure in the string-manipulation language" (25).

The novel repeatedly combines these moments of linguistic misunderstanding with arguments about the nature of comparison: Buddy Shock's definition of "identity" comes after Tim Flanders has been discussing the identity of Emmet Creed: "'Identity,' Buddy Shock said. 'An equality satisfied by all possible values of the variables for which the standardized expressions involved in the equality are quantitatively determined'" (57).

Likewise with Jimmy Fife, upon hearing the word "balance," in another context: "'Balance,' Fife said. 'The equality of effective values with respect to the applied number of reduced symbolic quantities on each side of an equation, excluding combined derivatives'" (207). These outbursts suggest that the links between disciplines need to be particularized in far more specific ways than just broad-scale analogy. To put it another way, the seemingly random use of language within the novel, when seen as a pattern, foregrounds questions of precision in comparison between objects, sets, or discourses. As a first step toward making a more precise comparison between disciplines, a closer look at *End Zone*'s game of football is in order; when we take that look, we realize how idiosyncratic its vision of the game really is.

For one thing, the kind of football that the Logos College team plays represents a game transformed by the arrival of the wholly new. The novel opens with Harkness's extended meditation on the arrival of Taft Robinson in the early fall: "Taft Robinson was the first black student to be enrolled at Logos College in West Texas. They got him for his speed" (3). While readers might anticipate (or, indeed, hope) that this is a precursor to an engagement with race in America, such is not to be the case. Rather, the novel will share the college's interest in speed rather than sociality, and, after noting that Taft went on to become one of the best running backs in the history of the region, Harkness undertakes an elaborate imagining of the might-have-been: "In time he might have turned up on television screens across the land, endorsing eight-thousand-dollar automobiles or avocado-flavored instant shave. His name on a chain of fast-food outlets. His life story on the back of cereal boxes. A drowsy monograph might be written on just that subject, the modern athlete as commercial myth, with footnotes. But this doesn't happen to be it" (3). While this passage indicates what the novel won't be about, without specifying what it will be about, two pages later Harkness gives us a possible indication of the book's subject, as well as why, perhaps, Taft Robinson is such a ghostly figure: "But mostly he could fly—a 9.3 clocking for the hundred. Speed. He had sprinter's speed. Speed is the last excitement left, the one thing we haven't used up, still naked in its potential, the mysterious black gift that thrills the millions" (5). The arrival of Robinson is marked as the one truly significant happening early in the novel—"an event, finally, in a time of incidents and small despairs"—and his arrival fundamentally transforms the nature of the football Logos plays, away from defense and toward offense, as they strive to take advantage of Robinson's gifts (5). This "event" of the fall semester is the arrival of a player whose talents allow an entirely new strategic culture to come into effect on the field.

With the arrival of Taft Robinson's speed, DeLillo begins drawing strict distinctions between offensive and defensive strategy and sport in ways that consistently privilege offense and pathologize defense. Rapturous descriptions of offensive plays are contrasted with the paradoxically indefensible nature of defense. Dennis Smee, the defensive captain, is a sadist who "likes to hurt people" (25). Paradoxically it doesn't seem to be a problem when you hurt a defensive player, only when they hurt you (Harkness can, without irony, take pride in his having really "wiped out that bastard Smee" precisely because Smee is a sadist and a "son of a bitch" who deserves it) (25). And Harkness really wants to drive the point home; after noting Smee's propensity for hurting people, he won't let us forget just what Smee does: "He's the defensive captain. He captains the defense" (25).

Likewise, the distinction in coaching staff couldn't be clearer. Even an assistant coach for the offense, Tom Cook Clark, "an expert on quarterbacking," is "known as a scholarly man," and the school mourns his death midway through the novel (27). As opposed to this quiet offensive genius, the coach of the defensive line, the absurdly named Rolf Hauptfuhrer, is loathsome, and his other duties make it clear how defense is valued: along with his coaching duties, Hauptfuhrer attends to matters of "grooming" for the team, as if the length of sideburns and the presence of beards were as important as the organization of defense. And that name, of course, brings with it a host of negative associations in a novel concerned with mass death: a head-führer responsible for defense reiterates the sadistic nature of defensive play.

But the most vivid, and most troubling, distinctions are those made between two particular players: Taft Robinson and Anatole Bloomberg. They are both minorities at the school—Robinson African American, Bloomberg Jewish—and DeLillo uses them to draw strict distinctions, as if to say that these two minority characters represent two extremes of body, attitude, and mind in an otherwise homogeneous campus population. Robinson, of course, is an offensive star because he is so fast. But he is also an ascetic who wears sunglasses indoors, eats alone, and rarely speaks. Bloomberg plays left tackle on the offensive line—in other words, his job is to defend the offensive players of his team. This distinction between Robinson's place as a purely offensive player and Bloomberg's place as a defensive block or protection for that offense is heightened by all the ways in which their characters differ. Bloomberg speaks constantly, snores loudly, wets the bed: the exact opposite of Robinson's cool self-possession. "Absolutely enormous" and in possession of slow feet that constantly anger the coaching staff, Bloomberg is the anti-Robinson, and Robinson the anti-Bloomberg (14). The stereotypes could scarcely be cruder: the "cool" and reserved African American with awe-inspiring athletic talent; the neurotic Jew. But to read this merely as uncritical racism on DeLillo's part would be to miss the larger project of pathologization of which this crudely rendered distinction is a part.

The novel asks us to do more than simply register differences between offense and defense; the disturbing glamorization of Robinson and denigration of Bloomberg is part of a larger project of judgment where we are asked to evaluate difference on a nearly metaphysical scale. Chapter 15 opens with Bloomberg engaging in one of his frequent (and odd) games of comparison, in this case with a visitor to his room, Andy Chudko:

"Who was the greater man?" Bloomberg said. "You get just one try. Sir Francis Drake or the prophet Isaiah? Take your time answering. It's not as obvious as it seems."

"How can you compare them?" Andy Chudko said. "They were in two different fields."

"The answer seems obvious only at first. Be very careful."

"I don't think it seems obvious at all," Chudko said. (75)

This exchange echoes Bloomberg's earlier interrogation of Gary Harkness, when he asks him if "Edward Gibbon or Archimedes" was the "greater man" (15). The idea that different fields don't prevent comparison and judgment as to the relative merit of their participants is just a heightened version of the redescription of football going on in the novel, where offense is seen as not simply different from defense but as qualitatively better and paradoxically more ethical. When, for instance, the player Onan Moley confronts one of the co-captains about some talk that "there might be a queer on the squad," Kimbrough's only response is to wonder whether this potentially "queer" player plays "offense or defense," and we are left to speculate as to why that distinction might matter so much in this case (25).

It comes as no surprise that in a novel about football, DeLillo might spend some time contrasting different positions, but here the attack, as it were, on defense is so overwritten that we can't help but notice the contrast between the two, especially when, just a page after a long conversation with Bloomberg that makes clear the distinction between Bloomberg and Robinson, and hence between defense and offense, Harkness tells us that he has received permission to audit the air force ROTC courses, and he refers to them by their acronym (AFROTC). The seemingly pointless and offensive racialization of the distinction between offense and defense thus emerges as a way for DeLillo to offer a new analogy, and one far more specific than the obvious one between football and war because it suggests that we might yet compare the impact Robinson is having on the team with contemporary strategic developments.

Such a reading is further invited by the bizarre discussion, midway through the novel, concerning Bloomberg's weight and his dieting. Bloomberg has been under strict orders to lose weight, so as to have fast feet, and his diet has produced a near-existential crisis for him since losing weight feels like losing himself: "I began to lose the idea of myself. I was losing the idea of my body, who it belonged to, what exactly it was, where all the different parts of it were located, what it looked like from different angles and during the various times of the day and evening. I was losing the most important part of my being. Obesity. What I had considered self-control was really self-indulgence. To make me pretty. To give me quick feet" (76). This rigorous training for defense is actually dangerous, causing as it does this radical spatial disorientation. But this speech about the problems of defense on the football field is introduced in ways that make us think more broadly about strategic culture; this speech comes right after Andy Chudko has asked Gary to explain Bloomberg to him, since Bloomberg has just mystified him with one of his comparative who-was-the-greater-man questions. In response to "what do you make of [Bloomberg]?" Gary gives a chilling response, claiming that Bloomberg is "our next secretary of defense" (76). Bloomberg, it would seem, is our next secretary of defense precisely because he doesn't believe in defense at all, even though it is supposedly his job, finding it dangerously self-delusional and totally indefensible. As we will see, this is precisely the paradoxical heart of strategic culture in the early 1970s.

The links (or elisions of the gap) between the discourse of war and the discourse of sport are brought home most fully in the course ("Aspects of Modern War") in which Gary is the star student. The course is taught by Major Staley, whose "father was the school's most famous alumnus, a three-letter man and a war hero, one of the crew on the Nagasaki mission" (71). The relative importance and priority of lettering in three sports and of having bombed Nagasaki is here apparently debatable. Especially debatable because at its most philosophical the course explores the same terrain as the football Harkness plays, in the ways that Major Staley tries to reimagine thermonuclear war. What Major Staley offers in his

AFROTC classes is a speculative imagination of war as purely offensive rather than defensive. The best defense for him is none at all:

> "I think what'll happen in the not-too-distant future is that we'll have humane wars. Each side agrees to use clean bombs. And each side agrees to limit the amount of megatons he uses. In other words we'll get together with them beforehand and there'll be an agreement that if the issue can't be settled, whatever the issue might be, then let's make certain we keep our war as relatively humane as possible. So we agree to use clean stuff. And we actually specify the number of megatons; let's just say hypothetically one thousand megs for each side. So then what we've got is a two-thousand-megaton war. We might go further and say we'll leave your cities alone if you leave ours alone. We make it strictly counterforce." (81)

As we saw in the last chapter, Staley's fantasy of a totally rational war requires no defense; in order for it to "work," both sides must have confidence in the ability of the limited number of weapons they will use to actually destroy their targets, and to "trade" destruction with an enemy. In making purely offensive games—of football and war—the subject of his elaborate analogy, DeLillo reveals the historical specificity of his interest in language during an era that could imagine war as a game. So when Harkness jokingly speaks of a "reordering of priorities" toward a "total offense concept," he really isn't joking at all, and could be describing both the game he plays for Logos and the strategy he studies in his classes (58).

"A Cute Little Ring"

Much as DeLillo's interest in the untellable emerges as a question of politics and ethics rather than linguistic competence, his interest in the shared vocabulary of offensive football and Staley's purely offensive war is a realization of what SALT 1 made possible, the supposed opportunity to wage rule-governed offensive wars again. As I previously suggested, the development of defensive weapons in the late 1960s was a threat to the possibility of limited nuclear wars: potential antimissile missiles virtually guaranteed that any nuclear exchange would necessarily be a large one. This was among the factors driving nuclear strategy in the late 1960s into the corner of assured destruction as McNamara moved from a counterforce to a city-killing strategy.

In 1972, DeLillo published a novel about a football player who positively transforms the nature of the game toward offense. What also arrived in 1972, however, was an arms-control treaty that made limited nuclear war—the kind of nuclear war that Major Staley imagines as a future possibility—possible again as an almost purely offensive conflict. Lawrence Freedman notes that the first account of "the 'defence is a dangerous thing' argument" was offered in 1964.[13] Because building more offensive weapons would always be cheaper than building defensive shields (think about the difference in guidance precision), defensive weapons threatened to escalate an arms race, and defensive weapons also threatened the delicate balance of terror that relied upon each side feeling confident that it could inflict at least as much damage to the other side as it might receive. Although for the next few years McNamara was able to resist calls for an ABM system by arguing that it likely wouldn't work, by 1966 advances in technology made an ABM system look feasible, and the military was eager to challenge McNamara's cost-control measures.[14]

The history of nuclear strategy is one in which offense and defense have been disproportionately valued at different times, and by 1967 it seemed that defense, despite its dangers, was ascendant.[15] After all, imagine the difficulty of making the case that defense was indefensible; it sounds like a virtually career-ending kind of political sophistry. Fred Kaplan recounts the chilling anecdote of McNamara trying to explain to Soviet premier Aleksei Kosygin why defensive weapons were so dangerous: "'When I have trouble sleeping nights,' he [Kosygin] told McNamara, 'it's because of your offensive missiles, not your defensive missiles.'"[16] In one of the more bizarre public speeches of the Cold War, McNamara was finally forced publicly to support the development of an ABM system he knew would never provide the security it promised. His 1967 speech in San Francisco, in which he argued for the deployment of an ABM system against the supposedly growing (but in reality nonexistent) threat from a Chinese arsenal, has been much discussed.[17] Designed to confuse, and confuse it did; McNamara's 1967 speech was part of a larger strategy designed to get the Soviets to the bargaining table, and slow things down by reaching agreement about defensive shields. Although the Nixon administration began the process of actually developing and deploying defensive missiles, it did so largely to escalate the pressure on the ongoing SALT process: the Safeguard missile project was at this point being sold to Congress as a "bargaining chip" in the ongoing negotiations.[18]

The major success of the arms-control agreements negotiated between 1969 and 1972 was the paradoxical limiting of defensive weapons in the ABM treaty, which restricted defensive shields to two locations in each country. The breakthrough of the meetings was thus the new understanding that what made defensive weapons indefensible was their destabilizing tendency. Arms control was so strange an enterprise as to make a ban on defensive shields a real breakthrough, an event that made the world safer from the threat of nuclear holocaust: since ABM shields could counterintuitvely generate all-out war, their banning made the world a safer place.[19] Defensive captains are in fact sadists after all, and secretaries of defense don't believe in defense: these were the "breakthroughs" of the negotiations.

What *End Zone* outlines, then, is the shift in strategy that the fall season brings to the Logos College team, and in doing so it also provides an exquisite account of strategic thinking's contemporary shift away from defense. The real horror of the novel is neither its anachronistic commentary on a bygone era of military thinking, nor its commitment to the erasure, via the linguistic, of real historical reference. Rather, its horrifying truth resides in its moment of publication, a moment that again made possible its central comparison of sport and nuclear war. DeLillo here anticipates the work of Paul Virilio, the foremost philosopher of speed, who proposes that the truly bizarre dimension of the ABM treaty was that it brought human decision, and hence the possibility of metaphors of gaming, back into the realm of possibility. SALT 1, he explained, "aims less at the quantitative limitation of weapons (as its adversary/partners claim) than at the preservation of a properly 'human' political power, since the constant progress of rapidity threatens from one day to the next to reduce the warning time for nuclear war *to less than one fatal minute*—thus finally abolishing the Head of State's power of reflection and decision in favor of a pure and simple *automation* of defense systems."[20]

Virilio's point is that the widespread deployment of defensive weapons, when combined with the very short warning time that new faster offensive weapons would have allowed, made the world far more dangerous. In order for defensive weapons to work, they would have to be launched almost immediately after the detection of enemy offensive weapon use. There would be no time for deliberation of any kind, and the last remaining shreds of human agency and oversight would necessarily disappear from the decision-making process. While not quite the doomsday machine of *Dr. Strangelove*, defensive weapons threatened to make nuclear war the province of machines. But perhaps even more importantly, they virtually guaranteed that if a nuclear war were to be fought, it would be a war of total destruction. Knowing that defensive weapons might destroy a proportion of one's offensive capability meant that one would be compelled to launch an excessive number of weapons in the first place, leading one's opponent to respond in kind—an end to any hope of fighting limited nuclear war.

DeLillo's narration of the public relations campaign that follows Logos's loss to West Centrex Biotechnical in the key game of the season makes the comparison with SALT even clearer. One of the recurrent features of the analysis of SALT has been the fact that though the acronym was well known, almost no one knew what it stood for; histories of the treaty note that the folksy title rarely implied related knowledge about what it meant.[21] And even if one knew that the acronym stood for *Strategic Arms Limitation Talks*, that knowledge wouldn't immediately suggest that the resulting ABM treaty limited *defensive* shields. The Logos College team has been on a winning streak all year when they suffer a devastating loss against their most feared opponent. The football team is on shaky ground, having only recently envisioned itself as a national force, and having only just convinced alumni to make that step financially possible—so the school is desperate to salvage something from the loss. The solution is spin, the spin an opaque acronym: "The next day we learned that the athletic department, meaning Creed, had hired a sports information director. Immediately I fashioned a theory based on the relationship between defeat and the need for publicity, or anti-publicity, the elevation of evasive news to the level of literature" (150). Obviously even the language of spin has a certain militaristic quality to it ("evasive news"), and Gary's first meeting with the new director, Wally Pippich, provides a lesson in the power of acronyms. Pippich wants to base a human-interest campaign around Harkness and Taft Robinson, and he wants to do it because of the linguistic possibilities this pair allows:

> "... Here's the approach as I conceive it. Taft Robinson and Gary Harkness. The T and G backfield. Taft and Gary. Touch and Go. Thunder and Gore."
> "A little word-play. A thing with letters."
> "We get the vital stats. We get action photos. We get background stuff. The T and G backfield. We release to newspapers, to sports pubs, to local radio and TV, to the networks. The whole enchilada. Taft Robinson and Gary Harkness. I like the sound of those names. Some names produce a negative gut reaction in my mind. Cyd Charisse. Mohandas K. Gandhi. Xerxes. But Taft-and-Gary has a cute little ring to it. I know I like it and I may even love it." (151)

The logic seems to be that the initial human interest in the racially binarized pair can then induce a logic of metaphoric substitution in the reader, turning a disastrous defeat into something entirely different, a team now defined by the yoking together of the team's two stars into a vision of an integrated America under the acronym, an integration that echoes the cooperation between the two superpowers that the SALT process supposedly represented. But the mere possibility of wordplay isn't enough; it is the innocuousness of Taft and Gary—the "cute little ring" that makes it sustainable as a strategy for winning back public and alumni support, provided the campaign finds channels in all available media. This "thing with letters" is DeLillo's ironic commentary on the acronym that, for him, signifies and covers up another loss, similar to SALT 1, a treaty that only made the world safe again for limited nuclear war.

Much has been made of the fact that Logos College loses the key game to West Centrex Biotechnical; the game signifies the victory of one kind of language (the scientific) over another (the religious) in most discussions of the novel. But the point I'd finally like to make is that more is at stake here than simply that particular opposition; Logos is of course not simply language but the Word itself, the language of divine revelation. To reduce it to language, and to elevate West Centrex Biotechnical (a school qualified by a direction that modifies a term that itself suggest only approximate centrality, and is furthermore distinguished not even by the more inclusive "polytechnic" but as an even more limited subset of such a school) abstracts too far away from the specificity of the loss. Even the most minor league of directionally identified subpolytechnics is able to trump Logos in this novel. This is not finally to reduce nuclear war to a linguistic game comparable to any other; rather, untellability in this novel is directly connected to the exercise of mass violence.

6 / The Dominant Tense: Richard Powers and Late Postmodernism

Born in 1957, Richard Powers is the most publicly visible heir to the tradition of postmodern self-reflexivity outlined in the preceding five chapters, and his stature as one of the most important writers of his generation now seems assured: his honors include a MacArthur "genius" grant and a National Book Award, he has a growing popular readership, and an emerging critical industry is devoted to his work. He came of creative age in the Reagan era when the Cold War was reheated (his first novel, *Three Farmers on Their Way to a Dance*, was published in 1985), and he has been profoundly influenced by the writers I have been discussing. Along with David Foster Wallace, he is the novelist most often imagined as the descendant of Pynchon and DeLillo, though that debt should not be taken to imply that Powers is merely a modernized version of the two, and he shares with Wallace and a long list of younger writers a sense of just how central the nuclear age was for the postmodernist writers who preceded him. Like those of Pynchon and DeLillo, Powers's complicated novels try to grasp the complex systems that obtain under conditions of globalization and global threat, and his fiction has continually returned to the intersections of the human and the technological in an era of big science, and to the guilty consciences that these intersections produce. Perhaps his most distinctive feature is his thematic and conceptual range: the history of corporate personhood, the history of visual art, the nature of consciousness, the possibilities of virtual reality, the history of race in the United States, the discovery and impact of DNA, the impact of epochal change, the world wars, the Cold War, and literary history.

But Powers, despite his capacious grasp of the realities that bind Americans to place, genetics, history, and structures of power, and despite his interest in some of the most pressing political issues of modern times, is also noticeably more committed to the ontological possibilities of aesthetic production than any of the writers I've discussed, with the exception of Barth, and more than any of these authors, he paradoxically locates his work precisely at the intersection of fabulous invention and the burdens of real history.[1] In his novels, concrete history intersects with the possibility of alternate worlds, and understanding how these two commitments—to the factual, historical, and tragic, and to the possibility of literary enchantment—interact is key to any attempt at understanding Powers's work. The possibilities of the imagination are central to his novels, and even at their most pessimistic moments, Powers and his characters find solace in fabulation. The aim of this chapter is to reveal Powers's implicit historicization of his interest in fabulation, and to grasp how Powers sees the intersection of concrete history and reflexive experimentation in political and ethical terms: as I will show, the nuclear age fundamentally shapes Powers's distinctive aesthetic, and explains his extraordinary commitment to the possibilities of the imagination.

It is in his 1988 novel *Prisoner's Dilemma* that Powers comes closest to explaining his interest in the intersection of "real" history (the history that, as Jameson says, always hurts) with fabulatory storytelling. The commitment to fantastic narrative invention in the novel becomes a way of surviving that history, and in *Prisoner's Dilemma* Powers explains his own narrative commitment to the combination of history and invention as a direct result of the Cold War. Narrative is powerless to enact change in the real world; narrative is the only tool we have to enact change in the real world. This is the paradox that emerges in Powers's work; and in *Prisoner's Dilemma*, which was published in the last full year of the Cold War, we see the links between narrativity and the maintenance of futurity as a potential zone of human affairs, and also the ways in which this intersection of ethics and escapism has been produced by the nuclear age. While less obviously autobiographical than *Galatea 2.2*, and less directly fanciful than *Operation Wandering Soul*, *Prisoner's Dilemma* is where Powers comes closest to explaining the origins of his particular brand of narrative styling, and this novel, with its active reflections on the relationship between the history of the first nuclear age and fabulatory storytelling, represents a perfect summary of the preceding chapters even as it extends them by imagining narrative as a place where a therapeutic rather than merely diagnostic relationship to nuclear history might be found.

"What Just One Bomb Did"

Prisoner's Dilemma, like much of Powers's fiction, is a multistranded contrapuntal narrative (with one anomalous section that I discuss at the end of this chapter). The first strand is a relatively straightforward account of the Hobson Family, consists of twenty-one numbered chapters, and is set in the fall and winter of 1978 (from a few weeks before Thanksgiving through to a few days after Christmas). The family (Eddie Sr., Ailene, and four children: Artie, Rachel, Lily, and Eddie Jr.) is trying to come to terms with the illness of Eddie Sr., who for years has suffered from periodic fainting attacks, and has consequently become a virtual invalid. The family has finally convinced him to see a doctor, and he has agreed to check himself into the VA hospital in Chicago just after a planned—and potentially final—family Thanksgiving. After admitting himself to the hospital, he "escapes" and begins a solitary journey back to the site of his illness's origin, and the family follows his progress west and south via occasional cryptic phone calls from the runaway paterfamilias. This relatively uncomplicated story of a complicated family is, however, overshadowed by the rest of the novel, which is anything but straightforward, particularly when we have to collate the multiple chapters and narrative lines into a single unified novel.

The second strand, told in italicized chapters, constitutes an elaborate counterhistory of the years between 1939 and 1945 that tries to rescue the twentieth century from the disasters those years brought, and tries to reconstruct the personal history that has, it appears, led Eddie Hobson to compose this counterhistory. Complicating matters is that these fourteen unnumbered italicized sections form at least two distinct narratives. The first story line is presented in chapters with words as titles ("Riddles," for instance), and in them one or more of the Hobson children (who remain unidentified, but it is most likely Artie) tells, in the first person and primarily in the past tense, the (or perhaps a) story of their father's life. We learn at the end of the novel that we can take these sections to be tape recordings made after their father's death, and after the children have listened to recordings that their father left behind. We assume that the other italicized sections (which always begin with dates) consist of the tape that Eddie Sr. left behind, and to which the children listen before beginning their own project of (re)recording their father's life.

Opening with the World's Fair of 1939, these italicized chapters (the ones we take to be dictated by Eddie Sr.) imagine a filmic project by Walt Disney that will bring all viewers into history itself, and make everyone understand that they are not mere objects of history but historical agents as well; the goal is to rescue history from scripted teleology, and so reveal that the Second World War and the half century of cold conflict that emerged from it were never inevitable. These sections tell alternate histories of the Manhattan Project and Japanese internment that turn these events against themselves, even as the shadow of retrospective prophecy makes them seem utterly fated. So the novel properly consists of three stories: the twenty-one numbered chapters tell a fairly straightforward (until the end) story of the Hobson family; the italicized chapters that begin with dates are part of the lifework of Eddie Hobson, who attempts to construct an alternative world in his imagination, and the italicized chapters that bear titles constitute attempts by the Hobson children to reconstruct their father's life in the light of his death and their discovery of his lifework. How these three narrative strands interact is the problem at the heart of the novel, and, as we will see in the complexities of their interaction, the counterhistory they collectively author amounts to more than simple nostalgia for a past that has been left behind. And while that counterhistory is by far the most interesting feature of the novel, the demands that motivate it suggest that we start with the family story. The particular history of the desire for a counterhistory of the midcentury (or, more properly, the desire for the possibility of counterhistory itself) turns out to be crucial.

The Hobsons of the twenty-one chapters are in many ways the typical "nuclear" family: postwar, large, and very patriarchal. The Hobson parents are demographically instantly recognizable as the kind of couple that produced the baby boom, and the characters even refer to theirs as a "nuclear" family. But Powers is playing with the multiple meanings of the term, of course; like his contemporary Rick Moody, Powers uses the term to show how the bonds that constitute the nuclear family are themselves a product of nuclear history.[2] For this family is "nuclear" in the most pessimistic sense. As Elaine Tyler May has influentially speculated, the postwar population boom was at least in part a psychic defense mechanism against the threat of the next war, and Eddie Sr. and Ailene certainly participate in this imaginative framework, identifying children as protection against undefined threats.[3] And these children are themselves growing up with the kind of nuclear unconscious that interested Tim O'Brien in *The Nuclear Age*: footballs are imagined as ICBMs, a household radio dates from the Bay of Pigs invasion, and a nuclear-age language suffuses the text. But the nuclear age acts upon this family in far more direct ways than merely as their unconscious background, and the nuclear homology, it turns out, is all too fitting.

The exact disease from which Eddie Sr. is suffering remains unspecified for most of the novel. However, his ill-health is the defining feature of the family's life: it means that the family has moved constantly, as Eddie Sr. loses job after job as a high-school history teacher after particularly alarming fainting episodes, and the children are continually recalled home to deal with their father. He suffers from periodic attacks in which he rolls his eyes skyward, passes out, and vomits, and is left weakened for a few hours or days (and physically he is gradually wasting away). The children come up with diagnosis after diagnosis, but none explains the full range of symptoms. Only near the end of the novel do we learn what has caused this combination of physical and mental illness, when, in one of the italicized chapters, one of the children reconstructs his wartime service: Eddie Sr., it turns out, was an inadvertent witness to the Trinity test in New Mexico in July 1945. Stationed across the Southwest at various airbases that are being shut down in the wake of Germany's surrender, he finds himself in the middle of the desert on the Jornada del Muerto in New Mexico.

On the (early) morning of the Trinity test, he is playing cards and eating peanuts with fellow soldiers when he decides to go outside for a smoke; as he finishes the cigarette and flicks it aside, the sky lights up with the Trinity test, and this artificial dawn at the birth of the nuclear age means that Eddie will never sleep properly again. Although Eddie has repeatedly told the story of his encounter with this fake sunrise to his family, it is only at the end of the novel, when Eddie has disappeared from the VA hospital, and tells his family over the phone that he is going home, that Artie realizes where his father is headed, and why he has suffered for so long; Eddie Sr. tells his daughter Lily that he has been awake for at least three decades. Postmodernity's iconic false dawn has left time out of joint.

Eddie Sr. meets the classic Freudian definition of trauma: he is witness to a catastrophic event that comes unexpectedly, remains unintegrated into consciousness, and leaves him with no physical injuries. His periodic attacks are thus flashbacks (which explains the movement of his eyes, and the wincing eye pain), and his physical symptoms are psychosomatic introjections of radiation sickness (we learn from his doctor that the symptoms that indicate radiation sickness have to be psychosomatic, since he is suffering them after more than thirty years, while an anecdote about the brain's ability to provoke physical symptoms is mentioned in the novel). Eddie's literal nuclear history thus produces a nuclear family as the bonds that hold the family together are produced by the effects of the splitting of the atom.

Cathy Caruth has argued that trauma is a problem of and for narrative: the past is never allowed to become historical, and keeps reemerging in the present, not as memory, but as repetitive experience; and conventional history, with its necessarily clear line between past and present, can thus scarcely exist as such.[4] But Powers makes it clear that this traumatized relationship to the past affects more than just Eddie Sr. The familial equivalent of his trauma is the foreclosure of futurity for his various children: the disease from which Eddie suffers produces a continual domestic present tense. As Lily recalls early in the novel, she was preparing to leave for college when her mother came into the room, and their conversation reveals a family living in a nuclear time when her mother notes, "If only you weren't starting off to school *just now*."[5] The italicized "just now" defines life as a nearly continual present tense that leaves Lily unable to move on, and to connect past, present, and future; this is the moment when "she was about to travel in two directions: forward into adulthood, and back to the place of her girlhood, the place she had loved before the Hobsons had started their long life of wagons west" (53). Instead of creating a life narrative that seamlessly connects past, present, and future, Lily stays at home, joining her father in the foreclosed futurity constitutive of traumatic experience. When Lily reflects on the decision some years later, she extends her father's condition to the whole family: "it was not her fault that the Hobsons were always in the middle of a 'just now.' It occurred to her that they were once again in a 'just now' just now" (57). This family's protracted nuclearity is literally produced by the nuclear; the children are unable to fully leave the nest because of the illness inflicted on their father by the nuclear age, and their bonds are produced out of a private trauma that replicates trauma's temporal dynamics in the very structure of the family. So the family lives, indirectly, under the conditions of nuclear time that, I have been arguing, constitutes one key version of the postmodern condition. And so the recovery of the history of this father and this family acts as a kind of coda to my project, as these histories make visible how completely daily life has been scripted by the nuclear age.

Powers complicates the idea of trauma at work in the text by unpacking the peculiar temporal dynamics of *nuclear* trauma. This isn't simply the story of someone traumatized by the Trinity test, and unable to integrate into their memory what they have witnessed; rather, in the italicized sections we get a critique of, rather than an example of, traumatic experience and the idea of working through. As Paul K. Saint-Amour notes, the nuclear poses a potential problem for theories of working through trauma: the nuclear could in fact threaten the very tense—the future—that is necessary for working through, and one could, in the most paradoxical of temporalities, be traumatized in advance of an event that could never be consigned to harmless memory. As I argued earlier in relation to Pynchon, if total war comes, there may not be time to work through the traumatic event because there will be no survival of it, and thus we are condemned to the endless "traumatic earliness" (Saint-Amour's phrase) constitutive of living in a nuclear age. The nuclear, then, presents a challenge to the axiomatic assumptions of the discipline of trauma theory. At its most extreme, the nuclear can produce only a traumatic experience from the future, in which symptoms paradoxically precede causes, since the only experience of nuclear war we can have is of a yet-to-be-realized occurrence. As Saint-Amour explains, this significantly complicates the idea that, following Caruth, we might access history through traumatic narrative. As Caruth argues in her now-classic account of trauma and narrative, traumatic experience and working through offer a potential model of how we might think of history outside the twin poles of a positivist discourse in which pure truth is accessed and the hopelessly relativistic possibilities of tropology, in which no event can ever be said to have a truth exterior to its narrative representation. But, crucially for Caruth, the problems raised by trauma are centrally ones raised by *surviving* an event, and how we relegate that event to the past helps to guide our understanding of history as a practice and discipline since trauma provides a model of an event that is witnessed, but cannot be immediately understood.[6]

This problem underlies Eddie Sr.'s illness; the traumatic event is less a single event and more an entry point into a nuclear era that has evolved long past the Trinity test into the possibility of a futureless future that renders impossible the activity of working through. The belatedness of his first symptoms certainly suggests that the traumatic event is at least partly a *future* trauma: the trauma of the Trinity test is not so much the event itself as the age it ushers in, an age that leaves no future in which to work through the past and to which we may never see a postscript. When Lily recounts her first memory of one of her father's bouts of illness (a bout which occured during a television broadcast of a travelogue), the reader gets a sense of what might be at stake in Eddie Sr.'s peculiar relationship to time and history: "Lily swelled and picked up speed. 'But when they showed footage of this lost temple, for some reason he shut up. I can still see the place, the camera moving over it. Amazing: a ruin, but intact. No human had touched a stone for hundreds of years. A pack of monkeys had taken the place over, colonized it. A temple given up to gibbons. I remember thinking, at age eight, that it looked like the last record of civilization. Then suddenly: bang. Dad went down behind me, flat on his back'" (33). I'd suggest that the particular traumatic trigger here is not civilization's "last record" but its survival. Whatever killed the original inhabitants of this temple left others untouched, and has turned the temple, crucially, into a kind of time capsule through which the future can look back, and understand, in however limited a way, a culture that predates it. In contrast, and as we shall see, what the Trinity test revealed to Eddie Sr. is an age that might not have a future at all; the present he lives in, he fears, may never be viewable to a future audience, no matter how carefully its time capsule is prepared. Just as in Hersey's revisions to *Hiroshima* in 1985, Powers and Eddie Sr. understand the dual problem of being a nuclear witness: one is a traumatized observer of a particular event (the initial blast), and yet one can also be traumatized in advance by the possibility of the future use of these weapons, weapons increasingly so powerful that their actual use would preclude trauma by ensuring that no one would live to be traumatized. It is this doubled sense of trauma—one that looks backward; another that looks forward—that produces the novel's doubled narrative.

The problems raised by escalation and the continued development of nuclear weapons are evidenced in the repeated reference to the real prisoner's dilemma, the game-theory problem central to Cold War strategy from which the novel takes its title. Eddie Sr. introduces the prisoner's dilemma in relation to these Cold War contexts at the family breakfast table, when he tells his family that he has been reading about it, and notes that it was invented at the RAND Corporation in 1951.[7] The dilemma was immensely important during the Cold War (even now, it almost immediately connotes a nuclear context) because it offered a distilled account of the value of cooperation in controlling both the escalation of arsenal size and in how one might conceptualize fighting a nuclear war.[8] Powers's example of the dilemma is this: two men are brought into Joseph McCarthy's office and told that the government knows they are both communists, but doesn't have quite enough evidence against either of them. So they are offered a deal: if one rats out the other, then that person goes free, and the one they have ratted out will get the death penalty. If they both stay silent, they both go to jail for two years. However, if they both rat out the other, they go to jail for ten years. Obviously the best outcome for both requires them to stay silent, but there is no system in place for one to communicate this to the other, and the only way you can know whether or not it is right to trust your opponent is to take the risk of trusting him or her.

In the nuclear context, however, the eventual scale of stockpiles renders the prisoner's dilemma more a utopian diagnosis than a viable strategy for thinking about conflict. Halfway through the novel, Eddie Jr. proposes a solution to the dilemma: "As ye give, so shall ye get. And verse-vica, you scratch my back, I'll scratch yours" (149). The appeal of what his father calls "Tit for Tat" is immediate, assuming as it does that one's opponent is every bit as decent and rational as oneself (149). Furthermore, the repeated iteration of the prisoner's dilemma has often been regarded as the solution to its otherwise seemingly intractable logic. But Eddie Sr. points out some problems: "this strategy requires that the dilemma occur not just once, but repeatedly. It doesn't help the one-shot event at all; you need retrials to make your policy known to the other guy. Retaliation won't enforce anything if there's no tomorrow" (150). Eddie Sr.'s imaginary scenario is implicitly nuclear war, of course, an event that might not leave time to assess the other's actions, and one in which the matrix starts to make little or no sense: the only outcome that might spare both of you the death penalty is mutual cooperation, but in cooperating you always have to trust the other not to betray the necessarily tacit agreement, and in the nuclear context, mutual defection no longer means ten years in prison, but universal death. As we saw in chapter 4, the assumption of an enemy just like yourself is problematic in the extreme; Eddie Jr.'s suggestion that the dilemma effectively provides the chance to get to know your opponent only works if the dilemma is ongoing, which already requires that your enemy be exactly like you. If they are not, you will likely resort immediately to full escalation. I can only trust my opponent, in other words, if I trust my opponent: hardly a solution to the dilemma. And this matrix gets infinitely more complex when the game incorporates more than two players.

Eddie Sr. goes on to demonstrate that political pseudo-imperatives dictate the military ones when he suggests: "There's an even bigger problem. True. In a world of independent vested interest, you need some threat to prevent the other guy from threatening you. But please tell me what threat is big enough to check the force we are *really* up against? PREZ SEZ

HE WILL NOT BLINK FIRST. How do you retaliate against something that size, little man?" (150, italics in original). The mock-newsprint that Eddie quotes suggests that even if the prisoner's dilemma works in theory, in practice the rhetorical demands and obligatory machismo of foreign policy may never allow the dilemma to become a reiterated pursuit (a point made by Nixon in his "madman theory" when he encouraged aides to let foreign officials think he was crazy enough to use nuclear weapons),[9] and Eddie Sr.'s reference to his son as "little man," combining as it does the names of the Hiroshima and Nagasaki weapons (Little Boy and Fat Man), makes the nuclear referent unambigious.

"I Have Seen the Future"

Saint-Amour's understanding of the peculiar temporality of nuclear trauma helps to account for much of the peculiarity of Powers's novel, and in particular for the striking counterhistory narrated in the novel's dated and italicized sections. We learn over the course of the novel that these sections are the postwar lifework of Eddie Sr., who has spent years dictating a fabulatory counterhistory into a tape machine, a project he began almost immediately after suffering his first traumatic flashback. The project makes apparent the contradictions of Eddie's life; as his daughter Lily says, he seems the least likely of people to engage in escapist fantasy: "Pop always insisted that one's only hope of salvation lay in finding out where history dropped you down. Yet the same man, trapped in phantoms, lived for Hobstown, a makeshift, escapist fantasy, as far as she could make out" (50). This tension between historical responsibility and escapist fantasy surfaces throughout the novel: Eddie Sr. is a gifted history teacher who can make the subject come alive for his students, and he is constantly quizzing his children about history, foreign policy, astronomy, and game theory. But he also loves the most generically constrained types of cinema:

> *Astonishingly, the professional educator, friendless, intent on discovering what was really going on, still loved the fables of moral fallen women and criminal moguls with hearts of gold. He fell victim to the cheapest narrative tricks. Until the end he was a secret fan of the possibility of* another *place, the* other *person's story. I always thought that intellect and sentiment formed the horns of an exclusive either-or. They do not. My father had them both in doses that he, as well as the rest of us, paid for healthily.* (78–79, italics in original)

Powers's own narrative emphasis here—the nonitalicized "another" and "other" in the otherwise italicized section—registers an almost Benjaminian concern with seeing history as something other than pure teleology and causality, a concern with brushing history against the grain. The alternate history the tapes recount is more than simply a different history from the one that textbooks offer; rather, it is an attempt to keep history and temporality alive: history as metahistory and a counterhistory of the possibility of counterhistory. And in this simultaneous embrace of concrete history and escapist fantasy, Powers comes closest to allegorizing his own practice as a novelist, since his novels repeatedly display those same commitments at one and the same time. The combination of intellect and sentiment that describes Eddie Sr. might equally well describe Powers: three parts brainy researcher, and one part soppy sentimentalist.

Before he leaves for the hospital, Eddie Sr. destroys all but one tape, the tape covering the years from 1939 to 1946, and it is this tape, interwoven with the commentary of his children about the tape, that constitutes the bulk of the italicized sections. When we consider these sections with Eddie's status as a nuclear veteran in mind, they begin to look like a very particular kind of nostalgic escapism. In fact, I would argue that the novel actually makes the case for a *progressive* nostalgia: Eddie Sr.'s look back on the 1940s is not an uncritical celebration of the "Greatest Generation"; on the contrary, it is a nostalgia not for the past as such, but for a past that could still imagine futurity. Indeed, his lifework is a counterhistory that preserves the possibility of history itself by preserving the future tense that enables the present to imagine itself becoming historical.

We learn early in the novel that Eddie Sr. is a "pure product" of the 1939 World's Fair (46). The William Carlos Williams reference ("The pure products of America / go crazy") is obvious, and Powers shows how a "pure product" of this World's Fair would have to go crazy after 1945. What characterizes the 1939 celebration in Powers's account is an insistent futurity. The first chapter describing Eddie's alternate world, "Hobstown: 1939," opens with a long description of a time capsule from the fair, imagined as a missile aimed fifty centuries into the future. The rest of the fair is just as insistently forward-looking, in keeping with its theme of "Building the World of Tomorrow." In retrospect, Artie can see what was wrong with his father, when he imagines his father's commitment to the future as a "virus" contracted at the World's Fair, specifically at *"the astonishing city of 1960"* of *"General Motors's Futurama,"* a *"pavilion that utterly floored him at the time, completely overhauled his life and therefore mine*" (83, 82, italics in original). The iconic pin that Eddie Sr. takes away from the fair and the Futurama exhibit bears the very message that will come to haunt him: "I Have Seen the Future." But the future that Eddie Sr. has seen is not the future that would come to be.

The 1939 World's Fair has been discussed at length by David Nye and Roland Marchand. As Nye points out, it was "the best-attended event in the United States during the first half of the twentieth century" and saw 45 million attendees (though some were, like Eddie, repeat visitors).[10] For Nye, the fair's immense power as a public event was derived from its imaging of utopian futures even in the wake of the Depression; the most successful displays "dramatized the future and presented it as a utopian landscape, usually in the form of a diorama or a miniaturized world." Nye compares the event to the sacred rituals of tribal societies, but with a crucial difference: rather than memorializing a collective past, the fair and its most successful exhibits pointed the populace toward the future.[11] The World's Fair presented a kind of ritualized collectivity that made futurity the national tense. As I argued in chapter 3, the persistence of futurity as a zone for national imagination was put under immense pressure by the nuclear age, and Coover's *The Public Burning* registers that pressure by revealing the incoherence of forms of sociality built around future perfection. But after the Depression, the future-tense utopia of the fair had immense appeal, even if the Second World War would prove its optimism ephemeral. At the heart of this orientation was Futurama, the massively successful General Motors exhibit that by all accounts was the runaway hit of the 1939 World's Fair, and that provides in miniature a picture of the culture of time and space that was to disappear with 1945.

As Nye and Marchand indicate, two key features distinguished the 1939 World's Fair: first, the centrality of corporate, rather than national, exhibits, and, second, the transformation of corporate displays from exhibits of the manufacturing process and new commodities into exhibits that emphasized the utopian possibilities of corporate technology as an experience of the future: "Corporations would henceforth entice fairgoers not to 'tour our factory' but to 'share our world.'"[12] The distinction between General Motors's 1934 display in Chicago and Futurama makes this transformation extraordinarily visible, and helps to account for Futurama's remarkable popularity. In Chicago, General Motors had offered a model Chevrolet assembly line as the centerpiece of its exhibit, in keeping with a corporate culture that emphasized commodities above all else. Although General Motors had initially planned an expanded version of the line for the 1939 exhibit, their plans were transformed by

Norman Bel Geddes, an industrial designer with a background in theater staging and lighting.[13]

Calling the exhibit that Bel Geddes ultimately designed a "world of the future" is almost too true: what he crafted was indeed a world, and one that made the promise of futurity rather than the commodities of the present its center. The building itself, with its "hook" shape that caught and then funneled the massive crowds that lined up, and with its triangular point that seemed to gesture metaphorically into the future, set the stage for a display of the inevitable progress toward an achieved utopia.[14] As fairgoers entered the building and adjusted to lower light, they saw a massive (60 by 100 feet) map that at first highlighted in red the nation's highway system in 1939, before moving on to represent the congestion of that system by 1960. The final step was another change: the illumination and representation of an imagined system of superhighways that solved the problems of congestion.[15] After being confronted with these two divergent futures, visitors left the map room.

They then entered a technological utopia. Visitors sat in padded chairs on a moving conveyor belt that took them on a fifteen-minute tour of the United States of 1960 as seen from a low-flying aircraft. Miniaturized at a scale of one inch to 200 feet, the nearly 36,000-square-foot model represented a huge swath of the nation, and contained several million structures, all constructed with an eye to radical verisimilitude of scale, yet ripe with utopian imaginations of a country of superhighways, peaceful cities, and perfect suburbs.[16] Bel Geddes's concern for detail led to smoke-generated clouds that hugged mountains, miniature waterfalls, and the complex manipulation of light so as to simulate afternoon light in orchards.[17] But it was the final step that served to imprint this technological utopia on the minds of so many of its visitors: "After gliding over a massive city (modeled on St. Louis), divided to contrast the 'old city' of 1939 with the spectacularly futuristic architecture and open space of the city of 1960, the spectators were brought down closer to one small segment of the new city, a particular intersection toward which the narrator directed their attention. Here they could admire from on high, yet in full and explicit detail, a rational new mode of urban planning in which pedestrians and auto traffic were segregated onto different levels."[18] The final step was key: after "arriving" on the conveyor belt at this intersection, the chairs swung around, and riders found themselves entering a full-sized version of the intersection and walking through it, where they received the iconic "I have seen the future" pin. So the full appeal of the Futurama display lay in neither its technical virtuosity, nor in the promises it made of a techno-utopian future; rather, it was in the ability of this world to come wholly alive for its viewers when they became actually, rather than figuratively, immersed in it.

It is this endless capacity for wonder inspired by the future that runs through Eddie's imaginary world of Disney, which seeks to do nothing less than rescue history by imagining forms of aesthetic production capable of actually intervening in the real world. This film is the symptom of the optimism "virus" that Eddie Sr. contracts at the World's Fair. In this imaginary world, with world war engulfing the planet, everyone is asked to play his or her part: even Walt Disney is figuratively drafted when he is ordered to start churning out propaganda pieces, and the novel tells the story of the success of such "actual" Disney films as *Victory through Air Power* and *Der Fuehrer's Face*. But for Disney, the merely technical accomplishment of blending animation and live-action isn't enough: "*Disney must create a film falling both squarely in this world and far, far outside it, a tough-as-steel fairy tale that will, for the first time, bring home to the GI and the Rosie Riveters and the Joint Chiefs as well as the shiftless teenagers in suburban Jersey just where they are in Time, just how urgent, critical, real, and present the present is, just how central each of them is to the larger picture*" (134–35, italics in original). To win this war means remembering that this war wasn't inevitable, which requires a film that can exceed merely technical accomplishment to become the kind of aesthetic experience that, like Futurama, literally brings the viewer into the text. Disney's title makes clear that he wants this film to suggest that we are agents as well as passive subjects of history: *You Are the War*. The idea that the war isn't simply the product of abstract forces or of diabolically evil enemies fought by pure-hearted allies is brought crushingly home when Disney convenes a meeting of his elite brain trust of illustrators, and notices that two of his best illustrators have been interned because of their Japanese ancestry. He withdraws into seclusion, meditating on lines of Rilke that suggest the power of the imagination, and realizes that any film that merely expresses the notion that we can all influence history will be worthless unless he acts within history to realize the film in such a way as to perform its message; if he looks away from the mass imprisonment of his fellow Americans in order to make a film that suggests we must never look away, then all is lost. He flies to Washington, pitches his idea to Secretary of War Henry Stimson, and tells him it will require a massive expenditure of money and unprecedented manpower—so much manpower, in fact, that he will need to free ten thousand of the Japanese Americans interned in camps. But this film is a kind of superweapon, a tool for assured victory, and one that, if properly realized, can keep the world safe for democracy well past the end of the war, even if the national enemy changes. Stimson relents only when this fictional Disney reminds him that he, Disney, has Japanese ancestry (in reality, Disney has no known Japanese ancestors, but this is, after all, a counterhistory) and will demand to be interned. Stimson demands that the film be made in a secret location, far from prying eyes, and furthermore gives Disney some creative advice: make a film without jingoism, since the "little scrap" with the Germans and the Japanese is nothing in comparison to what is yet to come.

Secret trips to Washington to pitch superweapons by a character of "questionable" ancestry, massive financial and manpower requirements, a need for an isolated location to work in total secrecy, and the hope that the weapon's usefulness might outlive the particular conflict it was designed to end—this should sound familiar. While Eddie Sr. never explicitly identifies this project as a version of the Manhattan Project, the parallel is clear: Mouse ears have replaced Oppenheimer's porkpie hat, and the most difficult quest of this filmic project turns out to be how to acquire enough of the magic "Fairy Dust" that can cause the film to come alive and actually create the living relationship to history that Disney craves. Fairy dust, it turns out, is the anti-plutonium, and he who wields it becomes not Oppenheimer's "Death, the destroyer of worlds" (the line from the *Bhagavad Gita* that Oppenheimer supposedly uttered at the moment of the first test) but instead an epic creator of worlds:

> *The corny voice-over elaborates:* "What you have just seen is almost half a kilogram of Fairy Dust, squirreled away in precious allotments obtained from private, international channels, kept under the most stringent safeguards and security, saved for the most urgent occasion. That occasion is now, with the whole globe pitched in a battle where everything of value is at stake. This potent substance can turn a lump of pasty papier-mâché into a terraced garden." *Proving the claim, the next shot shows one of the masked soldiers, fingers glowing with a pinch of the invisible stuff, standing in the middle of emptiness. He opens his hand with a colored flourish and, following a perfect jump cut, the fields around him transform into a bustling downtown. The sequence repeats in another open space: a sprinkling of powder, and up springs a mountain range. Three times in succession the protectively clothed creature creates,* ex nihilo, *factories, scenic gorges, and quiet residential streets.* (214, italics in original)

Neighborhoods, factories, and nature are created instantly, out of nothing: atomic bombing in reverse, as lumps of rocks are transformed into the Rockies. The freed Japanese Americans who make up the team even coin the name "World World" for the project, an antidote to Oppenheimer's world of death.

In his 1997 elegy for the Cold War, *Underworld*, Don DeLillo has the artist Klara Sax suggest that one of the enduring aesthetic legacies of the nuclear age is precisely that there is no enduring aesthetic legacy: "We all tried to think about war but I'm not sure we knew how to do this. The poets wrote long poems with dirty words and that's about as close as we came, actually, to a thoughtful response. Because they had brought something into the world that out-imagined the mind."[19] Sax's comment, particularly in its idea that the bomb's destructive power was simply too large to grasp, echoes many other comments on the bomb made by a diverse group of thinkers. But in Powers's alternate history, it isn't that plutonium leaves us unable to grasp its true power; rather, fairy dust has just the opposite effect: "This is no ordinary element. The dust derives its power by acting as the mind's prism. It is, in essence, imagination reified" (214). If one of the immediate postwar effects of the invention of the atomic age was the consensus of many members of the Manhattan Project that the only "solution" to the potentially divisive nature of the bomb was world government (the classic *One World or None* was first published in 1946), then fairy dust again looks like the anti-plutonium in its unifying imaginative power: "The secret subtext of the project, which must convince even the wartime censors, is: We man the trenches opposite ourselves" (216). Likewise, the slogan of the secret project tries not simply to create an alternate history but also to recover the very possibility of it: at one point, a group of craftsmen replaces the Holocaust-haunted "Work Will Set You Free" with "It Ain't Necessarily So." In other words, this alternate history sees links among the Manhattan Project, the Holocaust, and domestic internment, and seeks to imagine a world where none of these things could have happened, a world that lived up to the utopian longings of the World's Fair.

The film that Disney ends up making in Eddie Hobson's imaginary world is a grand-scale amplification of the idea at the heart of *It's a Wonderful Life*: we rescue time by showing that each of us affects it. When Disney finds that his originally desired lead actor—Bud Middleton, the "star" of the Westinghouse film from the 1939 World's Fair—has died at Guadalcanal, he replaces him with Eddie Hobson, and Eddie and Mickey Mouse (here playing the role of Clarence the angel), go on a whirlwind ride through the postwar years, with Disney determined to make a film that keeps the world trusting:

> *The world is not millions; it is one and one and one. It does not become an impasse until those* ones *start to renounce it. And they will have no cause to, if they stay tied to the good faith of others.* "That's where we come in," the cartoonist croons. "We show them how one life, yours, changes all the others it touches on. How the game remains worth the candle, so long as one walks by faith and not by sight." (265–66)

It is finally the explosion at Trinity that ends Disney's dream. Mickey Mouse has taken Eddie on a tour of the near future that reveals how the Supreme Court will uphold the legality of Japanese internment, and how Nazi scientists will be "rehabilitated" in the American push for leadership in the Cold War. The struggle to articulate a counterhistory that keeps the future front and center experiences its final defeat in the advent of the atomic age: Eddie Sr. "*lived through the specific moment of modern history when, in order to free ourselves, we locked ourselves away*" (250, italics in original).

As Nye points out, "The 1939 World's Fair, despite its emphasis on how technology could deliver Americans into a utopian future, failed to imagine how the rocket and the atomic bomb would reshape the real world by 1960."[20] The most obvious of these restructurings was of the visible world and the built environment; what we now might call the "urbanism" at the heart of Futurama was replaced by the decentered, postmodern city of *The Crying of Lot 49*, the visible symptom of the new possibilities of destruction that global conflict now made possible. But these massive demographic changes are really only the obvious signs of the destruction that the rocket and the atomic bomb brought; the most invisible and insidious of which might in fact be the destruction of the ability to imagine oneself within historical time in any meaningful way. It is of course a given, thanks to Fredric Jameson's work, that this inability to imagine the present historically is a hallmark of the postmodern. And it should be noted that the only "real" relationship to futurity in the novel is the work of Rachel, who spends her workday as an actuary, calculating "to eight significant digits how likely an individual was to die over a given period of years" (62). This may be the most authentic relationship to historical time in the novel, horribly depressing though it is.

But it is in Powers's implicit connection of the two narrative lines that we get something like the historicization of this ahistorical present. The novel suggests that the story of this family is the story of two competing and antithetical models of time and history. The virus of progress depends on the future; 1945 threatens, for the first time, the temporal underpinning that is a necessary—though by no means sufficient—condition of progress, and the development after 1945 of bigger weapons and new delivery systems only makes the problem worse. Perhaps the most poignantly awful aspect of all this is the technological underpinning of 1939's vision of utopia: industrial advances would usher in a new age of leisure. But by 1945, the same technological new age had given the world mass death rather than mass life, through the twin nightmares of the extermination camps and the atomic bomb. The conveyor belt that carried Futurama visitors into the future would have a very different association in the wake of World War Two. The "just now" that defines the Hobson family is the result: a present stuck in the present, and the counterhistory of Hobstown is an attempt to imagine a present linked to a past that could still imagine futurity; not Benjamin's angel facing the past's wreckage, but a temporal horizon that can look forward and help us locate ourselves within historical time.

Though Disney has been the heroic mind behind so much of the novel's counterhistorical imagination, the end of the film finds him broken. In the light of what the Mouse has shown Eddie, Disney decides to retreat from a shattered world. His solution? He builds Disneyland. Were the novel to end here, the point would be clear: in the face of the crushing catastrophes of the twentieth century, the only possible response is pure fantasy. But Powers isn't content to make Disneyland the postmodern condition. The Eddie Sr. of the tape makes a decision to keep trusting even after he listens to a recording in which Disney has explained his decision to turn his back on the world. So Eddie rewinds that tape and records over Disney a story of the family of the twenty-one chapters: "Let's start again, from scratch. Let us make a small world, a miniature of a miniature, say an even half-dozen, since we screw up everything larger. Let's model the daily workings of an unremarkable, mid-sized family, and see if we can't get it right. A family of six, who had one halfway happy summer vacation on the Pacific a decade and a half back" (333). This, of course, is the story we have been reading, and the first-person plural address of the recording, as well as the ways in which this story line intersects with the other strands of the novel, raises any number of characteristically postmodern questions about the ontological status of the entire narrative. But such ontological questions aren't the ultimate point. The real moral is clear: we have to keep writing, rewriting, and rereading. The novel's failure to definitively resolve the question of ontological priority among its three story lines isn't a mistake so much as an attempt to keep its motivating questions open.

At the end of the novel, Powers makes an extraordinary move that turns the mix of fabulation and history at the heart of *Prisoner's Dilemma* into a story of Powers's own method. Eddie Jr. has followed his father's path back to the White Sands Missile Range (the site of the Trinity test), and has undertaken an unofficial funeral for his presumably dead father by throwing some of the sand on the range into the air. Powers imagines it as a kind of reverse fallout, something like the fairy dust that replaces uranium and plutonium in the Disney movie: "The white sand whipped directly upward at an astounding rate, entered the trade winds, and instantly spread around the earth three times in a girdle of imperceptible thinness. As they fell back to earth, the grains, countless now, entered the eyes of the people of the sleeping kingdom, dislodging the spell that had hung there for hundreds of years. Some say it was at this moment that folks finally began to sit up and see things with some measure of sense" (341). But at this moment when the father seems finally at peace, Powers adds three short final sections in which he remakes the story we have been reading about the aesthetic development of the Hobson family into a story of Powers's own development as an artist. In the first of the final sections, we listen with the three older Hobson children to the last of the tape their father has left, and it initially seems as though the novel will end on a depressing note, when the hope of rescuing the future collapses in 1945: "The tape ran out. The fairy tale came to its end. Disney, the world of *You Are the War*, grew seamlessly into the world of NORAD and underground hardened silos. Brother and sisters sat stilled in the stilled room. Outside, shadows lengthened as the day disappeared into December afternoon, Snow thickened, wrapped them in the childhood mystery of winter" (343). The language here is insistently bleak; the repetition of "stilled" and these lengthened shadows suggest a descent into death, à la Joyce's "The Dead."

But here the paradoxes of storytelling disappear, as Artie recognizes his father's message: "*What we can't bring about in no way releases us from what we must*" (343, italics in original). Telling stories can neither prevent nor bring an end to the nuclear age, nor can it postpone war. But *not* telling stories, and *not* telling stories that imagine capacious historical time, can, in the end, make a nuclear end more possible; storytelling preserves a culture of temporality that refuses to accept at face value the nuclear predicament by helping us to imagine differences: another place, the other's story. This is the realization of the children at the end of the novel: storytelling is an ethical commitment. It makes nothing happen, but it just might prevent something else from happening. "Having listened in, they were now each of them condemned to do something about the ending" (344); with this realization, the children decide to keep the story going: "Slowly, deliberately, with the last reel still in position on the machine, in full and mutual knowledge of what they were about to do, Artie rewound the tape, reached forward, and hit record" (344). With this move Artie doesn't erase his father so much as commit to consigning him to memory in nonpathological ways, and the first line he records is, we realize, the first line of the novel. This may not be the capacious futurity of Hobstown, but it is certainly a gesture toward futurity, and toward the ongoing capacity to keep a story going; doing something about the ending means writing beyond it, and we now have to ask new questions about the presumptive time of narration. And this is not a loop that leaves us endlessly stuck within the space of the novel, or simply takes us back to the beginning, as some readings of *The Crying of Lot 49* would have it; rather, it is a loop that imagines forms of infinite rewriting as the means by which we avoid being conned into the trap of teleology, and the trap of misreading history's writtenness as the idea that the future is scripted in advance.

The next two sections productively extend such an idea of rewriting, even as they complicate an already complex text. In a short, single-page section that is exterior to the multiple plotlines that have animated the novel, but that bears a title suggestively redolent of one of the reconstructions of Eddie Sr.'s life, Powers tells the story of a family in DeKalb, Illinois (a mother, three sons, and two daughters) who have gathered at home on "one of those unrepeatable days in mid-May" (a phrase first appearing in the recording Eddie Sr. left) for a family meal: "Dad has just died, of cancer, the previous winter. No one is sure what caused the disease. Some of us blame his assignment at Alamogordo, thirty-three years before. Others think a more likely culprit to be the style of life he chose in response to a long and unrequited love affair with the world" (345). But this father is not Eddie Sr: "I have had an idea for how I might begin to make some sense of the loss. The plans for a place to hide out in long enough to learn how to come back. Call it Powers World" (345). This move reminds us that the multiple strands of the novel comprise in fact a novel written by Richard Powers.

The novel that Richard Powers has been writing becomes a novel about why Richard Powers writes. Powers has returned time and time again to those moments when everything changed: the discovery of DNA, for instance, or the 1914 of *Three Farmers on Their Way to a Dance*. But Powers here reveals the stakes of his own method: Eddie Sr.'s combination of strict history and fabulatory wonder is, in the end, Powers's own. And while in other Powers novels, storytelling becomes a way of escaping insanity or dealing with terminal illness, what his novels share is the idea that storytelling preserves futurity as potentiality, a potentiality that was and is most threatened by the chain of history that drew us into the atomic age. Storytelling keeps alive the past, but in keeping alive the past it also might—perhaps—preserve the future, at least as a possibility, rather than an inevitable (non)outcome. In "Powers World," stories make things happen: there is the depressing reminder in *Prisoner's Dilemma* of Alan Turing, of course, who found in Snow White's poisoned apple the "solution" to his own "disgrace." But then there are all the other characters in Powers (including Eddie Sr.) who survive only because of the stories they can and must tell in response to the awful burdens of disease, tragedy, political repression, and the weight of history. And in Powers's most ambitious novels set during the Cold War, the threat of nuclear ending always hangs over the narrative, reminding us of a possible destruction that conditions it.[21]

In his work on narrative form, Michael André Bernstein has argued compellingly against the idea of foreshadowing, finding in this interpretative convention not simply a description of narrative technique, but far-reaching implications for how we inhabit history, since it causes us to imagine narratives, and hence lives, as prescripted. Bernstein prefers the term "sideshadowing" as a more ethical relation to narrative, one that focuses on the paths that could have been taken, and thus avoids turning sequentiality into causality, causality into neccesity:

> Our instinctive gratitude to what frees us from the too strictly plotted, the too seamlessly coherent story, undoubtedly accounts for much of our pleasure in experimental fiction. But this responsiveness to the improvisatory is changed decisively at those moments when contemporary history and literature intersect, when the issue becomes one of representing an event with whose occurrence we are still attempting to come to terms. Especially in the face of catastrophe, there is an urge to surrender to the most extreme foreshadowing imaginable, thereby resisting sideshadowing altogether. We try to make sense of a historical disaster by interpreting it, according to the strictest teleological model, as the climax of a bitter trajectory whose inevitable outcome it must be.[22]

Bernstein's primary example is the Holocaust (he favors "Shoah," which carries none of the meaning-making connotations of the habitual English-language designation), and he resists those readings that see it as somehow inevitable, on the grounds that if the mass death of the camps was inevitable, mourning the lives it destroyed becomes an impossibility.

As the children reconstruct their father's life in the italicized sections, one of them discovers a folder of their father's documents, among them a school assignment dated September 1, 1939. The assignment asks students to name and explain their favorite poem, and Eddie Sr. chooses Rudyard Kipling's "If." But the assignment makes us think of a poem that Eddie Sr. couldn't have chosen on that day, since it was not yet written. Powers's substitution of Kipling's "If" for W. H. Auden's "September 1, 1939" is the place where Powers and Bernstein most fully connect. The two poems, taken together, can be seen as an intertextual coda to the novel, as Auden's poem famously is as at once an account and a critique of the seductions of retroactive prophecy, juxtaposing historical narratives of causal chains that reach far back into the past with the much simpler claim that "Those to whom evil is done / Do evil in return."[23]

Prisoner's Dilemma, finally, is the hope of Auden's last lines (in which he longs to offer an "affirming flame" despite the current state of the world) mixed with Kipling's insistence that no matter what surrounds us, we should act to create the world we want, rather than acquiesce to the world we have: this combination of acknowledging the evils of history while retaining the dream of potentiality, however difficult a balance it may seem, is exactly what explains Eddie Sr. A supremely gifted history teacher, yet closet lover of the happy ending; committed to "accurate scholarship," yet aware that the future might yet, if we try hard enough, be different from the destination to which the present tends. Nostalgic but never melancholic with regard to history, *Prisoner's Dilemma* leaves open the possibility of other novels and other lives.

It is hard, then, not to imagine that Eddie Jr.'s throwing the sand to the trade winds in 1978 isn't also Powers's hope in 1988; as the fairy dust enters the eyes of the world and it begins to wake up, one can't help but hear a prophetic hope that the end of the Cold War, becoming visible as Powers wrote the novel, might have marked the revival of the utopian dreams that seemed to have disappeared by 1945. "The End of History," Fukuyama famously imagined it, but it was also, paradoxically, the "Gift of Time" as the first nuclear age came to an end.[24]

Late in the novel, Artie visits his father at Hines, the gigantic VA hospital near Chicago into which Eddie Sr. has finally checked himself. When Artie arrives, his father asks him to guess what he has been up to, and we (and Artie) expect another classic battle of wits between the two of them. Artie is shocked when his father reveals he has been reading poetry, and Artie immediately starts speculating as to the poet:

> Dad at last came to his rescue. "What might have been and what has been / Point to one end . . ."
>
> In a rush of affection, Artie completed, "which is always present." He felt suddenly flushed, limitless, as if his father had just confessed to loving him. "*Eliot*, Dad? You going highbrow on me in your old age?" (259–60, italics in original)

These lines from T. S. Eliot's "Burnt Norton" are especially apt, gesturing as they do both to the history that produced the present and to the possibility of other histories creating other presents; like *Prisoner's Dilemma*, *Four Quartets* wants to believe that history isn't teleology. Registering Eliot's complex handling of time within *Four Quartets*, and his sense of parts interacting musically to complete the whole of the poem, helps to clarify why *Prisoner's Dilemma* should allude to it in this way, and make it the poem that connects father and son. Eddie Sr.'s interest in the poem is in how these abstract notions of literary form and the philosophy of history intersect with real events:

> "Somehow I knew you'd come through on that couplet. I used to hate that poem. Know why?" Artie shook his head. "Here's the leading poetic figure of the twentieth century. An air-raid warden during the Blitz. He's going to write the definitive literary statement on the world apocalypse. Comes out in '42. And he doesn't once mention the *real shooting*."
>
> "Oh, but he does," Artie objected.
>
> "That's what I have only now seen," Dad agreed. (260)[25]

A metafictional comment on metafiction's historicity, perhaps? In a novel that everywhere records the links between the most escapist forms of fantasy and real history, Powers is doing to the postmodern novel what Eddie Sr. here does to late modernism. For Eliot's poem isn't directly or mimetically about World War Two in the way that war poetry, conventionally understood, is "about" war. And historiographic metafiction, at times, can be hard to praise. But at the right time, and from the right angle, the links between Eliot's poem and World War Two become visible. In much the same way, Powers's novel reveals how certain forms of seemingly antirealist and fabulatory escapism are the direct result of a commitment to the real, and to the possibility of reality lasting just a bit longer.

Afterword: Critical Conventions / Postmodern Canons

In the third chapter of *Democracy* (1984), Joan Didion tells us that the novel she is "no longer writing" was to have been "a study in provincial manners, in the acute tyrannies of class and privilege by which people assert themselves against the tropics," focusing on a "family in which the colonial impulse had marked every member."[1] This is classic Didion in its narrative self-consciousness, but *Democracy* is also resolutely Didionesque in another way, since the novel she goes on to write is, like much of her fiction, interested in peeling away the veneer of civility to reveal what sustains it.[2] *Democracy* puts its anticipated reader in an uncomfortable place, as we are encouraged to sympathize not with the left-liberal Kennedyesque political figure of Harry Victor, but with Jack Lovett, Inez Victor's lover, and the one character who can, politically speaking, get things done. Things get sticky when we realize that Lovett works in the quasi-governmental realm. A man who "had access to airplanes" and saw "information as an end in itself" (31), Lovett is a shadow operator, with "the assignment to Vientiane, the missions to Haiti, Quebec, Rawalpindi" comprising "the traces of what intelligence people call 'interest'" (40). So a projected novel about class in Hawaii is replaced with one about the largely invisible underpinnings of hegemonic power, and done so in a way that asks us to love it (Lovett).

Democracy offers a suitable conclusion to this study in the ways in which it raises questions about novels both written and unwritten, and about the forces that impinge on the ability or desire to write. But most intriguingly for my purposes, Didion's attention to the differences between the novel she set out to write (about the machinery and rivalries of colonial history) and the novel she did actually write (about the realities of American involvement in world affairs) masks the third novel she could have written. For *Democracy* begins neither with colonial Hawaiian history nor with Jack Lovett's involvement in Vietnam. Rather, it begins with 1952 and 1953 thermonuclear tests ("Christ they were sweet," Lovett says (13)) in the Pacific, even though the rest of the novel will subsequently bracket this spectrally emergent nuclear theme:

> The light at dawn during those Pacific tests was something to see.
> Something to behold.
> Something that could almost make you think you saw God, he said. (11)

The dawn that makes one think of God, however, is not at this stage obviously natural or artificial; this could be either the naturally spectacular dawn of the tropics, or the artificial dawn of nuclear illumination (the "during" is ambiguous). If we assume that this dawn is a natural one, are we to take it that the dawn was something to see only because of the nuclear testing it preceded? Are all dawns seen from this atoll something to see, or do they need to be seen in relation to nuclear weapons? As Didion elsewhere notes, "dawned" was one of the "verbs favored for use with 'the atomic age.'"[3] When Lovett finally elaborates a few pages later by describing what he and his companions would do—"Watch for pink sky. And then the shot, naturally"—we get no real help, since it is unclear how we are to understand his use of "naturally" in this context (13). And, as Nadel has noted, the novel's first sentence raises the problems of narrative truth the novel will go on to explore, since the lack of context means we aren't sure how to take this: "Is it a claim about the light, given to us on the authority of Jack Lovett, or a claim about Jack's response to the light, given to us on the authority of Inez Victor, or a claim about Inez's conversation, given to us on the authority of Joan Didion, a character who narrates the story of *Democracy*?"[4]

While Nadel's identification of the formal ambiguity of this opening statement is instructive, I would add that the problem of narrative truth is further extended by the content of the novel's opening chapter. The passage goes on to record a problem for representation, though again the question of authority is raised: "He said: the sky was this pink no painter could approximate, one of the detonation theorists used to try, a pretty fair Sunday painter, he never got it. Just never captured it, never came close" (11). We are left to wonder whether the failure here is that of the "pretty fair Sunday painter" or painting in general, whether this subject stands outside of one painter's skill or outside of painting altogether, and how the cerebral logic of a detonation theorist might intersect with the aesthetic touch of the artist.

Likewise, what Lovett experiences during the testing is both a desire for and a problem of narration: "what you could do was, you could talk. You got to hear everybody's personal life story down there, believe me" (12). This storytelling energy, however, could end at any moment: "then the weather people would give the go and bingo, no more stories" (13). While there is a practical dimension to this—who would talk when a nuclear weapon was about to be detonated?—Didion goes further: on the atoll, "the point of the pen would go right through the paper" (12). Again there seems to be a deliberate double meaning here: the point of the pen referring both to the literal impossibility of writing on paper ruined by humidity, and to the inability to arrive at the "point" of this writing, the turning of witnessed experiences into narrative representations. So when we learn that "not much got written down on those islands" (12), we can understand both the practical problems that prevented writing as well as speculate as to more abstract problems of representation. In bypassing her novel of colonial manners for an incisive look at the contradictions of the national narrative of democracy, Didion also acknowledges only to bypass a novel about what helps constitute "conventional" U.S. military power.[5]

Lovett's representational problems are a more circumscribed version of one argument I have been making in *On Endings*: representation fails in the face of the "reality" of the bomb, and so to write about it is always to approach the subject indirectly; the bomb's reality demands plain speech, but plain speech is inadequate to the bomb. But after highlighting this issue, Didion goes on to write a novel not centrally concerned with the bomb's ultimate world-destroying power, focusing instead on other (non-nuclear) realities of U.S. foreign policy. Thus Didion raises a question that any reader of *On Endings* might ask. I've argued in the preceding chapters that high postmodernism was shaped by a new relation to historical time conditioned by the nuclear age, and that the techniques we traditionally associate with it—its substitution of ontological questions for epistemological ones, its relentless metafictionality, its problems with closure—reflect the potential futurelessness produced by those weapons. Furthermore, I've argued that total nuclear war also requires innovative aesthetic strategies if you seek to engage or critique its possibility; as Ballard revealed in the story I discussed in the introduction, conventional history fails in the face of the actual end of history's record. Although *On Endings* never set out to be a broad examination of the full range of nuclear anxiety during the period, nor a comprehensive account of postwar literature, it seems prudent to raise a few possible implications of and questions for its argument. How does this historicization of high postmodernism in relation to the Cold War's nuclear threat shed light on the larger field of the postwar novel? Does Didion's decision to bypass both her colonial and her thermonuclear novel in favor of a book about covert action tell us something about the politics or desires attendant on nuclear representation?

After all, references to the bomb are everywhere in postwar culture, and a fear of nuclear ending was widely shared. Daniel Cordle's *States of Suspense* has identified a pervasive nuclear anxiety across the literature of the period, admirably shifting our attention away from merely postnuclear disaster narratives, and toward a broader culture of nuclear fear and suspense. How then do we integrate into that larger history the argument I've made about how a legacy of narrative experimentation emerged out of a changed culture of time and space, and through a consideration of the world-destroying powers of the bomb? It isn't as if these postmodern authors were the *only* canaries in the coal mine, alert to apprehensions missed by others; to make that argument would be to elevate the writers I've been discussing into the realm of rare and prescient thinkers of the unthinkable, thereby repeating the exaltations of experimental writing performed by Barth in the 1960s, though, ironically, for referential rather than aesthetic reasons. So why did the bomb particularly influence the group of writers I've discussed, those who made potential nuclear ending into the structuring principle of their work rather than one thematic interest among many? Does this argument shed any new light on authors who, in contrast, have never needed exoneration from charges of ethical or historical nonresponsibility? Does this history of how postmodern metafiction is intimately tied to the nuclear allow us to understand in new ways why high postmodernism is overwhelmingly white and male? The answer to this last question is necessarily a complex one, turning as it does on the gendered and racialized dynamics of cultural investigation, capital, and prestige, as well as on individual careers and their links to particular institutions. These questions might be engaged in three ways: with reference to the particular relationship between the possibility of total nuclear war and a larger Cold War culture, to the racialized and gendered aspects of the broader Cold War, and to the politics of fictional experimentation.

And here we might note that what Didion keeps returning to in her own investigation of the nuclear condition is less the ontological problems caused by the potential wartime use of nuclear weapons, and more the actual reality of testing and development. This reflects a point made in "Pacific Distances," Didion's autobiographical essay about her life in California and her development as a writer. After recalling her time as a student in Mark Schorer's class at Berkeley in 1954, and her own 1975 teaching on campus, Didion's next section narrates her 1979 visit to the underground of the campus, the TRIGA Mark III nuclear reactor located in Etcheverry Hall that first achieved a sustained nuclear reaction in 1966. This leads her to a meditation on what the nuclear age has meant for her work, as she was "ten years old when 'the atomic age,' as we called it then, came forcibly to the world's attention": "it never occurred to me that I would not sooner or later—most probably sooner, certainly before I ever grew up or got married or went to college—endure the moment of its happening: first the blinding white light, which appeared in my imagination as a negative photographic image, then the waves of heat, the sound, and, finally, death, instant or prolonged, depending inflexibly on where one was caught in the scale of concentric circles we all imagined pulsing out from ground zero."[6] This isn't quite the fear of a necessarily instantaneous death I've been discussing (and Didion's double-negative—"it never occurred to me I would not"—is notable in making the bomb less an object of conscious contemplation and more a background assumption), though it does still imagine the severity of nuclear ending. What follows it is more interesting: after graduating and moving to New York, Didion "realized that I was no longer anticipating the blinding flash," dismissing that fear as "one of those ways in which children deal with mortality." Despite this feeling, Didion asserts that "this single image—this blinding white light that meant death, this seductive reversal of the usual associations around 'light' and 'white' and 'radiance'—became a metaphor that to some extent determined what I later thought and did."[7]

And yet even as Didion asserts that the threat of potential nuclear ending must have had a profound effect on her generation, her own reaction comes back not to things unexperienced, but to the reactor room in Etcheverry Hall: "yet something about the fact of the reactor still resisted interpretation: the intense blue in the pool water, the Cerenkov radiation around the fuel rods, the blue past all blue, the blue like light itself, the blue that is actually a shock wave in the water and is the exact blue of the glass at Chartres."[8] The language here recalls the opening of

Democracy, the "blue past all blue" in dialogue with the "pink no painter could capture," but the passage reveals that ultimately Didion is far more interested in what is literally and figuratively underground, and which resists representation/interpretation for that reason, than in something that could, but probably won't, happen.

From her first novel, *Run River* (1963), which notes the steady postwar increase of defense contracting around Sacramento, through *Democracy*, Didion is less interested in the deadly possibilities of World War Three than in what we have systematically disavowed; *Play It as It Lays* (1970), in which the Nevada Test Site has swallowed Maria Wyeth's former hometown, culminates with a nuclear test. Didion's interest in what can happen unremarked explains why nuclear testing and development constitute the focus of her interest in the nuclear national security state; while, obviously, a thermonuclear world war was never fought between the Soviet Union and the United States, a nuclear war of sorts was actually waged. Since 1945, more than 2,400 nuclear weapons have been tested on or in the planet, and the story of downwinders and victims is one that American culture has tried very hard to forget. I don't want to suggest here a kind of zero-sum equation in which any interest in the ontological reshaping of human experience caused by the bomb blinds you to its "real" politics, whereby an interest in politics as conventionally understood makes impossible an engagement with the abstract questions I've been asking. This is, rather, a matter of relative influence, but it does remind us why certain writers might have been far more interested in what did actually happen than in what didn't, and which in happening couldn't be recorded. We need not accept the Ivory Tower designation that Peck attaches to the writers I've discussed in order to suspect that novelists making the world-destroying power of nuclear weapons into their central interest (and thereby deemphasizing the political in favor of more metaphysical questions) is perhaps predicated on a relatively secure everyday life free of more direct political oppression. Molly Hite's influential *The Other Side of the Story*, for instance, begins with a "simple" question: "Why don't women writers produce postmodernist fiction?" a question she initially thought reflected a widely held feeling that "the important male fiction writers of the period after 1960 were characteristically engaged in certain kinds of stylistic and structural innovation and that the important female fiction writers of the period were engaged in no sort of innovation at all." As Hite realized, this depended on a strict divide between realism and a certain kind of experimentalism, as if to say that any writing that wasn't experimental in a particular way couldn't be experimental at all; uncovering the innovations of authors like Jean Rhys and Margaret Atwood, innovations directly in the service of political critique, does not mean that one should seek "to admit a select group of female—and feminist writers to the emergent canon of postmodernism" given the "recognizably distinct" quality of their writing.[9] Hite's work is a product of an era in which, in the interests of establishing the viability of the field or of individual authors, one might still have believed it necessary to argue for importance precisely on the criterion of formal innovation, a legacy no doubt of the cultural capital of modernism in the United States, and particularly in its system of higher education. But she is certainly correct to note both the experimental nature of much contemporary fiction by women and its differences from the formal strategies we associate with high postmodernism. And this importantly reminds us that the tradition I've been discussing in this book isn't simply distinct from realism, but also from other and vitally important forms of experimental writing more obviously committed to pointed political critique.

The long-running debate about whether or not Toni Morrison is a "postmodern" writer, for instance, often seems to rest, axiomatically, on the idea that it would be a good or bad thing if she were: if you believe that the term bears a host of positive or pejorative associations, then you want to make sure a writer you care about has the right set of credentials.[10] And regardless of whether or not you think Morrison's nonrealist (I intend the term neutrally) fiction is postmodern or not, you realize very quickly she certainly isn't experimenting with narrative in the same way that Barthelme was. As Morrison herself (as well as Madhu Dubey and Phillip Brian Harper) has pointed out, any celebration of self-conscious textuality that comes at the expense of reference looks very different for those communities who have been systematically denied their own histories, and who thus put fictional experimentation in the service of reclaiming those stories that have never been recorded[11] This may lead us to suppose that the archive-and-witness-erasing power of thermonuclear weapons might look somewhat different for those communities struggling to enter those archives in the first place, and to testify to the unrecorded facts of American history.[12]

(Un)containment

While recent criticism has revealed how porous the containment culture model turned out to be, it is worth remembering how proscriptive

American Cold War culture was if we seek to understand the gendered and racialized qualities of the version of high postmodernism I've been discussing. As Suzanne Clark has pointed out, the ideal "Cold Warrior" was engaged in a heavily masculinized struggle that attempted to erase questions of gender, sexuality, and race.[13] In this logic, the "correct" female response to the conflict was to avoid pondering the existential or policy questions raised by the period. One thinks here of Adlai Stevenson's notorious graduation speech to Smith College's class of 1955 (a class that included Sylvia Plath) in which he urged the graduating seniors to imagine their agency via domestic life: "marriage and motherhood" don't lead young women "away from the great issues of our day"; rather, they "bring you back to their very center" and are a responsibility "infinitely deeper and more intimate . . . than that borne by the majority of those who hit the headlines."[14]

To engage the geopolitics of the Cold War, whether as a personal interest or literary subject, was thus to violate enormous cultural assumptions about the "proper" role of female agency. The account offered by Buddy Willard's mother in Plath's *The Bell Jar* offers a Cold War–inflected reiteration of the divide between the political and the domestic, and between men and women: "What a man is is an arrow into the future and what a woman is is the place the arrow shoots off from."[15] Here the agency of archer and bow is erased, with the arrow imagined as a self-propelled rocket and the female body as merely a passive launch location. If this reveals the impossibility of ever separating the two realms and two sexes, it certainly isn't because Mrs. Willard intends it to, and it perfectly illustrates both the widespread diffusion and fundamental illogic of Cold War gender politics.

As I've already noted, Mark McGurl's work has revealed the self-consciousness of postwar fiction, all of which seems shaped by the ordinary reflexivity of life in the second half of the twentieth century. The chart offered by McGurl in which three circles (one representing what McGurl calls "technomodernism" in preference to postmodernism; one "high cultural pluralism," his preferred term for multicultural/ethnic literature; one "lower-middle-class modernism" instead of minimalism) partially overlap in a Venn diagram reminds us that stylistic designators are never absolute. The diagram encourages us to think about these categories in new ways; they retain utility neither as containers with single points of entrance nor as value judgments, but as shorthand designations.

We might utilize this Venn-diagram model with different terms, a point made when Ann Douglas maintains that three rival designations for the postwar period—postmodern, postcolonial, and Cold War—need to be seen as interrelated, though never in any straightforward relationship of cause-and-effect.[16] Ken Cooper more directly assesses the politics of periodization when he points out that "nuclear science and nuclear strategy have stood part from—and indeed above—racial politics. Nowhere has the color line more assiduously been monitored than between the separate-but-equal histories of postwar American politics, with the rubric of 'Cold War' on the one hand and 'Civil Rights' on the other."[17] While the intervening years have brought us a rich body of literary and cultural criticism that has begun to reveal the essential links between these two terms, the originality of that criticism attests to the fundamental truth of Cooper's insight.[18]

Indeed, Cooper identifies a substantial archive of minority writing interested in nuclear weapons, and in doing so complicates stories about what he calls "the whiteness of the bomb." But, importantly, in these texts Cooper locates the bomb less as an ontologically distinct development and much more on a continuum with prior forms of genocidal violence. For instance, Cooper discusses Ishmael Reed's *Mumbo Jumbo*, certainly one of the most extravagantly playful texts of the postwar period, yet also one whose experimental form is mobilized in the service of a larger argument about what the unrecorded history of African American culture is, and how it might be best recorded. After noting that Reed's book, set in 1920s Harlem, looks forward to more contemporary moments in America as well as back to ancient Egypt, Cooper points out that "atomic bombs are mentioned in all three periods, not as the 'subject' of the novel but rather as a shorthand for the violence implicit in Western Civilization's religious and cultural 'crusades.'"[19] Just as certain forms of postmodern textuality may have been less appealing to minority writers eager to claim rather than complicate reference, the bomb's extreme destructive power might not seem quite as ontologically distinct to those communities who had been on the receiving end of extreme, and even genocidal, violence for centuries.

Take the case of Leslie Marmon Silko's *Ceremony* (1977). It tells the story of Tayo, a half Native American veteran of the Second World War (he participated in the Bataan Death March and spent the rest of the war in a prison camp) suffering from what we would now call PTSD, the product primarily of witnessing his cousin Rocky's death. The novel seems initially to be a classic story of traumatic recovery. It opens, for instance, with narrative time out of joint, and with an aggressive insistence on registering that out-of-joint temporality; its multiple beginnings—one a creation story, one a description of a ritual (a ceremony spoken once by a man, once by a woman), one a sunrise, and one a description of Tayo actually waking up—are staged relative to the page in such a way as to make a reader anticipate that the novel's work will be to suture these divergent temporalities back together. And this makes us expect that the novel might come to be about the restitching together of personal, diurnal, ritual, and mythological time.

We learn early in the novel, however, that any recovery process that would properly align cause and effect is deeply compromised by recent history. Tayo's family enlists Ku'oosh, a traditional medicine man, to perform a healing ceremony, and Ku'oosh's vision of that healing is to reinsert the ailing Tayo back into a holistic culture: "He spoke softly, using the old dialect full of sentences that were involuted with explanations of their own origins, as if nothing the old man said were his own but all had been said before and he was only there to repeat it."[20] But the narrator reminds us that recent events make such a system impossible; in contrast to "the old way of warfare" which left you with visible evidence of whom you have killed, "white warfare" involves "killing across great distances without knowing who or how many had died. It was all too alien to comprehend, the mortars and big guns; ... Ku'oosh would have looked at the dismembered corpses and the atomic heat-flash outlines, where human bodies had evaporated, and the old man would have said something close and terrible had killed these people" (33–34). If there is a distinction to be drawn here, it is between an earlier era of warfare and a new ability to kill across great distances; the paradigm shift identified predates the invention of nuclear weapons, which are viewed here on a continuum with mortars and cannons.

The larger process of recovery is further complicated by the emergent realities of the atomic Southwest. Tayo's grandmother is blind, yet on the morning of the Trinity test she is able to "see" the flash. So if the novel begins by suggesting that the work of traumatic recovery is to realign both personal history and cultural mythology with the everyday temporalities of dawn and dusk, Silko complicates this process through her representation of a morning that saw two dawns. While interested in the problems of nuclear temporality (it shares with *Prisoner's Dilemma* a sense of how complicated the effects of artificial dawns might be), *Ceremony* doesn't make the threat of nuclear war the originating trauma of the novel. Rather, it is a culmination, as we learn at the end of the novel when Tayo, running from "friends" who seek to do him harm, finds himself at the mouth of a uranium mine, and realizes that "Trinity Site, where they exploded the first atomic bomb, was only three hundred miles to the southeast, at White Sands. And the top-secret laboratories where the bomb had been created were deep in the Jemez Mountains, on land the Government took from Cochiti Pueblo: Los Alamos, only a hundred miles northeast of him now" (228). The result is a humanist assertion of shared lineage ("human beings were one clan again, united by the fate the destroyers planned for all of them, for all living things, united by a circle of death") that no longer imagines acts of violence as discrete: "From the jungles of his dreaming he recognized why the Japanese voices had merged with Laguna voices, with Josiah's voice and Rocky's voice; the lines of cultures and worlds were drawn in flat dark lines on fine light sand, converging in the middle of witchery's final ceremonial sand painting" (228). This is the realization of the novel's larger argument that would link multiple forms of violence—forced Native American relocation, the Bataan Death March, Japanese internment—under the sign of "witchery."

Ceremony also helps us to understand the cultural capital of experimentation, canon formation, and historical reference when we interrogate its publication history. In her introduction to a recent edition of the novel, Silko reveals that there had been some disagreement between herself and her editor, the legendary Richard Seaver, though the example she offers is a seemingly minor one:

> Instead of the more proper "as if," I'd used the colloquial "like"— e.g., "He ran *like* a dog" vs. "He ran *as if* he were a dog." I checked a dictionary and found that Norman Mailer was allowed to use "like" in his novels, so I initially refused to make the changes. I didn't have an agent then, so when Dick Seaver hinted that if I didn't take the editorial advice on this point, he and Jeanette Seaver "could not get behind the book," I decided to agree to the change, in part because there were only about six instances where I used "like" instead of "as if." (xvii–xviii, italics in original)

This should raise a reader's eyebrow, since it is hard to imagine any editor seeing this substitution as a matter of life or death for the book, and it turns out that Silko's example is deliberately telling. Jeff Karem's research among her manuscripts and papers has revealed that the struggle with Seaver was about far more than grammar: Silko had to fight to include the "unconventional" sections that link Tayo's experience to larger world-historical forces, since, as Karem puts it, Seaver "wanted a more contained narrative of reservation life."[21] While Silko resisted Seaver's changes, Karem reminds us of the "horizon of expectations" established by the publishing industry for Native American writing. This is especially telling when we remember that Seaver was the editor who championed Coover's *The Public Burning*. In Coover's case, Seaver, in the face of sustained resistance from the press's legal staff, stood up for Coover's right to represent "real" and living Americans in highly experimental forms.[22]

Silko reminds us of the complicated relationship minority writers historically have had with fictional experimentation, both as a means to an end and as a form of cultural capital. For, following Morrison, we do well to remember that a metafictional suspicion of direct reference means something very different for those communities for whom reference isn't so much something to be transcended as something to be claimed for the first time. Likewise, the terrible Cold War possibilities of mass death can look different when one's cultural inheritance is substantially a history of violence. But Silko's case also reminds us that the choice of "experimental" literary form is never made in a vacuum; the complex network of patronage and publication through which contemporary texts pass on their way to becoming books is one that has been far more receptive to referentially playful work by authors who are white and male than it has been to similar work by women and minority writers.

And this is precisely the point of Percival Everett's recent parody of contemporary publishing, the novel *Erasure*, which is narrated by Thelonious Ellison, an African American author of experimental fiction. After delivering a paper at the "*Nouveau Roman*" society conference, he is accused by a journal editor of being merely a "mimetic hack" and returns to his hotel room to find a death threat ("*I'll kill you, you mimetic Philistine*") signed by "*The Ghost of Wyndham Lewis*."[23] But it turns out that a minority writer can't ever be enough of a "mimetic hack," so long as he or she understands the goal to be to return stereotypes of African American culture back to audiences; or, rather, to publish writing to broad acclaim—these two things turn out to be the same. Thelonious Ellison's new novel, "*in which Aristophanes and Euripides kill a younger, more talented dramatist, then contemplate the death of metaphysics*," has been rejected many times, despite being "*challenging and masterfully written and constructed*" (42, italics in original). His agent's supposition is that Ellison isn't "black enough" (43) in his recent fiction, since his one success was an earlier and more "realistic" work "about a young black man who can't understand why his white-looking mother is ostracized by the black community. She finally kills herself and he realizes that he must attack the culture and so becomes a terrorist, killing blacks and whites who behave as racists" (61).

We's Lives in Da Ghetto turns out to be the year's *"masterpiece of African American literature"*: the story of a fifteen-year-old girl pregnant with her third child by a third father, and living with a drug-addicted mother and her *"mentally deficient"* brother Juneboy (who is killed in a drive-by shooting), the novel is a potent racist cultural fantasy about African American urban life (39, italics in original). Ellison is incensed by its runaway success, and sits down one evening to write a response titled *My Pafology*, a subliterate rewriting of *Native Son* that ultimately earns Ellison millions in book and film rights (even after Ellison retitles it *Fuck*), since it is taken as even more of a "masterpiece" than the novel it was intended angrily to parody.

Beyond the Post

Although ending with Everett raises different forms of erasure than those caused by nuclear warfare, his novel reminds us of the multiple forces that impinge on literary history, and on how much work we still have to do to understand why the cultural production of our immediate past took the shapes that it did. What I've offered here is an account of how one strand of American fiction was influenced by a particularly vexed history of the possibility of history itself, and I hope this argument contributes to a larger rethinking of the period, both in terms of how we trace out the multiple effects of the Cold War and how we understand the content and contexts of postwar fictional experimentation. Now that what we used to call the contemporary is no longer contemporary in any meaningful sense, the work of understanding the pressures that produced it in the first place can begin. Now is a tremendously exciting time to be working in the field, as we uncover the range of ways in which fiction was both produced by and represents postwar culture.[24]

Understanding how the Cold War shaped fiction and habits of mind is also vital if we seek to engage imaginatively and responsibly a threatened world no longer principally defined by the Cold War's unique form of violence.[25] The conceptual inheritance of nuclear war is everywhere in 1990s and post–9/11 fiction, as authors struggle to come to terms both with the Cold War's end and with new acts of violence.[26] This is not the place to engage in a comprehensive survey of that fiction, of course, but rather to mention how reliant it has been on Cold War tropes. And understanding the particular ways that Cold War fears of total nuclear war produced certain fictional forms is essential if we are to imagine what a responsible post–9/11 fiction might look like.[27]

Notes

Introduction

1. Peck, "The Moody Blues," 33.
2. Ibid., 37.
3. Ibid.
4. See Franzen, "Mr. Difficult," as well as Myers, *A Reader's Manifesto*.
5. See Gardner, *On Moral Fiction*; Graff, *Literature against Itself*; and Newman, *The Post-Modern Aura*.
6. The bibliography on postmodernism is by now extensive, and a note on terminology seems in order. Part of the confusion in the use of the term stems from its deployment as both a stylistic and period designator. So, for instance, some critics will use it to refer to a historical epoch that emerges sometime in the second half of the twentieth century, while others will use it to refer more narrowly to a particular strand of cultural production generated during that period. My preference is for the latter usage, whereby postmodernism is only one response, and not the only response, to the condition of postmodernity.
7. Barth, *The Friday Book*, 195–96; Gardner, *On Moral Fiction*, 94.
8. Hutcheon, *A Poetics of Postmodernism*, 141 (hereafter cited parenthetically).
9. This circularity seems to me the most problematic feature of Hutcheon's account, as she is able to purchase the historical investigations of postmodernism only by dispensing with the work that many critics would see as the most postmodern. For examples, see Hutcheon, *A Poetics*, 40, 52.
10. See Elias, *Sublime Desire*.
11. See Cordle, *States*, 8; and Hungerford, *The Holocaust*, 13, for a discussion of how literary histories of the postwar have largely bracketed concerns about nuclear war.
12. By "thermonuclear weapons," I mean the hydrogen bomb, first tested by the United States in 1952 and the Soviet Union in 1953, weapons many times more powerful than those used against Japan.
13. See Brooks, *Reading for the Plot*.

14. Brian McHale, *Postmodernist Fiction*, 6–11. McHale has noted that nuclear war is a theme that runs through postmodern cultural production. McHale suggests that we can see the representational problems posed by nuclear war in a number of ways: in representations of more conventional notions of apocalypse in postmodern texts; in the displacement of nuclear war into either a distant future or the past; in a metafictional gesture that reveals that the text's representation of nuclear war isn't adequate; or in a breakdown of language that is supposed to mimic the damage of nuclear conflict (McHale, *Constructing Postmodernism*, 159–62). While I certainly agree with McHale about the centrality of nuclear concerns in the cultural production of the period, I disagree with him about the kind of representational problems posed by nuclear war, however, since he sees them on a continuum with other kinds of paradigmatically unrepresentable events.

15. See Jackson, "Postmodernism"; and McHale, "1966 Nervous."

16. For examples of how to think historically about recent fiction and postmodern experimentation, see DeKoven, *Utopia Limited*; Hoberek, *The Twilight*; and McClure, *Partial Faiths*.

17. McGurl, *The Program Era*.

18. As Patricia Waugh notes, the use of the term "metafiction" to describe a particular body of work that emerged in the 1960s is troubling, since metafictional devices can be found in texts that predate the decade, and indeed almost any novel can be said to be metafictional in that it displays or can be made to display some degree of self-consciousness about its status as fiction. I follow Waugh, however, in seeing a difference between those texts that relentlessly foreground their self-awareness, and those texts that merely display some degree of self-consciousness (Waugh, *Metafiction*, 1–19).

19. Jameson, *Postmodernism*, 1.

20. See Ermarth, *Sequel to History*; Heise, *Chronoschisms*; and Huehls, *Qualified Hope*.

21. Jameson, *Postmodernism*, iv.

22. *New York Times*, "Atomic Education Urged by Einstein," May 25, 1946.

23. For a comprehensive survey of early reactions to the arrival of the atomic age, see Paul Boyer, *By the Bomb's*.

24. Faulkner, *Essays*, 119.

25. Ballard, *War Fever*, 27.

26. Ibid., 23.

27. See Boyer, *By the Bomb's*, 14–15.

28. Ballard, *War Fever*, 23.

29. Derrida, "No Apocalypse," 23.

30. Berger, *After the End*, 5.

31. Schell, *The Fate*, 119.

32. Lifton and Mitchell, *Hiroshima in America*, 87–88.

33. Boyer, *By the Bomb's*, 209. For a fuller reception history of *Hiroshima*, see Yavenditti, "John Hersey."

34. This is not to say that critics have been uniformly in agreement about Hersey. For a discussion of how the text has generated surprisingly little critical commentary, see Torgovnick, *The War Complex*, 100. A number of critics have suggested that atomic weapons were presaged in countless works of science fiction that predate 1945 (see

Bartter, *The Way to Ground Zero*; Franklin, *War Stars*; and Wagar, *Terminal Visions*). For another survey of the legitimacy that Hiroshima gave to science fiction, see Seed, *American Science Fiction*, 8–9. As multiple critics have noted, Hersey's attempt at demographic representation is severely undercut by his choice of subjects: a German Catholic Priest, a Methodist minister, two doctors, a record keeper, and a widowed housewife are hardly demographically representative, and in many cases were chosen for their English-language ability, as well as their capacity to "humanize" an enemy for an American readership. For discussions of the role audience plays in *Hiroshima*, see Nadel, *Containment Culture*, 38–68; and Norris, *Writing War*, 190–91. For discussions of Japanese literary responses to Hiroshima, see Treat, *Writing Ground Zero*; and Yoneyama, *Hiroshima Traces*.

35. Dee, "The Art of Fiction," 226–27.
36. Hersey, *Hiroshima*, 2 (hereafter cited parenthetically).
37. McCarthy "The 'Hiroshima' *New Yorker*."
38. See Boyer, *By the Bomb's*, 14–15, for a discussion of how this kind of extrapolation from Hiroshima was very common in the immediate aftermath of the bombing.
39. Nadel, *Containment Culture*, 56.
40. Hersey's point is even more powerful when one realizes that these passages appear within the section of "The Aftermath" that details the post-1946 life of Kiyoshi Tanimoto. Tanimoto, one of the ministers on whom Hersey's 1946 text focuses, is the only Hibakusha (explosion-affected person) in the book who makes peace activism a principal activity of his or her post-bombing life. Though Hersey never narrates the precise relationship between the unframeable history of proliferation and the story of Tanimoto, the juxtaposition begs to be read as a commentary on the possible and actual legacies of Hiroshima. Albert Stone offers a more critical reading of "The Aftermath," finding in it merely a continuation of the same focus on the lives of the individual survivors, rather than on the expansion of the weapons. While I admire Stone's desire for a more direct and radical voicing of nuclear expansion, I find Nadel's reading of the earlier chapters more convincing than Stone's, and hence have a different reading of the end (Stone, *Literary Aftershocks*, 13).
41. Dee, "The Art of Fiction," 231.
42. Nadel, *Containment Culture*, 6.
43. For a discussion of some of the forms of metanarrativity that critics have adopted to narrate total thermonuclear war, see Seed, *American Science Fiction*, 5.
44. Shute, *On the Beach*, 3.
45. My thanks to Steven J. Meyer for this point. See Cordle, *States*, 36, for an elaboration of it.
46. The bibliography on Cold War culture is now extremely extensive, and I can cite only a few of the most important texts in addition to the texts engaged in later chapters. For discussions of Cold War literature, see Brunner, *Cold War Poetry*; Clark, *Cold Warriors*; Cornis-Pope, *Narrative Innovation*; and Schaub, *American Fiction*. For discussion of specifically nuclear culture, see Canaday, *The Nuclear Muse*; Davis *Stages of Emergency*; Dewey, *In a Dark Time*; Dowling, *Fictions of Nuclear Disaster*; Gery, *Nuclear Annihilation and Contemporary American Poetry*; Henricksen, *Dr. Strangelove's America*; Weart, *Nuclear Fear*; and Winkler, *Life under a Cloud*.
47. See, for instance, Cordle's recent *States of Suspense*, an ambitious attempt to put nuclear anxiety at the center of much post-1945 American culture. We differ, however, in

how we understand the links between postmodernism and the nuclear age. For Cordle, nuclear anxiety is apparent in a range of texts, from science-fiction novels directly about the bomb through to the wider culture, or, as he puts it, in "'mainstream,' particularly postmodern, literature" (1). Obviously we disagree about the extent to which "postmodern" fiction is the mainstream of postwar fiction, at least in part because Cordle uses "postmodernism" as a much broader stylistic marker. Where we primarily differ is in scale; since Cordle is interested in atomic anxiety more broadly, he finds it as a thematic preoccupation in works of postmodern fiction, whereas I see it as a shaping force on the forms those fictions took. While Cordle finds "postmodern texts to have concerns overlapping with a culture of nuclear anxiety" (2) and notes that "the nuclear subject . . . reveals fundamental limitations to the realist mode in which it is rendered" (7), he doesn't offer a causal account of the rise of postmodernism, preferring instead to note its contiguities with the nuclear age. I am indebted to Nadel's argument in *Containment Culture* that the questions raised by the nuclear age help explain postmodernism more generally by raising the distinction between events and history in striking ways. See also Chow, *The Age*, Davis, *Deracination*; and Schwenger, *Letter Bomb*. Schwenger's book is the most powerful examination of Derrida's thinking on nuclearity, and what it can teach us about literature more generally. For a suggestive account of how "Cold War nuclear anxiety" contributed to the "emergence of postmodernism" by stressing the importance of chance, see Jackson, "Postmodernism," 325.

48. "Containment culture" refers to the widespread critical consensus that much of domestic political culture during the Cold War imported the idea of containing dissent internally from a foreign policy dedicated to containing Soviet expansion. For a key statement of this paradigm, see Nadel, *Containment Culture*.

49. See, for instance, Belletto, "Curbing Containment"; and Dickstein, *Leopards*, 8.

50. Recent revisionist documentary work has argued that in effect nuclear war was fought, but "ironically" it was a war in which the United States and the Soviet Union bombed their own citizens during the decade-plus period of above-ground testing; I mention this because the immense costs, in every sense, of the Cold War risk being erased in a contemporary, post–9/11 culture of Cold War nostalgia. See, for instance, Fradkin, *Fallout*; Gallagher, *American Ground Zero*; Masco, *The Nuclear Borderlands*; Miller, *Under the Cloud*; Shambroom, *Face to Face with the Bomb*; Solnit, *Savage Dreams*; Welsome, *The Plutonium Files*; and Williams, *Refuge*.

51. Boyer, *By the Bomb's*, offers the most coherent argument about the episodic nature of American nuclear fear.

52. Quoted in Boyer, *By the Bomb's*, 250.

53. See, for instance, Luckhurst, "Review," 88–89, as well as the introductions to Schwenger, *Letter Bomb*; and Stone, *Literary Aftershocks*. For an account of what nuclear criticism could look like today, see Cordle, "Cultures of Terror."

54. Brians, "Farewell," 1.

55. See, for instance, Engelhardt and Linenthal, eds., *History Wars*.

56. For a variety of conflicting positions on the threats posed by nuclear weapons today, see Cirincione, *Bomb Scare*; Langewiesche, *The Atomic Bazaar*; and Schell, *The Seventh Decade*.

57. Cohen, *After*.

58. Boyer, *Fallout*, xi.

59. See Hoberek, "Introduction," for a discussion of the end of "postmodernism" as a useful term for describing contemporary fiction.

1 / Institutionalizing Postmodernism

1. See McGurl, "The Program Era"; and Punday, "John Barth's Occasional Writing."
2. Hungerford, "On the Period," 412.
3. Hepburn, *Intrigue*, 251.
4. Schaub, *American Fiction*, 164.
5. For readings that claim them as essentially realist texts, see Stark, *The Literature of Exhaustion;* and Stonehill, *The Self-Conscious Novel*.
6. John Barth, *The Floating Opera*, v (hereafter cited parenthetically).
7. Barth, *The Friday Book*, 56.
8. Ibid., 55.
9. Barth, *Giles Goat-Boy*, v, vi.
10. The quotation used in the heading is from Dirda, "Dirda on Books."
11. Scholes, *The Fabulators*, 153 (italics in original).
12. Though in a less extreme way than Scholes, Alan Lindsay exemplifies much of the criticism when he treats the novel, and by extension much of Barth's midcareer, as having a contemporary setting but no critical relationship to it: "These texts, even if they did not ignore the contemporary political situation (e.g., Barth's use of feminism in *Chimera*, the Cold War in *Giles Goat-Boy*) did not attend to their own politics" (Lindsay, *Death in the Funhouse*, 138). For a characteristic example of archetypal criticism, see Olderman, *Beyond the Waste Land*, 72–93.
13. Barth, *The Friday Book*, 55 (italics in original).
14. Ibid.
15. See, for instance, Lois Parkinson Zamora's chapter on Barth ("The Apocalypse of Style: John Barth's Self-Consuming Fiction"), which understands the principal problem of apocalypse as a literary one (Zamora, *Writing the Apocalypse*, 97–119). See also Robinson, *American Apocalypses*, 224–32.
16. Harris, *Passionate Virtuosity*, 17–18 (italics in original).
17. McHale, *Postmodernist Fiction*, 192.
18. Zamora, *Writing the Apocalypse*, 99.
19. Ibid.
20. Engelhardt, *The End of Victory Culture*, 46.
21. It was Stanley Baldwin, former prime minister, who made this claim in a 1932 speech to the House of Commons (Patterson, *Guernica*, 75).
22. Fussell, *The Great War*, 64.
23. Patterson, *Guernica*, 2.
24. Fussell, *The Great War*, 21.
25. See Nadel, *Containment Culture*, 157–203, for a divergent account of how a distinct postmodern turn is in evidence slightly earlier.
26. McHale, "1966 Nervous," 408 (italics in original).
27. Mark McGurl, "The Program Era," 107. For a more extended discussion of the Cold War and the university, see Schiffrin, ed., *The Cold War and the University;* and Lowen, *Creating the Cold War University*.

2 / The Crying of Lot 49, Circa 1642

1. Pynchon, *The Crying of Lot 49*, 58 (hereafter cited parenthetically).
2. Dollimore, *Radical Tragedy*, xvii–xviii.
3. Moretti, *Signs Taken for Wonders*, 42–82.
4. Hutcheon, *The Politics of Postmodernism*, 59–88.
5. For an exemplary discussion of the complex doubled (at a minimum) eras of Pynchon's fictions, see Hinds, ed., *The Multiple Worlds of Pynchon's Mason & Dixon*.
6. Entropic decay is one of the most commonly cited themes of Pynchon's fiction, despite his own attempt in the introduction to *Slow Learner* to distance himself from the term. For readings of his work that emphasize possibility and potentiality over entropy, see Bové, "History and Fiction"; Schaub, *Pynchon*, 21; and Levine, "Risking the Moment."
7. Seed, *The Fictional Labyrinths*, 129.
8. Pynchon, *Slow Learner*, 22.
9. Tanner, *Thomas Pynchon*, 56.
10. Wilde, *Middle Grounds*, 99.
11. Hayles, "A Metaphor," 97.
12. This absence of Pynchon's usual historiographic negotiation has often been overstated as the idea that *The Crying of Lot 49* has no interest in history; as several critics have pointed out, the novel is actually quite situated within the historical moment of its setting and publication, and we can learn much about the 1960s from it. See, in particular, Cowart, "Pynchon and the Sixties."
13. Tanner, *Thomas Pynchon*, 56.
14. In his perceptive study of revenge tragedy, John Kerrigan notes that the nuclear age renders the possibility of tragedy untenable "by removing altogether the possibility of individual endeavor and survival"; in other words, the "faceless administrator" of Pynchon's play would himself be engulfed in the destruction he unleashed (Kerrigan, *Revenge Tragedy*, 311).
15. Lewis, *Blasting and Bombardiering*, 4, italics in original.
16. This is not to say that Pynchon's invented generation of poets didn't privately imagine themselves as important prior to their own public recognition; rather, that it is only in 1956 that it makes sense to put on paper an account of Maijstral's 1937 sense that "A sure wind of Greatness" was flowing over his shoulders" and that "Maratt, Dnubietna and I were to be the cadre for a grand School of Anglo-Maltese Poetry" (305). Likewise, no reader of Lewis could be unaware of his self-evaluation, and it was hardly news that he, along with his other core men of 1914, had been doing important work in the earlier part of the century.
17. Pynchon, *V.*, 307 (hereafter cited parenthetically).
18. For a fuller account of the "American rocket state" in relation to *Gravity's Rainbow*, see Carter, *The Final Frontier*.
19. Readings of *Gravity's Rainbow* that make the ICBM central include: Berger, "Merrill and Pynchon"; Hamill, "Confronting the Monolith"; Hume, *Pynchon's Mythography*; McHoul and Wills, *Writing Pynchon*; Milesi "Postmodern Ana-Apocalyptics"; Robson, "Frye, Derrida, Pynchon"; Schwenger, *Letter Bomb*; and Smith and Tölölyan, "The New Jeremiad."
20. Dugdale, *Pynchon: Allusive Parables*, 148–65.

21. Edward Mendelson's description of the religious imagination of the novel in its buildup to Pentecostal revelation (fifty being the number of the Pentecost) remains one of the most influential articles in Pynchon scholarship (see Mendelson "The Sacred, The Profane").

22. Derrida, "No Apocalypse," 23

23. Ibid., 27.

24. Alperovitz, *The Decision*, 240.

25. Ibid., 259-60. Act 4 of the *The Courier's Tragedy* accelerates in intensity: "It is about this point in the play, in fact, that things really get peculiar, and a gentle chill, an ambiguity, begins to creep in among the words. Heretofore the naming of names has gone on either literally or as metaphor. But now, as the Duke gives his fatal command, a new mode of expression takes over. It can only be called a kind of ritual reluctance. Certain things, it is made clear, will not be spoken aloud; . . . The Duke does not, perhaps may not, enlighten us. Screaming at Vittorio he is explicit enough about who shall *not* pursue Niccolò. . . . But who then will the pursuers be? Vittorio knows: every flunky in the court, idling around in their Squamuglia livery and exchanging Significant Looks, knows" (55).

This description echoes at least one account of the Potsdam Conference, where the bomb was the proverbial elephant in the room. Much speculation has focused on how to "read" Stalin's reaction to Truman's private announcement (on July 24) of the development of a new weapon, which was, apparently, curiously blasé. Part of the reason for the muted reaction, however, may well have been that Stalin knew about the Manhattan Project thanks to espionage, and in fact likely knew about it before Truman did, since Truman was only briefed on it when he took office (see Alperovitz, *The Decision*, 387).

26. Hayles, "A Metaphor," 117.

27. Peter Schwenger has noted the frequency with which novels about nuclear war return to the postal as a key emblem of the problem they face: the problem of how to imagine the communication of an event that resists narrativity immediately summons its analogue in the breakdown of the postal system, and in post–nuclear-war fiction, the postal system's reemergence becomes a central trope for imagining survival (Schwenger, *Letter Bomb*, 3-23).

28. Siebers, *Cold War Criticism*, 142.

29. Dugdale, *Pynchon: Allusive Parables*, 146.

30. Pynchon, "A Journey," 35.

31. Galison, "War," 7.

32. Ibid., 8, 30.

33. Ibid., 14, 26.

34. Kaplan, *The Wizards*, 201-19. "City-killing" meant that a nuclear war had moved past the point where each side was targeting only strategic sites of enemy military concentration; that previous stage of escalation was known as "counterforce," a fact that suggestively echoes Pynchon's use of the term in *Gravity's Rainbow*. For a discussion of that novel in the light of nuclear strategy, see Hamill, "Confronting the Monolith," 433-35.

35. Dugdale, *Pynchon: Allusive Parables*, 9.

36. Ibid., 125

37. In "Bombing and the Symptom: Traumatic Earliness and the Nuclear

Uncanny," Paul K. Saint-Amour offers a provocative reading of how the threat of total nuclear war complicates our understanding of trauma theory. For further discussion of Saint-Amour's contribution to the study of nuclear representation, see chapter 6 of this book.

38. The task of differentiating Pynchon's early novels has perhaps only grown more difficult in recent years, since *Mason & Dixon* and *Against the Day* present a much more optimistic Pynchon, whose career is now routinely divided into pre- and post-*Vineland* phases. Even as the more recent novels catalogue a variety of evils and gross historical injustices, they extend the affirmative dimensions of Pynchon's earlier work. If in Pynchon's early fiction we were able to occasionally glimpse the possibilities of humanist sociality, *Mason & Dixon* and *Against the Day* significantly highlight that possibility, particularly in their (quite moving) endings. While I believe that the end of the Cold War did have an impact on Pynchon's imagination of community, I also believe that we should be wary of too quickly imagining his career as having only two stages: *The Crying of Lot 49* and *Gravity's Rainbow* are, in the end, very different novels in how they imagine the links between finitude and community. For examples of criticism that sees an important break in Pynchon's career, see Cohen, 33–59; and Punday "Pynchon's Ghosts."

39. For a discussion of Pynchon's work at Boeing, see Wisnicki, "A Trove."

40. Boyer, *By the Bomb's*, 352–67.

41. *The Day After* is a notable exception, in that despite its incredibly horrifying representation of nuclear attack, the film ends with a message that alludes to the paradoxes of nuclear representation: "The catastrophic events you have just witnessed are, in all likelihood, less severe than the destruction that would actually occur in the event of a full nuclear strike against the United States."

42. Pynchon, "Is It O.K.," 41. This is not to propose that American science fiction didn't produce novels about nuclear war, or that Pynchon was a naïve reader of the genre. Rather, Pynchon's argument in the essay is that Luddite fictions (and despite the counterintuitive nature of the claim, he sees much modern science fiction as Luddite) frequently take the form of what he calls the "countercritter" narrative, novels in which a monster of some kind both embodies and critiques contemporary technology (Frankenstein's monster being the most obvious example). Obviously, however, no countercritter can mark the absence of all forms of life, and the form has to change in the nuclear age.

43. See Jackson, "Postmodernism."

3 / The Time of the Nation, the Time of the State

1. Coover, *The Public Burning*, 94 (hereafter cited parenthetically).

2. See Mazurek, "Metafiction," 143–56.

3. I borrow the term "national symbolic" from Lauren Berlant's work on Hawthorne, in which she sees it as "the order of discursive practices" that "provide an alphabet for a collective consciousness of national subjectivity" (Berlant, *Anatomy*, 20). More broadly, I'm indebted to Berlant's continuing work on national fantasy and temporality.

4. See McEnaney, *Civil Defense*, 3–10, for an account of how the rhetoric of civil defense combined both extreme strength and an always-threatening weakness.

5. Carmichael's *Framing History* offers the best survey of the uses to which

novelists have put the Rosenberg story. For a suggestive account of the multiple ways we can read the Rosenberg case, see Garber and Walkowitz, *Secret Agents*.

6. Walsh, "Narrative Inscription," 332.
7. See Melley, *Empire of Conspiracy*.
8. Giorgio Agamben's recent critical genealogy of the notion of the state of exception is useful for explicating the peculiarity of making Nixon the subject of national violence. Agamben famously argues that sovereignty derives its principal power not from the ability to make and enforce law but from the ability to suspend law, to create the state of exception in which, in order to save democracy, law is suspended. Agamben's formulation has enormous explanatory power in dealing with Cold War political excess, as well as more recent political developments (such as the Patriot Act), and helps to explain the structure of the Rosenbergs' execution in the novel. What is crucial, however, in Coover's account, is that Sam, as a metaphysical embodiment of America, is the one able to authorize the suspension of the law, making the concrete analysis of state power in the novel difficult.
9. Whitfield, *The Culture of the Cold War*, 146–47.
10. Slotkin, *Gunfighter Nation*, 395.
11. A point I owe to Jessica Baran.
12. See Gaddis, *The Cold War*, 48–82, for an argument about the importance of the years between 1950 and 1954 for any attempt to understand how the Cold War evolved into a conflict that could have such drastic consequences.
13. Stanley Corkin has noted the ways in which Westerns released during the Korean War systematically debate the ethics of violence, in contrast to earlier films, where the value of violence was taken as self-evident. He relates this generic development to the fact that Korea was the first conflict where there was a public awareness of the possibility of nuclear conflict (Corkin, *Cowboys*, 127–63).
14. Henriksen, *Dr. Strangelove's America*, 68.
15. Ibid.
16. Klein, "The Future of Nuclear Criticism," 81.
17. Here I am indebted to Christian Moraru's formulation of the novel as a public burning of Habermasian notions of the public sphere (Moraru, "Rewriting").
18. Breitwieser, *National Melancholy*, 14, 12–13.
19. Miller, "The End of the World," 189–91.
20. Bercovitch, *The American Jeremiad*.

4 / Unthinking the Thinkability of the Unthinkable

1. Peter Schwenger argues that the motivations for Cowling's hole may be more complicated than simple protection, since Cowling starts to imagine the hole as the compensation for other forms of absence in his life (Schwenger, *Letter Bomb*, 107-8). Jacqueline Foertsch notes the homoerotics at the core of Cowling's desire for salvation; in her reading, the hole becomes a kind of idealized anus, which helps to explain the comprehensive lack of female agency in the novel (Foertsch, *Enemies Within*, 107–10).
2. Kenneth D. Rose's history of the fallout shelter in America makes the case that it functioned largely as a symbolic device; shelters were never built in large numbers and would, in any case, have offered little protection (Rose, *One Nation*).
3. Hugh Gusterson remarks that the sudden end of the Cold War shocked even

security studies analysts; 1985 would manifestly not have felt like the end of the conflict (Gusterson, *People*, 100–120).

4. O'Brien, *The Nuclear Age*, 4 (hereafter cited parenthetically).

5. See chapter 5 for a discussion of nuclear language.

6. Gusterson, *People*, 38–39.

7. Boyer, *By the Bomb's*, 352–67.

8. See Cordle, *States of Suspense*, 127–36, for an account of just how completely Cowling reflects the nuclear reality of his era.

9. Albert E. Stone observes that Cowling's fallout shelter construction indicates how completely his childhood has been colonized by the bomb, since the construction suggests a "nuclear cave, tree house, snow fort, den, bomb shelter" (Stone, *Literary Aftershocks*, 86).

10. Kaplan, *The Wizards*, 52.

11. Ibid., 26.

12. De Landa, *War in the Age*, 3. Tracy C. Davis's *Stages of Emergency* reads civil defense and war-planning during the Cold War through a performance studies methodology, which helpfully contextualizes and theorizes this commitment to simulation.

13. Kahn is such a fascinating figure that it is tempting to spend more time with him here. *On Thermonuclear War* provides a good sense of Kahn's encyclopedic and digressive imagination, and Sharon Ghamari-Tabrizi's *The Worlds* does a compelling job of placing Kahn within a larger intellectual and cultural milieu.

14. See Belletto, "The Game Theory," for a literary-cultural history of the role game theory played in America during the Cold War.

15. Ghamari-Tabrizi, *The Worlds*, 161.

16. Kaplan, *The Wizards*, 10.

17. Ghamari-Tabrizi, *The Worlds*, 5.

18. Kahn, *On Thermonuclear War*, 19.

19. Ibid., 20.

20. The classic example of this is how a supposed "operational but undetected" capability was possessed by the Soviet Union in the period from 1958–1961. In this period, the absence of evidence of Soviet missile fields was taken as evidence of their creativity in hiding those missiles rather than of the more obvious likelihood that they didn't actually have them; this led to the notorious "missile gap" of the 1960 presidential election (Ghamari-Tabrizi, *The Worlds*, 108–23).

21. Kaplan, *The Wizards*, 45–49.

22. Ibid., 174–84.

23. Ibid., 271.

24. Ibid., 185–200.

25. Ibid., 196.

26. Ibid., 248–57.

27. For an explanation of counterforce as a strategy, see Kaplan, *The Wizards*, 201–19.

28. McNamara had to balance a wide variety of interests during the 1960s, not least of which were the economic consequences of targeting dispersed military sites; as a result, counterforce was valorized and yet sometimes called into question even as it remained a dominant targeting plan. For a history of these negotiations, see Kaplan, *The Wizards*, 315–27.

29. Ibid., 347, 357.
30. Ibid., 271
31. McGurl, *The Program Era*, 12.
32. Hutcheon, *A Poetics of Postmodernism*, 40, 52.
33. For a discussion of how the canon of contemporary fiction has evolved, see Hungerford, "On the Period."
34. Barthelme, *Not-Knowing*, 3–10.
35. McGurl, *The Program Era*, 213–14.
36. Lasch, *The Culture of Narcissism*, 19.
37. See, for instance, Belletto, "The Zemblan"; Mizruchi, "*Lolita*"; and Piette, *The Literary*, 74–105.
38. Waugh, *Metafiction*, 34. Hutcheon offers a parallel account in *Narcissistic Narrative*, 82.
39. Donald Barthelme, *Sixty Stories*, 63–67. I follow Susan Strehle and Alan Wilde here in complicating the identification of Barthelme as a metafictionist. Unlike Strehle and Wilde, however, I'm less interested in taking apart the metafictional/referential divide than I am in seeing the metafictional interest in created worlds as itself a form of referential content (see Strehle, *Fiction in the Quantum Universe*, 190–217; and Wilde, *Middle Grounds*, 161–72). Paul Maltby's formulation of a Barthelme who puts self-reflexivity to political ends strikes me as the most useful (Maltby, *Dissident Postmodernists*, 43–81). For a reading of Barthelme that emphasizes his metafictional interest, see McCaffery, *The Metafictional Muse*, 99–150.
40. Philip Mirowski has pointed out that Oskar Morgenstern, one of the authors of the seminal *Theory of Games and Economic Behavior*, kept a copy of Barthelme's story in his papers. My thanks to Steven Belletto for this (Mirowski, "When Games Grow Deadly Serious," 227).
41. An earlier version of this fear obviously informs *Dr. Strangelove* (1964) and thus circulated quite publicly.
42. Barthelme, *Sixty Stories*, 63.
43. By the midpoint of the story, the narrator has furthermore reversed cause and effect: "one of us watches the console at all times and if the bird flies then that one wakes the other and we turn our keys in the locks simultaneously and the bird flies" (Barthelme, *Sixty Stories*, 65).
44. Ibid., 64.
45. This took the form of the problem of "thinking red." That is, how do I, based on the assumption of an implacable ideological divide between myself and my enemy, think like my enemy during simulated combat? This was especially important given that these simulations and games weren't simply academic exercises; rather, their outcomes came to guide defense policy. For a discussion of "Thinking Red," see De Landa, *War*, 100.
46. Galison, "The Ontology."
47. Ibid., 230
48. Ibid., 264.
49. Edwards, *The Closed World*, 15.
50. Barthelme, *Sixty Stories*, 63.
51. Ibid., 66.
52. As Ghamari-Tabrizi, *The Worlds*, 165–74, notes, this question of when a simulation

could be said to be real enough was a central one for war-gamers; she goes on to describe it as a primarily literary problem of the reality-effect.

53. De Landa, *War*, 101.

54. Coover, *The Universal Baseball Association, Inc.*, 19–20 (hereafter cited parenthetically).

55. Arendt, *On Violence*, 6–7 (italics in original).

56. Ghamari-Tabrizi, *The Worlds*, 126.

57. Ibid., 10, 76.

58. Barth, *Friday Book*, 56.

59. Ghamari-Tabrizi, *The Worlds*, 204

60. See, for instance, the description of *The Joke*, which is pure metafilm (Wallace, *Infinite Jest*, 397–98; hereafter cited parenthetically).

61. By Wallace's own admission (in an unpublished letter to DeLillo) the game is indebted to DeLillo's description, in *End Zone*, of war-gaming.

62. Baudrillard, *Simulacra*, 32.

5 / Trying to Understand *End Zone*

1. DeLillo, *End Zone*, 21 (hereafter cited parenthetically).

2. The bibliography on the language of nuclear war strategizing is extensive, and I can mention only a fraction of it here. For a quick introduction that reveals some of the ways this language helps participants ignore what they are "actually" talking about, see Cohn, "Sex and Death" as well as Chaloupka, *Knowing Nukes*.

3. DeLillo, *White Noise*, 117.

4. This is not to say that other readings don't exist. For examples of DeLillo criticism that place him in other traditions, see Maltby, *The Visionary Moment*, 73–84, as well as McClure, *Partial Faiths*, 63–99 .

5. Reading the novel from a masculinity studies perspective, Donald L. Deardorff's survey of much of the scholarship on the novel finds critics uniformly interested in the linguistic as the novel's primary focus (Deardorff, "Dancing").

6. Heise, "Toxins, Drugs."

7. LeClair, "An Interview," 5.

8. My reading differs from Cowart's insofar as I read the analogy in historical rather than metaphysical terms, but I sympathize with Cowart's attempt to move the discussion away from the applicability of postmodern linguistic theory to DeLillo's work. Cowart's point about criticism not engaging the analogy is correct, but perhaps could be extended to note that much of the criticism barely even acknowledges that nuclear war is one of the novel's subjects. A notable exception is Mark Osteen's reading of *End Zone*, where he identifies evidence of Herman Kahn's thought in the novel's discussion of nuclear strategy (Cowart, *Don DeLillo*, 20; Osteen, *American Magic*, 31–45).

9. Agamben, *Remnants of Auschwitz*, 64.

10. For an extended account of the links between mass death and Rilke's poetry, see Wyschogrod, *Spirit in Ashes*.

11. For a provocative and quite different reading of the presence of Rilke in the novel, see Cowart, *Don DeLillo*, 26–27. Rilke's poem is, among other things, a lament for the fact that animals have an access to a realm of pure experience—the open— from which human self-consciousness excludes us; it is a celebration of the animal at the expense of the human. While Rilke's ontological division provoked a severe

critique in Heidegger's work, which suggested that brute animality never has the world-disclosing power of the human, and hence could never have access to the open, both Rilke and the traditions of critique inherited from him make that animal/human distinction central to the worlds they invent or try to diagnose. Agamben's work, however, reveals how central such distinctions are to the anthropological machine that produces humans as such; in other words, the human/animal distinction is crucial to the biopolitical terrain on which the major twentieth-century ethical questions emerge, namely the issue of bare life: "This is also why Auschwitz marks the end and the ruin of every ethics of dignity and conformity to a norm. The bare life to which human beings were reduced neither demands nor conforms to anything. It itself is the only norm; it is absolutely immanent. And 'the ultimate sentiment of belonging to the species' cannot in any sense be a kind of dignity" (Agamben, *Remnants*, 69). Rather than producing the animal out of humans—the view of the Holocaust that Agamben is out to challenge—the camps expose, at least in Agamben's ongoing analysis, the unworkability and complicity of a system that makes the distinction central; an ethics that thinks through the events of the twentieth century would have to imagine a new terrain on which to conduct its investigations.

12. Osteen, *American Magic*, 39.
13. Freedman, *The Evolution*, 238.
14. Ibid., 239.
15. Ibid., 242.
16. Kaplan, *The Wizards*, 346.
17. Ibid., 347–48, Freedman, *The Evolution*, 240–42.
18. Kaplan, *The Wizards*, 354.
19. Smith, *Doubletalk*, 19.
20. Virilio, *Speed and Politics*, 139 (italics in original).
21. Newhouse, *Cold Dawn*, 1.

6 / The Dominant Tense

1. Joseph Dewey proposes that Powers should be properly contextualized as synthesizing the formal achievements of high postmodernism—as displayed in the work of Pynchon, Gaddis, Gass, and Barth—with the more direct social commentary of Updike, O'Hara, Styron, and Cheever. While I largely agree with Dewey's contextualizing, I'm not sure "synthesis" is the right word; rather, and as I argue in this chapter, part of Powers's project is to historicize postmodern experimentation as precisely a commitment to a reality that has been derailed by the bomb (Dewey, *Understanding*, 3). For a situating of Powers in relation to the work of high postmodernism, see LeClair, "The Prodigious Fiction." I borrow the idea of "late postmodernism" from Jeremy Green (Green, *Late*).
2. Moody has contextualized his *Purple America* as an attempt to uncover the links between the nuclear age and particular structures and pathologies of domestic life (Goldstein, interview with Rick Moody).
3. May, *Homeward Bound*, 17–18.
4. Caruth, *Unclaimed Experience*, 1–9.
5. Powers, *Prisoner's Dilemma*, 53, italics in original (hereafter cited parenthetically).
6. Caruth, *Unclaimed Experience*, 10–24; Saint-Amour, "Bombing and the Symptom," 62–65.

7. Eddie Sr. is only slightly wrong; the dilemma was first identified in 1950.
8. For a concise history of the dilemma, see Poundstone, *Prisoner's Dilemma*.
9. Ibid., 212–13.
10. Nye, *American*, 203.
11. Ibid., 215.
12. Marchand, *Creating*, 302.
13. Ibid.
14. Ibid., 303.
15. Ibid., 304.
16. Marchand notes that, among other research tools, Bel Geddes contracted with Eddie Rickenbacker to do fly-overs of Pennsylvania with his key staff members, so they would have an idea of the level of detail that could be visible at various heights (303).
17. Ibid., 306.
18. Ibid., 307.
19. DeLillo, *Underworld*, 76.
20. Nye, *American*, 225.
21. Both *The Gold Bug Variations* (1991) and *The Time of Our Singing* (2003) stress the endless possibilities of the future. In *The Gold Bug Variations*, the future is the time when the continuing and ongoing evolution of the human can take place, and in *The Time of Our Singing*, it offers the necessary condition for a postracial world. But both novels also stress the immense threat that conditions our relationship to the future.
22. Bernstein, *Foregone Conclusions*, 9.
23. Auden, *Selected Poems*, 95.
24. *The Gift of Time* is the title of Jonathan Schell's moving account of the chance for total disarmament offered by the end of the Cold War.
25. Eddie Sr. has his date slightly off, as *Four Quartets* was not published as a complete collection until 1943. Eddie Sr. is, of course, quoting from "Burnt Norton," which originally appeared in 1936.

Afterword

1. Didion, *Democracy*, 29, 22, 26 (hereafter cited parenthetically).
2. One thinks of the ways in which genteel Sacramento life is undergirded by adultery in her first novel, *Run River* (1963), through to how unofficial and extralegal forms of power are the basis for the illusion of democratic citizenship in novels such as *Democracy* and *The Last Thing He Wanted* (1996).
3. Didion, *We Tell Ourselves*, 598.
4. Nadel, *Containment Culture*, 278.
5. See ibid., 275–96, for a reading that suggests the two-novel model is to be read as an elegy for the very idea of democracy.
6. Didion, *We Tell Ourselves*, 598–99.
7. Ibid., 599.
8. Ibid., 599–600.
9. Hite, *The Other Side of the Story*, 1, 2.
10. For an overview of this debate, see Davis, "Postmodern Blackness."
11. See Dubey, *Signs*; Harper, *Framing*; and Morrison, "Living Memory."

12. See Morrison, "The Future of Time," 172–73, for her account of how the nuclear age is but one force among many impinging on our sense of the future.
13. See Clark, *Cold Warriors*.
14. Quoted in Nelson, "Plath, History," 29.
15. Plath, *The Bell Jar,* 72.
16. Douglas, "Periodizing," 74–75.
17. Cooper, "The Whiteness," 81.
18. See, for instance, Dudziak, *Cold War*.
19. Cooper, "The Whiteness," 89.
20. Silko, *Ceremony,* 31 (hereafter cited parenthetically).
21. Karem, "Keeping the Native," 21.
22. Coover, "One Hot Book," 18–19.
23. Everett, *Erasure,* 18, 19 (italics in original; hereafter cited parenthetically).
24. See Hungerford, "On the Period," for an account of the field's broad shift to historical accounts.
25. This is not to say that the weapons have disappeared—indeed, their use may be more likely than ever before; rather, it is to say that if they are used, it will likely not be in a global exchange.
26. See Cohen, *After,* esp. 191–202; and Cordle, *States,* 139–54, for discussions of the nuclear inheritance of post–Cold-War literature.
27. See Gray, "Open Doors," for an account of the conceptual failure of much 9/11 fiction.

Bibliography

Agamben, Giorgio. *Remnants of Auschwitz: The Witness and the Archive.* Translated by Daniel Heller-Roazen. New York: Zone, 1999.
———. *State of Exception.* Translated by Kevin Atell. Chicago: University of Chicago Press, 2005.
Alperovitz, Gar. *The Decision to Use the Atomic Bomb.* New York: Vintage, 1996.
Arendt, Hannah. *On Violence.* San Diego: Harvest, 1970.
"Atomic Education Urged by Einstein," *New York Times,* May 25, 1946.
Auden, W. H. *Selected Poems.* Selected and edited by Edward Mendelson. New York: Vintage, 2007.
Ballard, J. G. *War Fever.* New York: Farrar, Strauss, Giroux, 1990.
Barth, John. *"The Floating Opera" and "The End of the Road."* 1967. Rev. ed. New York: Bantam, 1988.
———. *The Friday Book: Essays and Other Nonfiction.* New York: Putnam, 1984.
———. *Giles Goat-Boy; or, The Revised New Syllabus.* New York: Bantam, 1987.
Barthelme, Donald. *Not-Knowing: The Essays and Interviews.* Edited by Kim Herzinger. Berkeley: Counterpoint, 1997.
———. *Sixty Stories.* New York: Penguin, 1993.
Bartter, Martha A. *The Way to Ground Zero: The Atomic Bomb in American Science Fiction.* New York: Greenwood Press, 1988.
Baudrillard, Jean. *Simulacra and Simulation.* Translated by Sheila Glaser. Ann Arbor: University of Michigan Press, 1994.
Belletto, Steven. "Curbing Containment: Cold War Studies in the Twenty-First Century." *Contemporary Literature* 48, no. 1 (2007): 150–64.
———. "The Game Theory Narrative and the Myth of the National Security State." *American Quarterly* 61, no. 2 (2009): 333–57.

———. "The Zemblan Who Came in from the Cold, or Nabokov's *Pale Fire*, Chance, and the Cold War." *ELH* 73, no. 3 (2006): 755–80.
Bercovitch, Sacvan. *The American Jeremiad*. Madison: University of Wisconsin Press, 1978.
Berger, Charles. "Merrill and Pynchon: Our Apocalyptic Scribes." In *Thomas Pynchon: Modern Critical Views*, edited by Harold Bloom, 203–15. New York: Chelsea House, 1986.
Berger, James. *After the End: Representations of Post-Apocalypse*. Minneapolis: University of Minnesota Press, 1999.
Berlant, Lauren. *The Anatomy of National Fantasy: Hawthorne, Utopia, and Everyday Life*. Chicago: University of Chicago Press, 1991.
Bernstein, Michael André. *Foregone Conclusions: Against Apocalyptic History*. Berkeley and Los Angeles: University of California Press, 1994.
Bové, Paul. "History and Fiction: The Narrative Voices of Pynchon's *Gravity's Rainbow*." *Modern Fiction Studies* 50, no. 3 (2004): 657–80.
Boyer, Paul. *By the Bomb's Early Light: American Thought and Culture at the Dawn of the Atomic Age*. Chapel Hill: University of North Carolina Press, 1994.
———. *Fallout: A Historian Reflects on America's Half-Century Encounter with Nuclear Weapons*. Columbus: Ohio State University Press, 1998.
Breitwieser, Mitchell. *National Melancholy: Mourning and Opportunity in Classic American Literature*. Stanford: Stanford University Press, 2007.
Brians, Paul. "Farewell to the First Atomic Age." *Nuclear Texts and Contexts* 8 (1992): 1–3.
———. *Nuclear Holocausts: Atomic War in Fiction, 1895–1984*. Kent, Ohio: Kent State University Press, 1987.
Brooks, Peter. *Reading for the Plot: Design and Intention in Narrative*. Cambridge: Harvard University Press, 1992.
Brunner, Edward. *Cold War Poetry*. Urbana: University of Illinois Press, 2001.
Canaday, John. *The Nuclear Muse: Literature, Physics, and the First Atomic Bombs*. Madison: University of Wisconsin Press, 2000.
Carmichael, Virginia. *Framing History: The Rosenberg Story and the Cold War*. Minneapolis: University of Minnesota Press, 1993.
Carter, Dale. *The Final Frontier: The Rise and Fall of the American Rocket State*. London: Verso, 1988.
Caruth, Cathy. *Unclaimed Experience: Trauma, Narrative, and History*. Baltimore: Johns Hopkins University Press, 1996.
Chaloupka, William. *Knowing Nukes: The Politics and Culture of the Atom*. Minneapolis: University of Minnesota Press, 1992.
Chow, Rey. *The Age of the World Target: Self-Referentiality in War, Theory, and Comparative Work*. Durham: Duke University Press, 2006.
Cirincione, Joseph. *Bomb Scare: The History and Future of Nuclear Weapons*. New York: Columbia University Press, 2007.

Clark, Suzanne. *Cold Warriors: Manliness on Trial in the Rhetoric of the West*. Carbondale: Southern Illinois University Press, 2000.
Cohen, Samuel. *After the End of History: American Fiction in the 1990s*. Iowa City: University of Iowa Press, 2009.
Cohn, Carol. "Sex and Death in the Rational World of Defense Intellectuals." *Signs* 12, no. 4 (1987): 687-718.
Cooper, Ken. "The Whiteness of the Bomb." In *Postmodern Apocalypse: Theory and Cultural Practice at the End*, edited by Richard Dellamora, 79-106. Philadelphia: University of Pennsylvania Press, 1995.
Coover, Robert. "One Hot Book: Richard Seaver and *The Public Burning*'s Wild Ride." *Humanist* 70, no. 3 (2010): 16-21.
———. *The Public Burning*. New York: Grove, 1998.
———. *The Universal Baseball Association, Inc., J. Henry Waugh, Prop*. New York: Plume, 1971.
Cordle, Daniel. "Cultures of Terror: Nuclear Criticism during and since the Cold War." *Literature Compass* 3, no. 6 (2006): 1186-99.
———. *States of Suspense: The Nuclear Age, Postmodernism, and United States Fiction and Prose*. Manchester: Manchester University Press, 2008.
Corkin, Stanley. *Cowboys as Cold Warriors: The Western and U.S. History*. Philadelphia: Temple University Press, 2004.
Cornis-Pope, Marcel. *Narrative Innovation and Cultural Rewriting in the Cold War Era and After*. New York: Palgrave, 2001.
Cowart, David. *Don DeLillo: The Physics of Language*. Athens: University of Georgia Press, 2002.
———. "Pynchon and the Sixties." *Critique* 41, no. 1 (1999): 3-12.
Davis, Kimberly Chabot. "'Postmodern Blackness': Toni Morrison's *Beloved* and the End of History." *Twentieth Century Literature* 44, no. 2 (1998): 242-60.
Davis, Tracy C. *Stages of Emergency: Cold War Nuclear Civil Defense*. Durham: Duke University Press, 2007.
Davis, Walter A. *Deracination: Historicity, Hiroshima, and the Tragic Imperative*. Albany: State University of New York Press, 2001.
Deardorff, Donald L. "Dancing in the End Zone: Don DeLillo, Men's Studies, and the Quest for Linguistic Healing." *Journal of Men's Studies* 8, no. 1 (1999): 73-82.
Dee, Jonathan. "The Art of Fiction XCII: John Hersey." *Paris Review* 100 (1986): 210-49.
DeKoven, Marianne. *Utopia Limited: The Sixties and the Emergence of the Postmodern*. Durham: Duke University Press, 2004.
De Landa, Manuel. *War in the Age of Intelligent Machines*. New York: Zone, 1991.
DeLillo, Don. *End Zone*. New York: Penguin, 1986.
———. *Underworld*. New York: Scribner, 1997.
———. *White Noise*. New York: Penguin, 1985.

Derrida, Jacques. "No Apocalypse, Not Now (full speed ahead, seven missiles, seven missives)." *Diacritics* 14, no. 2 (1984): 20–32.

Dewey, Joseph. *In a Dark Time: The Apocalyptic Temper in the American Novel of the Nuclear Age.* West Lafayette, Ind.: Purdue University Press, 1990.

———. *Understanding Richard Powers.* Columbia: University of South Carolina Press, 2002.

Dickstein, Morris. *Leopards in the Temple: The Transformation of American Fiction 1945–1970.* Cambridge: Harvard University Press, 2002.

Didion, Joan. *Democracy.* New York: Vintage, 1995.

———. *Play It As It Lays.* New York: Noonday, 1990.

———. *Run River.* New York: Vintage, 1991.

———. *We Tell Ourselves Stories in Order to Live: Collected Nonfiction.* New York: Alfred A. Knopf/Everyman's Library, 2006.

Dirda, Michael. Transcript of "Dirda on Books." *Washingtonpost.com* June 9, 1999. www.washingtonpost.com/wp-srv/style/talk/dirda/dirda0609.htm.

Dollimore, Jonathan. *Radical Tragedy: Religion, Ideology, and Power in the Drama of Shakespeare and His Contemporaries.* Durham: Duke University Press, 1993.

Douglas, Ann. "Periodizing the American Century: Modernism, Postmodernism, and Postcolonialism in the Cold War Context." *Modernism/Modernity* 5, no. 3 (1998): 71–98.

Dowling, David. *Fictions of Nuclear Disaster.* Iowa City: University of Iowa Press, 1987.

Dubey, Madhu. *Signs and Cities: Black Literary Postmodernism.* Chicago: University of Chicago Press, 2003.

Dudziak, Mary L. *Cold War Civil Rights: Race and the Image of American Democracy.* Princeton: Princeton University Press, 2000.

Dugdale, John. *Thomas Pynchon: Allusive Parables of Power.* New York: St. Martin's Press, 1990.

Eden, Lynn. *Whole World on Fire: Organizations, Knowledge, & Nuclear Weapons Devastation.* Ithaca: Cornell University Press, 2004.

Edwards, Paul N. *The Closed World: Computers and the Politics of Discourse in Cold War America.* Cambridge: MIT Press, 1996.

Elias, Amy J. *Sublime Desire: History and Post-1960s Fiction.* Baltimore: Johns Hopkins University Press, 2001.

Engelhardt, Tom. *The End of Victory Culture: Cold War America and the Disillusioning of a Generation.* Amherst: University of Massachusetts Press, 2007.

Engelhardt, Tom, and Edward T. Linenthal, eds. *History Wars: The Enola Gay and Other Battles for the American Past.* New York: Owl Books, 1996

Ermarth, Elizabeth. *Sequel to History: Postmodernism and the Crisis of Representational Time.* Princeton: Princeton University Press, 1992.

Everett, Percival. *Erasure: A Novel.* Hanover, N.H.: University Press of New England, 2001.

Faulkner, William. *Essays: Speeches & Public Letters.* Edited by James B. Meriwether. New York: Modern Library, 2004.
Foertsch, Jacqueline. *Enemies Within: The Cold War and the AIDS Crisis in Literature, Film, and Culture.* Urbana: Illinois University Press, 2001.
Fradkin, Philip. *Fallout.* Boulder: Johnson Books, 2004.
Franklin, H. Bruce. *War Stars: The Superweapon and the American Imagination.* Oxford: Oxford University Press, 1988.
Franzen, Jonathan. "Mr. Difficult: William Gaddis and the Problem of Hard-to-Read Books." *New Yorker*, September 30, 2002.
Freedman, Lawrence. *The Evolution of Nuclear Strategy.* 3rd ed. London: Palgrave, 2003.
Fussell, Paul. *The Great War and Modern Memory.* Oxford: Oxford University Press, 1977.
Gaddis, John Lewis. *The Cold War: A New History.* New York: Penguin, 2005.
Galison, Peter. "The Ontology of the Enemy: Norbert Wiener and the Cybernetic Vision." *Critical Inquiry* 21, no. 1 (1994): 228–66.
———. "War against the Center." *Grey Room* 4 (2001): 6–33.
Gallagher, Carole. *American Ground Zero: The Secret Nuclear War.* Cambridge: MIT Press, 1993.
Garber, Marjorie, and Rebecca L. Walkowitz, eds. *Secret Agents: The Rosenberg Case, McCarthyism, & Fifties America.* New York: Routledge, 1995.
Gardner, John. *On Moral Fiction.* New York: Basic Books, 1978.
Gery, John. *Nuclear Annihilation and Contemporary American Poetry: Ways of Nothingness.* Gainesville: University Press of Florida, 1996.
Ghamari-Tabrizi, Sharon. *The Worlds of Herman Kahn: The Intuitive Science of Thermonuclear War.* Cambridge: Harvard University Press, 2005.
Goldstein, Bill. Audio interview with Rick Moody. *New York Times on the Web*, February 1, 2001.
Graff, Gerald. *Literature against Itself: Literary Ideas in Modern Society.* Chicago: University of Chicago Press, 1979.
Gray, Richard. "Open Doors, Closed Minds: American Prose Writing at a Time of Crisis." *American Literary History* 21, no. 1 (2009): 128–48.
Green, Jeremy. *Late Postmodernism: American Fiction at the Millenium.* New York: Palgrave, 2005.
Gusterson, Hugh. *People of the Bomb: Portraits of America's Nuclear Complex.* Minneapolis: University of Minnesota Press, 2004.
Hamill, John. "Confronting the Monolith: Authority and the Cold War in *Gravity's Rainbow*." *Journal of American Studies* 33, no. 3 (1999): 417–36.
Harper, Phillip Brian. *Framing the Margins: The Social Logic of Postmodern Culture.* Oxford: Oxford University Press, 1994.
Harris, Charles B. *Passionate Virtuosity: The Fiction of John Barth.* Urbana: University of Illinois Press, 1983.
Hayles, N. Katherine. "'A Metaphor of God Knew How Many Parts': The Engine

That Drives *The Crying of Lot 49*." In *New Essays on "The Crying of Lot 49*," edited by Patrick O'Donnell, 97–126. Cambridge: Cambridge University Press, 1991.

Heise, Ursula K. *Chronoschisms: Time, Narrative, and Postmodernism*. Cambridge: Cambridge University Press, 1997.

———. "Toxins, Drugs, and Global Systems: Risk and Narrative in the Contemporary Novel." *American Literature* 74, no. 4 (2002): 747–78.

Henriksen, Margot. *Dr. Strangelove's America: Society and Culture in the Atomic Age*. Berkeley and Los Angeles: University of California Press, 1997.

Hepburn, Allan. *Intrigue: Espionage and Culture*. New Haven: Yale University Press, 2005.

Hersey, John. *Hiroshima*. New York: Vintage; 1989.

High Noon. Directed by Fred Zinneman. Republic Entertainment, 1952. DVD. Artisan, 2002.

Hinds, Elizabeth Jane Wall, ed. *The Multiple Worlds of Pynchon's Mason & Dixon*. Rochester: Camden House, 2005.

Hite, Molly. *The Other Side of the Story: Structures and Strategies of Contemporary Feminist Narratives*. Ithaca: Cornell University Press, 1989.

Hoberek, Andrew. "Introduction: After Postmodernism." *Twentieth Century Literature* 53, no. 3 (2007): 233–38.

———. *The Twilight of the Middle Class: Post–World War II American Fiction and White-Collar Work*. Princeton: Princeton University Press, 2005.

Huehls, Mitchum. *Qualified Hope: A Postmodern Politics of Time*. Columbus: Ohio State University Press, 2009.

Hume, Kathryn. *Pynchon's Mythography: An Approach to Gravity's Rainbow*. Carbondale: Southern Illinois University Press, 1987.

Hungerford, Amy. *The Holocaust of Texts: Genocide, Literature, and Personification*. Chicago: University of Chicago Press, 2003.

———."On the Period Formerly Known as Contemporary." *American Literary History* 20, no. 1–2 (2008): 410–19.

Hutcheon, Linda. *Narcissistic Narrative: The Metafictional Paradox*. Waterloo, Ontario: Wilfrid Laurier University Press, 1980.

———. *A Poetics of Postmodernism*. New York: Routledge, 1988.

———. *The Politics of Postmodernism*. London: Routledge, 1989.

Jackson, Tony. "Postmodernism, Narrative, and the Cold War Sense of an Ending." *Narrative* 8, no. 3 (2000): 324–37.

Jameson, Fredric. *Postmodernism, or, The Cultural Logic of Late Capitalism*. Durham: Duke University Press, 1991.

Kahn, Herman. *On Thermonuclear War*. New Brunswick, N.J.: Transaction, 2007.

Kaplan, Fred. *The Wizards of Armageddon*. Stanford: Stanford University Press, 1983.

Karem, Jeff. "Keeping the Native on the Reservation: The Struggle for Leslie Marmon Silko's *Ceremony*." *American Indian Culture and Research Journal* 25, no. 4 (2001): 21–34.

Kerrigan, John. *Revenge Tragedy: Aeschylus to Armageddon.* Oxford: Clarendon, 1996.

Klein, Richard. "The Future of Nuclear Criticism." *Yale French Studies* 77 (1990): 76–100.

Kushner, Tony. *Angels in America: A Gay Fantasia on National Themes.* New York: Theatre Communications Group, 1993.

Langewiesche, William. *The Atomic Bazaar: The Rise of the Nuclear Poor.* New York: FSG, 2007.

Lasch, Christopher. *The Culture of Narcissism: American Life in an Age of Diminishing Expectations.* New York: Norton, 1979.

LeClair, Thomas. "An Interview with Don DeLillo." In *Conversations with Don DeLillo*, edited by Thomas DePietro, 3–15. Jackson: University Press of Mississippi: 2005.

———. "The Prodigious Fiction of Richard Powers, William Vollmann, and David Foster Wallace." *Critique* (Fall 1996): 12–37.

Levine, George. "Risking the Moment: Anarchy and Possibility in Pynchon's Fiction." In *Mindful Pleasures: Essays on Thomas Pynchon*, edited by George Levine and David Leverenz, 113–36. Boston: Little, Brown, 1976.

Lewis, Wyndham. *Blasting and Bombardiering.* London: John Calder, 1982.

Lifton, Robert Jay, and Greg Mitchell. *Hiroshima in America: A Half-Century of Denial.* New York: Avon Books, 1995.

Lindsay, Alan. *Death in the Funhouse: John Barth and Poststructuralist Aesthetics.* New York: Peter Lang, 1995.

Lowen, Rebecca S. *Creating the Cold War University: The Transformation of Stanford.* Berkeley and Los Angeles: University of California Press, 1997.

Luckhurst, Roger. "Review: Nuclear Criticism: Anachronisms and Anachorism." *Diacritics* 23, no. 2 (1993): 89–97.

Maltby, Paul. *Dissident Postmodernists: Barthelme, Coover, Pynchon.* Philadelphia: University of Pennsylvania Press, 1991.

———. *The Visionary Moment: A Postmodern Critique.* Albany: State University of New York Press, 2002.

Marchand, Roland. *Creating the Corporate Soul: The Rise of Public Relations and Corporate Imagery in American Big Business.* Berkeley and Los Angeles: University of California Press, 1998.

Marcus, Ben. "Why Experimental Fiction Threatens to Destroy Publishing, Jonathan Franzen, And Life as We Know it: A Correction." *Harper's*, October 2005, 39–52.

Masco, Joseph. *The Nuclear Borderlands: The Manhattan Project in Post–Cold War New Mexico.* Princeton: Princeton University Press, 2006.

May, Elaine Tyler. *Homeward Bound: American Families in the Cold War Era.* New York: Basic Books, 1999.

Mazurek, Raymond A. "Metafiction, the Historical Novel, and Coover's *The Public Burning.*" *Critique* 23, no. 3 (1982): 143–56.

McCaffery, Larry. *The Metafictional Muse.* Pittsburgh: University of Pittsburgh Press, 1982.
McCarthy, Mary. "The 'Hiroshima' *New Yorker.*" *Politics* 3, no. 10 (November 1946): 367.
McClure, John A. *Partial Faiths: Postsecular Fiction in the Age of Pynchon and Morrison.* Athens: University of Georgia Press, 2007.
McEnaney, Laura. *Civil Defense Begins at Home: Militarization Meets Everyday Life in the Fifties.* Princeton: Princeton University Press, 2000.
McGurl, Mark. "The Program Era: Pluralisms of Postwar Fiction." *Critical Inquiry* 32, no. 1 (2005): 102–29.
———. *The Program Era: Postwar Fiction and the Rise of Creative Writing.* Cambridge: Harvard University Press, 2009.
McHale, Brian. *Constructing Postmodernism.* London: Routledge, 1992.
———. "1966 Nervous Breakdown; or, When Did Postmodernism Begin?" *Modern Language Quarterly* 69, no. 3 (September 2008): 391–413.
———. *Postmodernist Fiction.* London: Methuen, 1987.
McHoul, Alec, and David Wills. *Writing Pynchon: Strategies in Fictional Analysis.* Urbana: University of Illinois Press, 1990.
Melley, Timothy. *Empire of Conspiracy: The Culture of Paranoia in Postwar America.* Ithaca: Cornell University Press, 2000.
The Day After. DVD. Directed by Nicholas Meyer. 1983. Santa Monica: MGM, 2004.
Mendelson, Edward. "The Sacred, the Profane, and *The Crying of Lot 49.*" In *Pynchon: A Collection of Critical Essays,* edited by Mendelson, 112–46. Englewood Cliffs: Prentice Hall, 1978.
Milesi, Laurent. "Postmodern Ana-Apocalyptics: Pynchon's V-Effect and the End (of Our Century)." *Pynchon Notes* 42, no. 3 (1998): 213–43.
Miller, Perry. "The End of the World." *William and Mary Quarterly,* 3rd ser., 8, no. 2 (1951): 171–91.
Miller, Richard. *Under the Cloud: The Decades of Nuclear Testing.* New York: Free Press, 1986; The Woodlands, Tex.: Two-Sixty Press, 1991.
Mirowski, Philip. "When Games Grow Deadly Serious: The Military Influence on the Development of Game Theory." In *Economics and National Security,* edited by Craufurd D. W. Goodwin, 227–55. Durham: Duke University Press, 1991.
Mizruchi, Susan. "*Lolita* in History." *American Literature* 75, no. 3 (2003): 629–52.
Moraru, Christian. "Rewriting Horatio Alger: Robert Coover and the Public Burning of the Public Sphere." *LIT: Literature, Interpretation, Theory* 10, no. 3 (1999): 235–54.
Moretti, Franco. *Signs Taken for Wonders: Essays in the Sociology of Literary Form.* New York: Verso, 1988.
Morrison, Toni. "The Future of Time: Literature and Diminished Expectations."

In *What Moves at the Margin: Selected Nonfiction*, edited by Carolyn C. Denard, 170–86. Jackson: University Press of Mississippi, 2008.
——. "Living Memory." City Limits (March 31–April 7, 1988): 10–11.
Myers, B. R. *A Reader's Manifesto*. Hoboken: Melville House, 2002.
Nadel, Alan. *Containment Culture: American Narratives, Postmodernism, and the Atomic Age*. Durham: Duke University Press, 1995.
Nelson, Deborah. "Plath, History, and Politics." In *The Cambridge Companion to Sylvia Plath*, edited by Jo Gill, 21–35. Cambridge: Cambridge University Press, 2006.
——. *Pursuing Privacy in Cold War America*. New York: Columbia University Press, 2002.
Newhouse, John. *Cold Dawn: The Story of SALT*. Washington: Pergamon-Brassey's, 1989.
Newman, Charles. *The Post-Modern Aura: The Act of Fiction in an Age of Inflation*. Evanston: Northwestern University Press, 1985.
Norris, Margot. *Writing War in the Twentieth Century*. Charlottesville: University of Virginia Press, 2000.
Nye, David. *American Technological Sublime*. Cambridge: MIT Press, 1994.
O'Brien, Tim. *The Nuclear Age*. New York: Penguin, 1996.
Olderman, Raymond. *Beyond the Waste Land: A Study of the American Novel in the Nineteen Sixties*. New Haven: Yale University Press, 1972.
Osteen, Mark. *American Magic and Dread: Don DeLillo's Dialogue with Culture*. Philadelphia: University of Pennsylvania Press, 2000.
Patterson, Ian. *Guernica and Total War*. Cambridge: Harvard University Press, 2007.
Peck, Dale. "The Moody Blues." *New Republic*, July 1, 2002, 33–38.
Piette, Adam. *The Literary Cold War: 1945 to Vietnam*. Edinburgh: Edinburgh University Press, 2009.
Plath, Sylvia. *The Bell Jar*. New York: Bantam Books, 1979.
Poundstone, William. *Prisoner's Dilemma: John von Neumann, Game Theory, and the Puzzle of the Bomb*. New York: Anchor Books, 1993.
Powers, Richard. *Prisoner's Dilemma*. New York: Harper Perennial, 1988.
Punday, Daniel. "John Barth's Occasional Writing: The Institutional Construction of Postmodernism in *The Friday Book*." *American Literature* 77, no. 3 (2005): 591–619.
——. "Pynchon's Ghosts" *Contemporary Literature* 44, no. 2 (2003) 250–74.
Pynchon, Thomas. *The Crying of Lot 49*. New York: Perennial Classics, 1999.
——. "Is It O.K. to Be a Luddite?" *New York Times Book Review*, October 28, 1984.
——. "A Journey into the Mind of Watts." *New York Times Magazine*, June 12, 1966.
——. *Slow Learner*. Boston: Little, Brown, 1984.
——. *V.* New York: Harper Perennial, 1986.
Robinson, Douglas. *American Apocalypses: The Image of the End of the World in American Literature*. Baltimore: Johns Hopkins University Press, 1985.

Robson, David. "Frye, Derrida, Pynchon, and the Apocalyptic Space of Postmodern Fiction." In *Postmodern Apocalypse: Theory and Cultural Practice at the End*, edited by Richard Dellamora, 61–78. Philadelphia: University of Pennsylvania Press, 1995.

Rose, Kenneth D. *One Nation Underground: The Fallout Shelter in American Culture*. New York: New York University Press, 2001.

Saint-Amour, Paul K. "Bombing and the Symptom: Traumatic Earliness and the Nuclear Uncanny." *Diacritics* 30, no. 4 (2000): 59–82.

Schaub, Thomas Hill. *American Fiction in the Cold War*. Madison: University of Wisconsin Press, 1991.

———. *Pynchon: The Voice of Ambiguity*. Urbana: University of Illinois Press, 1981.

Schell, Jonathan. *The Fate of the Earth and the Abolition*. Stanford: Stanford University Press, 2000.

———. *The Gift of Time: The Case for Abolishing Nuclear Weapons Now*. New York: Metropolitan Books, 1998.

———. *The Seventh Decade: The New Shape of Nuclear Danger*. New York: Holt, 2007.

Schiffrin, André, ed. *The Cold War and the University: Toward an Intellectual History of the Postwar Years*. New York: New Press, 1997.

Scholes, Robert. *The Fabulators*. Oxford: Oxford University Press, 1967.

Schwenger, Peter. *Letter Bomb: Nuclear Holocaust and the Exploding Word*. Baltimore: Johns Hopkins University Press, 1992.

Seed, David. *American Science Fiction and the Cold War: Literature and Film*. Edinburgh: Edinburgh University Press, 1999.

———. *The Fictional Labyrinths of Thomas Pynchon*. Iowa City: University of Iowa Press, 1988.

Shambroom, Paul. *Face to Face with the Bomb: Nuclear Reality after the Cold War*. Baltimore: Johns Hopkins University Press, 2003.

Shute, Nevil. *On the Beach*. New York: Ballantine Books, 1997.

Siebers, Tobin. *Cold War Criticism and the Politics of Skepticism*. Oxford: Oxford University Press, 1993.

Silko, Leslie Marmon. *Ceremony*. New York: Penguin, 2006.

Slotkin, Richard. *Gunfighter Nation: The Myth of the Frontier in Twentieth-Century America*. New York: Athenaeum, 1992.

Smith, Gerard. *Doubletalk: The Story of the First Strategic Arms Limitation Talks*. Garden City, N.Y.: Doubleday, 1980.

Smith, Marcus, and Khachig Tölölyan. "The New Jeremiad: *Gravity's Rainbow*." In *Thomas Pynchon: Modern Critical Views*, edited by Harold Bloom, 139–56. New York: Chelsea House, 1986.

Smith, Shawn. *Pynchon and History: Metahistorical Rhetoric and Postmodern Narrative Form in the Novels of Thomas Pynchon*. London: Routledge, 2005.

Solnit, Rebecca. *Savage Dreams: A Journey into the Landscape Wars of the American West*. Berkeley and Los Angeles: University of California Press, 1999.

Stark, John O. *The Literature of Exhaustion: Borges, Nabokov, and Barth*. Durham: Duke University Press, 1974.

Stone, Albert. *Literary Aftershocks: American Writers, Readers, and the Bomb.* New York: Twayne, 1994.
Stonehill, Brian. *The Self-Conscious Novel: Artifice in Fiction from Joyce to Pynchon.* Philadelphia: University of Pennsylvania Press, 1988.
Strehle, Susan. *Fiction in the Quantum Universe.* Chapel Hill: University of North Carolina Press, 1992.
Tanner, Tony. *Thomas Pynchon.* London: Methuen, 1982.
Torgovnick, Marianna. *The War Complex: World War II in Our Time.* Chicago: University of Chicago Press, 2005.
Treat, John Whittier. *Writing Ground Zero: Japanese Literature and the Atomic Bomb.* Chicago: University of Chicago Press, 1995.
Virilio, Paul. *Speed and Politics.* New York: Semiotext(e), 1986.
Wagar, W. Warren. *Terminal Visions: The Literature of Last Things.* Bloomington: Indiana University Press, 1982.
Wallace, David Foster. *Infinite Jest.* New York: Little, Brown, 1996.
Walsh, Richard. "Narrative Inscription, History, and the Reader in Robert Coover's *The Public Burning*." *Studies in the Novel* 25, no. 3 (1993): 332–46.
Waugh, Patricia. *Metafiction: The Theory and Practice of Self-Conscious Fiction.* New York: Routledge, 1988.
Weart, Spencer R. *Nuclear Fear: A History of Images.* Cambridge: Harvard University Press, 1988.
Welsome, Eileen. *The Plutonium Files: America's Secret Medical Experiments during the Cold War.* New York: Delta, 1999.
Whitfield, Stephen J. *The Culture of the Cold War.* 2nd ed. Baltimore: Johns Hopkins University Press, 1996.
Wilde, Alan. *Middle Grounds: Studies in American Fiction.* Philadelphia: University of Pennsylvania Press, 1987.
Williams, Terry Tempest. *Refuge: An Unnatural History of Family and Place.* New York: Vintage, 2001.
Winkler, Allan M. *Life under a Cloud: American Anxiety about the Atom.* Oxford: Oxford University Press, 1993.
Wisnicki, Adrian. "A Trove of New Works by Thomas Pynchon? *Bomarc Service News* Rediscovered." *Pynchon Notes* 46, no. 9 (2000): 9–34.
Wyschogrod, Edith. *Spirit in Ashes: Hegel, Heidegger, and Man-Made Mass Death.* New Haven: Yale University Press, 1985.
Yavenditti, Michael. "John Hersey and the American Conscience: The Reception of *Hiroshima*." *Pacific Historical Review* 43, no. 1 (1974): 24–49.
Yoneyama, Lisa. *Hiroshima Traces: Time, Space, and the Dialectics of Memory.* Berkeley and Los Angeles: University of California Press, 1999.
Zamora, Lois Parkinson. *Writing the Apocalypse: Historical Vision and Contemporary U.S. and Latin American Fiction.* Cambridge: Cambridge University Press, 1989.

Index

ABM missiles, 84, 120
ABM treaty, 22, 120, 121–22
Acker, Kathy, 6
Adorno, Theodor, 11
Agamben, Giorgio, 111, 171n8, 174–75n11
Alperovitz, Gar, 169n25
anxiety, nuclear, 6, 12, 56, 152, 165–66n47
apocalypse: definition of, 11–12, 50; as literary problem, 29, 167n15; in relation to nuclear war, 26, 50, 164n14
Arabian Nights, 26, 97
Arendt, Hannah, 96–97
Atwood, Margaret, 155
Auden, W. H., 145
authenticity, concept of, 111

Baldwin, Stanley, 167n21
Ballard, J. G., 12, 14, 16, 151; "The Secret History of World War 3," 8–11
Barth, John, 19–20, 23–41, 46, 47, 54, 57, 86, 125, 152, 167n12, 167n15, 175n1; *Chimera*, 24, 167n12; *The End of the Road*, 24, 25, 26, 29; *The Floating Opera*, 25, 26, 29–40, 47, 54; *Giles Goat-Boy*, 20, 25, 26–28, 39–40, 167n12; "The Literature of Exhaustion," 25, 28; *Lost in the Funhouse*, 24; "Muse, Spare Me," 25–26, 28; reputation of, 23; *Sabbatical*, 24; shape of career, 23–27; *The Sot-Weed Factor*, 26

Barthelme, Donald, 1, 6, 21, 85, 86–92, 94, 96–97, 103, 155, 173nn39–40; "After Joyce," 85; "The Balloon," 85; "Game," 21, 86–92, 94; *Unspeakable Practices, Unnatural Acts*, 86
Bartter, Martha A., 165n34
battlefield, changes in nature of, 36–37
Baudrillard, Jean, 103, 105, 106
Beck, Ulrich, 85, 106
Bel Geddes, Norman, 136, 176n16
Belletto, Steven, 166n49, 172n14, 173n37, 173n40
Bellow, Saul, 4
Benjamin, Walter, 5, 134, 141
Bercovitch, Sacvan, 75
Berger, Charles, 168n19
Berger, James, 12
Berlant, Lauren, 170n3
Bernstein, Michael André, 144–45
biopolitics, 174–75n11
Bové, Paul, 168n2
Boyer, Paul, 12, 19, 77, 164n23, 164n27, 165n38, 166nn51–52, 170n40
Breitwieser, Mitchell, 74–75
Brians, Paul, 18
Brodie, Bernard, 80, 82
Brooks, Peter, 5
Brunner, Edward, 165n46

Canaday, John, 165n46

192 / INDEX

Carmichael, Virginia, 170n5
Carter, Dale, 168n18
Caruth, Cathy, 129–30
Chaloupka, William, 174n2
Chandler, Raymond, 53
Chow, Rey, 166n47
Cirincione, Joseph, 166n56
city, Cold War effects on, 52–53, 140
"city-killing," strategy of, 54, 119, 169n34
civil defense, 60, 170n4, 171n2, 172n12
civil rights, 157
Clark, Suzanne, 156, 165n46
Cohen, Samuel, 19, 170n38, 177n26
Cohn, Carol, 174n2
Cold War: allegories of, 26–29, 66–71; beginning of, 51; cultural criticism concerning, 17–18, 165–66nn46–48; effect of end, 18–19, 145, 161, 166n50; effects of, 17–19, 20, 26, 29, 39, 40–41, 48, 51–53, 55–56, 58, 60–75, 76, 87, 98–103, 124, 125, 131–33, 139–40, 144, 152, 156–57, 160, 161
containment culture, 17, 60, 62–63, 155, 166n48
Cooper, Ken, 157
Coover, Robert, 6, 21, 59–62, 63–67, 69–75, 86, 92–97, 103, 135, 160; *The Public Burning*, 21, 59–62, 63–67, 69–75, 135, 160; *The Universal Baseball Association, Inc., J. Henry Waugh, Prop.*, 21, 92–96
Cordle, Daniel, 152, 163n11, 165n45, 165–66n47, 166n53, 172n8, 177n26
Corkin, Stanley, 171n13
Cornis-Pope, Marcel, 165n46
counterforce strategy, 83–84, 88, 119, 169n34, 172nn27–28
Cowart, David, 109, 168n12, 174n8, 174n11,
Cuban Missile Crisis, 18, 26, 56, 78
cybernetics, 88–89

Davis, Kimberly Chabot, 176n10
Davis, Tracy C., 165n46, 172n12
Davis, Walter A., 165–66n47
The Day After, 57, 170n41
Deardorff, Donald L., 174n5
death, changes in nature of, 7–8, 12, 14, 19, 29–40, 45–46, 81, 97, 111, 141, 153, 157–59, 160
defense: contracting, 52, 55; intellectuals, 21, 27, 79–85; strategy, 56, 79–85, 96, 105, 115–19; is a dangerous thing, 120–21

DeKoven, Marianne, 164n16
De Landa, Manuel, 92, 173n45
Deleuze, Gilles, 53
DeLillo, Don, 1, 4, 5, 6, 22, 85, 104–23, 124, 139, 174n4, 174n8; *Americana*, 105; *End Zone*, 22, 104–23; *Great Jones Street*, 105; language as subject in 104–12; *Libra*, 4; reception of, 85, 105–6; relation to risk, 104–6; *White Noise*, 105–6; *Underworld*, 139, 174n61
Demilitarized Zone, the, 98
demographics, Cold War changes in, 52–53, 140
Derrida, Jacques, 11–12, 13, 14, 18, 49–50, 57–58, 67, 166n47
Dewey, Joseph, 165n46
Diacritics, 18
Dickstein, Morris, 166n49
Didion, Joan, 149–54; *Democracy*, 149–54, 176n2, 176n5; *The Last Thing He Wanted*, 176n2; "Pacific Distances," 153; *Play It as It Lays*, 154; *Run River*, 154
Dirda, Michael, 167n10
Doctorow, E. L., 3
Dollimore, Jonathan, 43
Doomsday Clock, the, 69, 73
Douglas, Ann, 156–57
Dowling, David, 165n46
Dr. Strangelove, 49, 57, 121, 173n41
Dresden, bombing of, 82
Dubey, Madhu, 155
Dudziak, Mary L., 177n18
Dugdale, John, 48–49, 55
Dulles, John Foster, 82

Eden, Lynn, 81–82
Edwards, Paul N., 89
Einstein, Albert, 8
Eisenhower administration, 82–83; fictional representation of, 59–67, 69–71
Elias, Amy J., 4, 7
Eliot, T. S., 46–47, 146–47
enemy, concept of, 80, 83–84, 86, 88–89, 95, 131–32
Engelhardt, Tom, 32, 166n55
Ermarth, Elizabeth, 7
Everett, Percival, 160–61
existentialism, 24; critique of, 37

fallout shelter, 76, 78, 171n2, 172n9

Fascism, 36
Faulkner, William, 8
Foertsch, Jacqueline, 177n1
Fradkin, Philip, 166n50
Franklin, H. Bruce, 164-65n34
Franzen, Jonathan, 2
Freedman, Lawrence, 120
frontier thesis, 72
Fukuyama, Francis, 145
Fussell, Paul, 37, 39
Futurama exhibit, 134-37, 140-41
futurity: changes in nature of, 4-5, 11-12, 16-17, 27, 39, 45-46, 49-50, 60, 71-75, 129-31, 135, 140-41, 151, 176n21, 177n12; relation to American nationality, 72-75; in relation to 1939 World's Fair, 134-37; as scripted, 143, 144, 145
futurology, 97

Gaddis, John Lewis, 171n12
Gaddis, William, 1-2, 175n6
Galison, Peter, 53, 88-89
Gallagher, Carole, 166n50
game theory, 80, 89, 101, 131-33, 172n14, 173n40
Garber, Marjorie, 170-71n5
Gardner, John, 2
Gass, William 2, 175n1
Gery, John, 165n46
Ghamari-Tabrizi, Sharon, 80, 97, 172n13, 172n15, 172n17, 172n20, 173n52, 174n57, 174n59
Giddens, Anthony, 85
Ginsberg, Allen, 74
Goldstein, Bill, 175n2
Graff, Gerald, 2
Gray, Richard, 177n27
Green, Jeremy, 175n1
Guernica, 36-37
Gusterson, Hugh, 76-77, 171-72n3

Hamill, John, 168n19
Harper, Phillip Brian, 155
Harris, Charles B., 30
Hawkes, John, 1
Hayles, N. Katherine, 45
Heidegger, Martin, 111, 174-75n11
Heise, Ursula K., 7, 105-06
Henriksen, Margot, 69
Hepburn, Allan, 24

Hersey, John, 12-16, 131, 164nn33-34, 165n40; *Hiroshima*, 12-16, 165n40; reception of, 13-14, 164nn33-34, 165n40
High Noon, 21, 66-71
highway system, interstate, 53, 136
Hinds, Elizabeth Jane Wall, 168n5
historiographic metafiction, 3, 21, 44, 85, 146; relation to modernism, 3, 85
Hite, Molly, 154-55
Hoberek, Andrew, 164n16, 167n59
Hudson Institute, 80
Huehls, Mitchum, 7
Hume, David, 34
Hume, Kathryn, 168n19
Hungerford, Amy, 4, 6, 23, 163n11, 173n33, 177n24
Hutcheon, Linda, 2, 3-4, 7-8, 44, 85, 163n9, 173n38
hydrogen bomb: development of, 14, 26, 67, 163n12; effects of on city, 54

ICBM: effects of, 5, 16, 20, 26, 31, 48, 120, 168n19

Jackson, Tony, 5, 57-58, 165-66n47
Jameson, Fredric, 3-4, 7-8, 125, 140
jeremiad, 72, 75
Johnson administration, 83
joint chiefs of staff, the, 80

Kahn, Herman, 80-81, 97, 172n13
Kaplan, Fred, 120, 169n34, 172nn10-11, 172n16, 172-73nn21-30; 175n18
Karem, Jeff, 159
Kaufmann, William, 82
Kennedy administration, 82-83
Kermode, Frank, 57-58
Kerouac, Jack, 74
Kerrigan, John, 168n14
Kipling, Rudyard, 145
Klein, Richard, 50, 73
Korea, war in, 67, 171n13
Kushner, Tony, 61

Langewiesche, William, 166n56
language, nuclear, 76-77, 87, 104, 106-7, 112, 174n2
Lasch, Christopher, 86
LeClair, Thomas, 108, 175n1
LeMay, Curtis, 82

Levine, George, 168n6
Lewis, Wyndham, 46–48, 160, 168n16
Liberalism, 17
Lifton, Robert Jay, 12
Limited Test Ban Treaty, 57
limited war, 56, 82–84, 112, 119–20, 122–23,
Lindsay, Alan, 167n12
Los Angeles, 49
Lowen, Rebecca S., 167n27
Luckhurst, Roger, 166n53
Lucky Dragon incident, 15

Maltby, Paul, 173n39, 174n4
Manhattan Project, 127, 138–39, 169n25
Marchand, Roland, 135, 176nn12–18
Marcus, Ben, 2
Masco, Joseph, 166n50
May, Elaine Tyler, 127
Mazurek, Raymond A., 170n2
McCaffery, Larry, 173n39
McCarthy, Mary, 13–16
McCarthyism, 17, 60, 62, 65, 66, 131
McClure, John A., 164n16, 174n4
McEnaney, Laura, 170n4
McGurl, Mark, 6, 41, 85, 156
McHale, Brian, 5, 28, 30, 40, 164n14
McHoul, Alec, 168n19
McNamara, Robert, 83–85, 119–20
Melley, Timothy, 63
Mendelson, Edward, 169n21
Metafiction, 2–3, 16, 20–21, 23–41, 44, 59, 61, 71–72, 79, 86, 96–98, 103, 105, 146, 151, 152, 160, 164n18, 173n39; critiques of 1–2, 21, 86, 96; emergence of, 23–41; relation to nuclear strategy, 85–98
Milesi, Laurent, 168n19
Miller, Perry, 75
Miller, Richard, 166n50
minimalism, 6, 156
Mirowski, Philip 173n40
missile age. *See* ICBM
missile gap, 172n20
Mizruchi, Susan, 173n37
Modernism, 1, 5, 40, 46–48, 57, 85; cultural capital of, 155; late 30, 146. *See also* Postmodernism: definition of; relation to modernism.
Moody, Rick, 1, 127, 175n2
Moraru, Christian, 171n17
Moretti, Franco, 43

Morrison, Toni, 6, 155, 160, 177n12
Myers, B. R., 163n4

Nabokov, Vladimir, 86
Nadel, Alan, 14, 16, 17, 150, 164–65n34, 165n40, 165–66n47, 166n48, 167n25
narrative theory, 5, 40, 57–58
national identity, American, 21, 55, 59–75
Nelson, Deborah, 62–63
Nevada Test Site, 154
New Left, the, 76
Newhouse, John, 175n21
Newman, Charles, 2
9/11 fiction, 161
Norris, Margot, 164–65n34
nostalgia, 3, 125, 127; progressive version of, 134
"Nuclear Criticism," 18, 166n53
nuclear family, 127
nuclear testing, 14, 56, 67, 150–54, 166n50
Nuclear Texts and Contexts, 18
Nye, David, 135, 140

O'Brien, Tim: *The Nuclear Age*, 76–79, 85, 100, 106, 108, 127
Olderman, Raymond, 167n12
Oppenheimer, J. Robert, 27, 138–39
Osteen, Mark, 112, 174n8

Patterson, Ian, 37, 167n21
Peck, Dale, 1–2, 6, 154
periodization: in relation to war, 31–38, 45–48
Piette, Adam, 173n37
Plath, Sylvia, 61, 156
Postmodernism: city in, 52–54; critical reaction to, 1–3; debates concerning, 1–5, 86, 154–55; definition of, 1–5, 7, 28, 163n6; emergence of, 4–5, 20, 40–41, 167n25; end of 19, 167n59; and gender, 154–56; late, 22; and postwar literature, 152–66; and publishing industry, 159–61; relation to future periods, 17; relation to modernism, 7, 85, 155–56; relation to postcolonialism, 157; relation to race and ethnicity, 155–66.
Potsdam Conference, 51–52, 169n25
Potsdam Declaration, 51
Poundstone, William, 176n8
Power, Tommy, 82

INDEX / 195

Powers, Richard, 6, 22, 106, 124–47, 158, 175n1, 176n21; *Gain*, 106; *Galatea 2.2*, 125; *The Gold Bug Variations*, 176n21; *Operation Wandering Soul*, 125; *Prisoner's Dilemma*, 22, 125–47, 158; relation to postmodernism, 124–25, 175n1; *Three Farmers on Their Way to a Dance*, 124, 144; *The Time of Our Singing*, 176n21
prisoner's dilemma, 131–32
privacy, 62–66
proliferation, problem of, 14–15, 19, 76, 165n40,
Punday, Daniel, 167n1, 170n38,
Pynchon, Thomas, 1, 2, 4, 5, 6, 20, 38, 40, 42–58, 75, 85, 124, 130, 140, 143, 168nn5–6, 168n8, 168n12, 168n16, 168nn18–19, 169n34, 170n38, 170n42; *Against the Day*, 44, 170n38; city in, 52–53; creation of reader's expectations in, 44–45, 49, 52; *The Crying of Lot 49*, 20, 40, 42–46, 48–58, 140, 143, 168n12, 170n38; and entropy, 44, 168n6; *Gravity's Rainbow*, 20, 40, 43, 45, 48, 51, 55–56, 168nn18–19, 169n34, 170n38; historiographic imagination of, 4, 43–48, 56; "Is It O.K. to Be a Luddite?" 57, 170n42; "A Journey into the Mind of Watts," 52; literary generations in 46–48, 168n16; *Mason & Dixon*, 44–45, 168n5, 170n38; nuclear content in 48–58; paranoia in, 43; *Slow Learner*, 168n6, 168n8; *V.*, 45–48, 168n16

RAND Corporation, 80, 97, 131
Reagan, Ronald, 9–11, 18, 28, 57, 124
realism, 2, 5, 25, 39, 97, 154–55
Reed, Ishmael, 6, 157; *Mumbo Jumbo*, 157
reflexive modernity, 85
revenge tragedy, 42–43, 45, 168n14
Rhys, Jean, 155
Rilke, Rainer Maria, 110–12, 137, 174n10, 174–75n11,
Robinson, Douglas, 167n15
Robson, David, 168n19
romance thesis, 72
Rose, Kenneth D., 171n2
Rosenberg, Ethel and Julius, 21, 59–64, 66, 74, 170–71n5, 171n8

Saint-Amour, Paul K., 130, 133, 169–70n37

Schaub, Thomas Hill, 24–25, 165n46, 168n6
Schell, Jonathan, 12, 166n56, 176n24
Scholes, Robert, 27–28
Schwenger, Peter, 165–66n47, 166n53, 168n19, 169n27, 171n1
science fiction, 18, 38, 57, 97, 164–65n34, 165n43, 165–66n47, 170n42
Seaver, Richard, 159–60
Seed, David, 164–65n34, 165n43, 168n7
Shambroom, Paul, 166n50
Shute, Nevil: *On the Beach*, 16
Siebers, Tobin, 51–52
Silko, Leslie Marmon: *Ceremony*, 157–60
simulation, 21, 79, 81, 84, 86, 88, 90–92, 94–103
Slotkin, Richard, 66
Smith, Gerard, 175n19
Smith, Marcus, 168n19
Smith, Shawn, 45
Smithsonian, controversy at, 19
Solnit, Rebecca, 166n50
sport, nuclear war as, 22, 77–79, 85, 92–103, 106–23
Sputnik, 16, 26
Stark, John O., 167n5
Stein, Gertrude, 18
Stevenson, Adlai, 156
Stone, Albert, 165n40, 166n53, 172n9
Stonehill, Brian, 167n5
Strategic Air Command (SAC), 82
Strategic Arms Limitations Talks (SALT), 22, 108–9, 119, 120, 121–23
Strehle, Susan, 173n39

Tanner, Tony, 44–45, 58
Targeting, nuclear, 55, 82–84, 119, 168n34, 172n28
time, *see* futurity
Tölölyan, Khachig, 168n19
Torgovnick, Marianna, 164n34
total war: emergence of as concept 36–38; nuclear version of, 11, 18, 49–50, 55, 130.
trauma, 128–30, 157–58; nuclear 129–31, 133, 169n37
Treat, John Whittier, 164–65n34
Trinity: site, 49, 142, 158; test, 51, 128, 130–31, 140, 158

Uncle Sam, 21, 59–62, 64–66, 71–74

university system, relationship to Cold War of, 41, 167n27
untellability, concept of, 110–12, 123
Updike, John, 74

victory culture, 32
Vietnam, war in, 49, 86, 150
Virilio, Paul, 121
von Braun, Wernher, 48
von Neumann, John, 80

Wagar, W. Warren, 164–65, n34
Walkowitz, Rebecca L., 170–71n5
Wallace, David Foster: *Infinite Jest*, 98–103
Walsh, Richard, 61
war games, 80–83, 173n45, 173–74n52, 174n61; critiques of, 21, 85–103, 113, 119
Waugh, Patricia, 86, 164n18
Weart, Spencer, 165n46
Welsome, Eileen, 166n50
Westerns, effect of Cold War on: 66–71, 171n13
Whitfield, Stephen J., 66
Wiener, Norbert, 89

Wilde, Alan, 45, 173n39
Wilder, Thornton, 12
Williams, Terry Tempest, 166n50
Wills, David, 168n19
Winkler, Allan M., 165n46
Wisnicki, Adrian, 170n39
world government, concept of, 139
World War One: effects of, 29, 31–32, 37–39, 46–47, 54; relation to modernism, 46–47
World War Two, effects of 29, 36–37, 47, 48, 79–80, 82–83, 88, 127, 135, 137, 141, 146–47, 157
World War Three, imagination of, 8–12, 16–17, 20, 45, 48, 50, 58, 80, 91, 97, 104, 154
Woolf, Virginia, 46
World's Fair, 1939, 127, 134–37, 139–40
writing programs, 6, 85
Wyschogrod, Edith, 174n10

Yavenditti, Michael, 164n33
Yoneyama, Lisa, 164–65n34

Zamora, Lois Parkinson, 31, 167n15

www.ingramcontent.com/pod-product-compliance
Lightning Source LLC
Chambersburg PA
CBHW011750220426
43670CB00018B/2928